Unsprawl

Remixing Spaces as Places

by Simmons B. Buntin
with Ken Pirie

Introduction by Galina Tachieva

Published by **PLA**NETIZEN PRESS

Unsprawl: Remixing Spaces as Places

© 2013 by Urban Insight, Inc.

PLANETIZEN PRESS

Published in the United States by Planetizen Press (www.planetizen.com), an imprint of Urban Insight, Inc.

Authors: Simmons B. Buntin with Ken Pirie
Editor: Jonathan Nettler
Introduction by: Galina Tachieva
Book design: Mindy Oliver

ISBN: 978-0-9789329-7-8

Second Edition

PLANETIZEN is an online resource for news and information, with daily news stories, features, job listings and opinion pieces exploring the world of city planning. You can find us at www.planetizen.com.

Cover photo: Ron Pollard

Table of Contents

Introduction

by Galina Tachieva

Prospect New Town in Longmont, Colorado combines traditional and modernist architecture with a New Urbanist town design, making it one of the nation's most distinct new communities.

Despite its title, this book is not about sprawl. In fact, sprawl is rarely mentioned. *Unsprawl* is about built places—real, human-scale communities created by people and for people, not for cars. It diligently surveys the struggles and rise of twelve innovative communities that were built despite the heavy tide of zoning, lending and marketing that were created to encourage sprawl. Simmons Buntin and Ken Pirie are urban thinkers who have analyzed the existing predicament and present an optimistic, diverse and common-sense direction for the future.

Centered on projects and how they were built, *Unsprawl* is above all about the people shaping these places, their efforts and passion for good urbanism. These people were the leaders, the thinkers and doers who made things happen through persistence and talent for practical application. It is encouraging that these visionaries came from a broad range of professions: urban designers, architects, developers, builders, local officials, and city staff. These are the people who will carry the change of our built environment beyond our current sprawling habits. The common thread through their accounts is that the obstacles were abundant, but the rewards were well worth the effort.

We live in a time of transition for urbanism. Our society is slowly awakening to a new economic reality of post-recession downscaling. A new demographic shift is upon us, with a new class of buyers (Baby Boomers, Millenials and immigrants) changing the suburbs with their preferences for more urban environments. There is a new awareness about the environment, health and aging, and how all of these issues are dependent on the form of our built habitats. Sprawl has been failing as a built habitat for decades, but its inadequacy has become apparent with the recent economic meltdown. Rising energy costs make long commutes prohibitive and the expansion of suburban infrastructure unfeasible. Sprawl is expensive, and we cannot afford it anymore.

The good news we gather from *Unsprawl* is that the transformation from sprawl's auto-dependent, single-use environments to complete and walkable, human-scale communities has begun. The renaissance of great and diverse urbanism is not only imminent, but is already a reality—one qualitative change at a time, project by project, the transition has amounted to hundreds of built places all around America, and they are the models for the future. Whether they are downtown redevelopments, new greenfield villages, retrofits, or ambitious sustainability experiments, the projects in this book demonstrate the long-needed revival of our thinking about urbanism. Good public realm as a setting for human interaction, convenient amenities in proximity, and harmony with the natural settings were once considered elemental requirements of city-making, but they have been obliterated by the madness of building wasteful sprawl for half a century. But these principles have now been recovered.

A few years ago some of the ideas behind the projects—tearing down a highway, transforming a mall into an urban core, bringing agriculture to the forefront of real estate—might have seemed bold and unconventional. Today these concepts are becoming the norm and are seen simply as a return to common sense. *Unsprawl* traces the trajectory of this change.

The value of this book is not only in its encyclopedic efficiency in describing the facts in precise detail. It also connects the goals and thought processes of governments and community groups, and carries them through to the final product. This is not a smooth process; it is full of peaks and valleys, conflicts and rough moments. The stories are fascinating, told with great specifics and with much empathy for the protagonists struggling to create good urbanism. *Unsprawl* is a great compendium of information rarely available to the wider public. (Buntin and Pirie went to great lengths to assemble and make available a long list of references for each project.) It shows their curiosity about every step of the process of conceptualizing, designing and executing each project, about every square foot of use and how it was financed and built, who helped and who didn't, and how the projects ultimately came to life. It is the documentation of this particular moment when a project becomes a true place that brings the reportage to life.

The Q&A sessions with the important players in these projects are intriguing; honest and personal, the assessments show the often-heroic battles fought by private developers, city staffers and officials to turn plans into built reality. Some of them chose to not comply with the usual bureaucracy and protocol, and bravely decided to do what they thought was needed to create better places. Lots of educating of the public about this new phenomenon called good urbanism was also required.

The writing in this book is concise and pragmatic, but we can detect a poetic sensibility in the photographs of the projects—well-framed moments that capture a calm balance between manmade urbanity and nature. The photographers have an eye for the human-scale detail that is essential to making good urbanism. Excellent two-dimensional plans are important as blueprints for a place, but the real thing depends on the execution of three-dimensional structures, including utilitarian details such as an awning, the shape of a window, or the slope of a roofline, and the case studies represent these details well.

Unsprawl presents two primary ways of initiating and building better places: public-sector redevelopments, done over many years, involving a complex network of organizations and decision makers, and private-sector development where one individual, a family, or a small group of investors shapes the vision for a new place. The book also articulates the possibilities of positive interaction between the public and private sectors. For example, in the Second Street District of Austin, Texas, the city provided expedited permitting, development fee waivers, and funding for streetscape among other incentives for private investment. The strategies of a wide range of implementation processes and civic financing mechanisms can be successfully used in future projects.

These built projects are well-suited for today's economic instability: they are diverse and flexible, easily adaptable to changing needs. These places are centered on walkability and a public realm for a more socially engaged population. Smaller housing types are introduced for shrinking households, organic farms replace old-time amenities such as golf courses, malls are demolished and substituted with town centers.

The featured communities give us hope for a recovery from sprawl. Many of them are still maturing, providing "a great big classroom," for study and instruction, as one town founder put it. None of them are perfect: some of them come up short on urban and architectural design; others are exhibiting the usual defects of highly desirable places–little economic or racial diversity. What is essential is their structural shift towards a walkable, human scale. The truth is that even if the American development industry is never going

to be the same after the recent recession and real estate bust, quality projects (in our cities as well as our suburbs) will still be in high demand. They will hold their value not only as investments, but also as healthy human environments that will attract younger and older generations.

Though it is essential to be frugal and economical today, austerity should not preclude excellence and permanence. In contrast to the disposable and wasteful exuberance of suburban sprawl, the best sustainability is achieved in places and buildings that are built to last. Let's Unsprawl by building–and rebuilding–well!

Galina Tachieva, AICP, LEED AP, is a Partner at Duany Plater-Zyberk & Company. Originally from Bulgaria, she is an expert in form-based codes, urban redevelopment, and sprawl retrofit.

New Communities

Live/work units in the heart of Nashville's award-winning traditional neighborhood development, Lenox Village.

Home is not where you have to go but where you want to go; nor is it a place where you are sullenly admitted, but rather where you are welcomed—by the people, the walls, the tiles on the floor, the followers beside the door, the play of life, the very grass.

Scott Russell Sanders, *Staying Put*

If you could create your neighborhood anew, how would you craft the walls and tiles–how would you direct the unrehearsed play of life? For new communities, the script appears to be unwritten; the stage swept clear. But as the three case studies of this section demonstrate, that's never the case: though these greenfield developments face the preconceptions, histories, and cultural tendencies of any place, they also face additional obstacles, be they a reluctant municipality, a challenging economy, or an environmental trial.

The debate in rural Longmont, Colorado, appears to center on style–until one recognizes that Prospect New Town's modernist design is a fitting evolution both of the town plan

and the historic industrial structures of the pioneering West. Built on a former tree farm, Prospect features a colorful, eclectic mix of residential and commercial buildings. NorthWest Crossing in the eastern Oregon mountain town of Bend likewise takes advantage of the pioneering spirit to advance bold design among a dynamic mix of homes, businesses, schools and open space. A forested environment and mountain views are critical to the expanding community's sense of place. Located in the suburban hills south of Nashville, Tennessee, Lenox Village is rich in Southern vernacular, with a formal village green, thriving town center and a mix of housing types. By restoring a farm pond to create a natural stream and central greenway, and subsequently enhancing habitat for an endangered species, Lenox Village expands the discussion and perhaps the definition of community ecosystem.

These projects highlight the essence of good urban design, even, and perhaps especially, in suburban and rural locations. They similarly speak to the form, texture and malleability of place–how our communities and citizens mature, how we can build more responsibly on the land and how we can make new and distinct places that respect economy and heritage.

Prospect New Town
Longmont, Colorado
by Simmons B. Buntin

Prospect New Town is defined in part by its colorful, eclectic architecture in a mix of traditional and modern styles.

Photo: Simmons Buntin

Prospect New Town is located on an 80-acre former tree farm south of Longmont, Colorado, a rapidly suburbanizing agricultural town northeast of Boulder. Designed by Duany Plater-Zyberk & Company (DPZ), Colorado's first New Urbanist development is perhaps best known for its architectural evolution from traditional to modern styles based loosely on the historic building types of Colorado mine towns, railroad structures, barns and silos–a style that architectural critic Randolph Stewart has called "Prospect Contemporary Vernacular." In *Council Report III* for the Congress for the New Urbanism, prepared early in the project's development, town planner Bill Dennis writes, "Prospect represents a noble experiment in the ongoing testing of New Urbanism." Though some critics and

early buyers were less enthusiastic about the design transition, today Prospect features an eclectic mix of boldly colored homes, a mixed-use downtown, and a passionate developer and town architect.

The town plan calls for narrow, tree-lined streets with views of 14,259-foot Longs Peak, the Indian Peaks Wilderness, and the Colorado Rockies Front Range. A mix of single-family detached homes, townhouses, live/work units, condominiums and carriage homes all lie within a short walk of the central square, which hosts a bandstand and regular gatherings. Mature trees have been planted along streets and in the town's parks to provide the appearance of an established community. Though at one time buildout was anticipated as early as 2004, as of December 2012 the

3

JUST THE FACTS

- 80-acre site of a former tree farm located 15 miles northeast of Boulder, Colorado
- Designed in 1994, construction began in 1996; four of seven phases complete
- 610 predominantly custom-built residential units at buildout: To date, 145 single-family detached homes (about 65% include carriage houses), 50 attached homes and 98 condominiums, most in mixed-use buildings
- 150,000 square feet of ground-floor commercial space anticipated at buildout
- "Downtown" incorporates a mix of street-level retail, professional offices, restaurants and live/work units, including Ion Place (a wind-powered, mixed-use building containing three high-end condos) and Solar Village Prospect (a solar- and wind-powered, super-efficient complex of 16 lofts, flats and two-story condos)
- Nine parks planned (six currently built), including swimming pool, playground and community garden
- Distinctive for its land use and modern architectural design
- Called "America's Coolest Neighborhood" by *Dwell* magazine, named a "Best of the West" by *Sunset* magazine and awarded the Colorado Governor's Smart Growth Award in 1996
- Master plan by Duany Plater-Zyberk & Company
- Town architect: Mark Sofield, Prospect Land Company
- Developed by Kiki Wallace and Dale Bruns

development is in its fifth of seven phases and completion of the project is not likely to occur for several more years.

Project History: From Tree Farm to "Cranky" Plan

The idea for Prospect New Town was born in the early 1990s, when Kiki Wallace decided to give new life to his family tree farm just south of Longmont. Inspired by a 1993 *Wall Street Journal* article featuring Andrés Duany, principal of DPZ and one of the leaders of the New Urbanist movement, and seeking to develop the land in a way that would avoid the typical, front-loaded subdivisions appearing on Longmont's periphery and across the Front Range, Wallace formed a partnership with local developer Dale Bruns. He then began studying neighborhood and community types across the region. Wallace wanted to create a community that prioritized people over cars, respecting the historic architecture of Old Longmont while retaining the mature landscaping of the tree farm.

In January 1994, Wallace invited Duany to conduct a design charrette that would enable DPZ to develop the plan for the "Wallace Addition," as the City of Longmont called it. Over a span of seven days at the Longmont Opera House, charrette participants–the design team, city planners, citizens, and other stakeholders–crafted three plans for Prospect New Town, one of which emerged as the favored plan. In addition to the physical placement of streets, parks and the higher-density downtown area, the participants drafted detailed urban and architectural design guidelines intended to provide a cohesive framework for the overall community.

In the layout, streets bisect and radiate outward from a primary horseshoe-shaped loop, and are aligned to take advantage of mountain views. The result is what Duany calls a "cranky" plan full of odd-shaped lots. "One of the major challenges in the development of

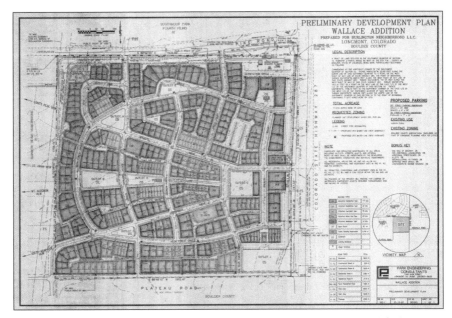

The Prospect New Town site plan, where lot shapes have proved to be an unexpected challenge for building single-family residences, fostering the project's distinct architecture.

the master plan," says the project's tear sheet, "was the restriction of access to the two arterial roads to the north and east of the project. Originally slated to become an expressway, the charrette demonstrated that expansion of the north artery was unnecessary." Still, negotiations with the city were challenging. Bruns and Wallace teamed with Duany to "fight tooth and nail," according to the *Boulder County Business Report*, to devise an agreement that would make Prospect a reality. The plan as first presented did not mesh with many of the city's zoning ordinances, including those addressing open space (not enough), streets (too narrow), traffic patterns (too complex) and curb cuts (too many, according to the Colorado Department of Transportation). The challenge of getting the project approved is reflected in many of Prospect's street names–Tenacity Drive and Incorrigible Circle, for example.

In October 1995, the Longmont Planning Board finally approved the project, stating that "this is what people want," despite the fact that

"city staff detested New Urbanism," says Wallace. In approving the Wallace Addition, the city created a new designation in its Municipal Code, the "Planned Unit Development-Mixed Use," or PUD-MU. The PUD itself is "intended to encourage innovative land planning and site design concepts that conform with community quality of life benchmarks and that achieve a high level of environmental sensitivity, energy efficiency, aesthetics, high-quality development and other community goals." It aims to encourage these concepts by:

1. Reducing or eliminating the inflexibility that sometimes results from strict application of zoning and development standards that were designed primarily for individual lots;

2. Allowing greater freedom in selecting the means to provide access, light, open space and design amenities;

3. Allowing greater freedom in providing a mix of land uses in the same development, including a mix of housing types,

Because Longmont lacks a true regional vernacular, Prospect New Town's designers looked to Colorado's industrial past for design cues, resulting in an architecture that reflects the region's agricultural and mining past, as this farmhouse-inspired home demonstrates.

Photo: Simmons Buntin

lot sizes, densities and/or supporting commercial uses in residential PUDs;

4. Promoting quality urban design and environmentally sensitive development by allowing development to take advantage of special site characteristics, locations and land uses; and

5. Encouraging quality urban design and environmentally sensitive development by allowing increases in base densities or floor area ratios when such increases can be justified by superior design or the provision of additional amenities such as public open space.

In return for this flexibility, the Code states that, "PUDs are expected to include exceptional design that preserves critical environmental resources; provide above-average open space and recreational amenities; incorporate creative design in the layout of buildings, open space and circulation; assure compatibility with surrounding land uses and neighborhood character; and provide greater efficiency in the layout and provision of roads, utilities and other infrastructure."

Based on the successful implementation of the PUD-MU at Prospect and other locations, Longmont's city council approved a Mixed Use District Ordinance in June 2009. The new ordinance builds on the PUD-MU to "support pedestrian-friendly, mixed-use and transit-oriented development while helping to foster reductions in vehicle trips [and] create new opportunities for lifestyle choices in places that are centers for social interaction in mixed residential, retail, workplace and civic settings."

The Prospect Contemporary Vernacular

Prospect's design guidelines cover such parameters as building placement, elements, height and parking for each of six building types established in the Prospect Urban Regulations finalized by DPZ in 1996. Implementing the architectural design guidelines in the early phases felt "like trying to get a change

Photo: Simmons Buntin

There is no "typical" streetscape in Prospect New Town, nor any singular architectural style, making the neighborhood among the most distinct in the country.

approved in a designated historic district," said one local housing expert. "We're not building something for people to disappear into the interior of," said Wallace in response. "We're building something that when you are outside the exterior, you feel like you are part of something and that you enjoy the experience of walking outside."

The architectural guidelines were so stringent that DPZ reviewed and approved the architectural drawings for each house from its office in Miami before construction could begin. For self-described "control freak" Wallace, that was a plus; for architects and builders, it proved to be tedious and in some cases unattainable–several builders were forced out for failing to follow the town's design principles. Many of Prospect's earliest residents were at first wary of Wallace's approach, but when the initial ring of traditional houses was built they appreciated his insistence on design and architectural integrity.

To foster that integrity and enhance the design review process, Wallace hired Mark

Sofield as town architect in 1998. Sofield moved to Longmont from Connecticut. He did not find much of a regional vernacular in Longmont, echoing Duany's statement that "all of the older architecture was imported from elsewhere." With Wallace he visited a number of other notable New Urbanist projects, primarily in the South, including Seaside. "In the end," he says in *Fast Company* magazine, "we both felt strongly that we needed to break out of the 'cute' mode," referring to the "traditional" architecture found at Seaside and other New Urbanist projects.

After the first 20 houses at Prospect had been built (including the preservation and relocation of three historic farm homes into the new neighborhood, one of which is the home of Sofield and his family), Wallace and Sofield decided to expand beyond traditional architecture–Queen Anne, Tudor, Victorian, Craftsman–to allow for a greater variety. The resulting mixture of styles included a modern interpretation of the area's historical structures: the buildings of Colorado mining towns and

7

railroad facilities, as well as the barns and silos that dot the plains around Longmont. What resulted, slowly at first and more widely as the project has matured, is an eclectic but distinct Prospect vernacular.

"Contemporary architecture offered a new direction, one inspired in part by our visit to Seaside," says Wallace. "Our inclusion of new architectural styles didn't seem like a seismic shift at the time, though it was perceived that way, particularly by our first residents. I think of it as an evolution, one that brings more exposure to Prospect and broadens the possibilities for homebuyers."

More than 35 lots were sold before the project broke ground. However, when the first modernist single-family homes were built, "predictably, quite a few buyers were furious about the buildings to the point of feeling betrayed," says Duany. Sofield recalled in 2002 that the architectural shift was undertaken not just for the sake of stylistic change, but also as a result of the town plan itself. "Some lots are so oddly shaped that getting any sort of traditional architecture on them became an exercise in half measures," he says in *Places*. Still, the early homeowners formed a coalition with builders and tried to force Wallace and Sofield out. The developers had to bring Duany out for a special town meeting to "talk neighbors down," Sofield says.

"When I finally found out about [the transition in styles], I very much approved of it," says Duany. "I succeeded in laying it to rest among the residents." Duany assured homeowners that a contemporary architectural style could support the New Urbanist town plan—that indeed the success of the community depended on architectural variety and growth.

Once Sofield joined the project, however, the architectural guidelines developed by DPZ were implemented only selectively. He, Wallace and another Prospect Architectural Committee member approved designs on a case-by-case basis. Sofield did recognize, however,

that the ad-hoc standard of review needed to be documented. In October 2003, he created the revised Prospect Architectural Regulations, with a goal of seeking "to inspire, for Prospect, an architecture of individual and situational relevance." Though they do not alter Prospect's urban regulations—which address building placement and bulk—the new guidelines speak to building appearance, providing the "aesthetic sensibilities of Prospect's founder and designers . . . an aesthetic characterized by a desire for congruence of form and content; a dislike of contrivance; a preference for simplicity—not for its own sake, but for the coherence of the inevitably complex whole; and an appreciation for underlying, formal consistency."

Wallace and Duany both call the document a "manifesto" more than a set of amended architectural guidelines. Duany says, "It is, in fact, the protocol of a dictatorship, where there are no rules. Rules or laws protect the designer and the citizens because they know where you stand. Because there are no rules [at Prospect] everything is subject to the opinions of the town architect. . . . Known rules protect the designer from the arbitrary notions of the town architect."

"I acknowledge the need for directive guidance and, to that end, the last three of five pages of the 2003 Prospect Architectural Regulations still are prescriptive," counters Sofield. "I tried, though, to contextualize those prescriptions in the first two pages, which seem to be the only ones the document's critics are reading."

Wallace's concern lies more in the fact that design review is conducted by a limited group than in the idealistic nature of much of the document. "We end up not following the specific codes already in place." It's an outcome that Wallace takes responsibility for; as developer, he fostered Prospect's unique, individualized process of review and approval. So in March 2011, Wallace added another architect to the committee. It's important to note, too, that Prospect is not like most other

Photo: Ron Pollard

Homes feature a mix of traditional and modern architecture in Prospect New Town's first phase.

communities, because every home is custom-built and therefore requires individual review and approval. "Prospect has 'clients,'" says Duany, "those who have met the architect and were brought along to a level of sophistication. . . . It is a jewel of a project but it is not typical of what confronts the New Urbanism."

The new Prospect Architectural Guidelines include sections on Order, Context, Tradition and Dissent, as well as General Requirements (urban position, environmental conditions, programmatic requirements, formal interests and technological realities) and Additional Specifications (ranging from exterior elements and finishes to doors, rainwater controls and interior finishes). In "Order," for example, the document states, "Real places, we believe, accommodate the real differences in the ways that people conduct their lives. To this end, individual architectural expression of those differences is essential to the idea of Prospect, as is the tectonic invention necessary to achieve it."

In the context of Tradition, the narrative states, "The most useful way to regard history, in Prospect, is to recognize that it cannot be frozen, that it is never over. We generally prefer architecture that engages history critically to that which seeks to copy it exactly–though we find faithful reproduction less disruptive than clumsy novelty. We encourage a similarly critical view of modernity. No vision is ever unprecedented and an appreciation of the past's presence is essential to successful innovation. Nothing can be truly different without an awareness of what it is different from."

The guidelines conclude with a section titled "Dissent," which seems an apt and unifying theme for the stylistic evolution of Prospect's commercial and residential buildings: "We consider criticism and dissent to be essential to the process of communal creation. We ask that it be civil, informed and exercised for the greater good. This document, like the community it envisions, will always be a work in progress. A neighborhood's continuing vitality is largely dependent on its capacity for adaptation and evolution."

One result of Prospect's architectural adaptation and evolution is that contractors who are "content to work on speculative houses designed from scratch have stepped in and a corps of local architects are happily becoming adept at working in Prospect," says Todd W. Bressi in *Places*. Yet in 2007 Sofield estimated that 70% of architectural plans need "extensive" alterations while 25% need "at least moderate changes"–perhaps an inevitable outcome given Prospect's modified review process. "It sounds harsh," Sofield says in the *Fast Company* article. "But somebody's taste has to prevail, or else it would be anarchy."

Some New Urbanist practitioners believed early on that Prospect was creating a kind of architectural anarchy. "The 'Prospect Vernacular' that evolved, though well designed in its own right, ignored earlier patterns and began a competition among the design professionals, at the expense of the relationship of the variety of styles that previously existed within Prospect," writes Randolph Stewart in 2003's *Council Report III*. "This created conflict

9

Townhomes built in the first phase of Prospect New Town reflect the development's initial adherence to traditional design.

Photo: Simmons Buntin

within the neighborhood and confusion in the public realm. . . . The woven mosaic that was intended went awry."

In the same *Council Report*, town planner and architectural critic Bill Dennis, in calling Prospect an "experiment," writes that the project is trying to answer three questions: Is there one style that is more appropriate to our time and this particular location? Do we live in a certain way today that calls for a new expression of style? How do we allow freedom of individual expression and still create community? In considering Prospect in 2003, his answers echoed Stewart's: "It seems as though neither [the traditional nor modern] camp is particularly happy with the crazy quilt of styles, which seems to mock the 'realness' of either style. The cooks at Prospect have started out making a pot roast and in the middle of dinner have brought in sushi. Both can be good, but not together."

Karrie Jacobs, editor of *Dwell*, disagrees. Noting that Prospect doesn't rely on "a kind of fake historical feel," she wrote in 2002 that the community instead serves as "a laboratory for a new generation of American modernism," one that particularly appeals to city-lovers settling down to raise families.

For Wallace and Sofield, the caliber of the architecture is more important than any particular design dictum. "What we are trying to do is encourage quality building designs, no matter what the style, that work together to develop the excellent land plan," Sofield says. "We still build plenty of traditional houses, which speaks to our larger goal for Prospect's buildout: architectural variety. The trick, though, is keeping that variety cohesive enough to not work against the land plan. Well implemented, the prescriptive rules create a consistent rhythm across styles and along any given streetscape."

Ten years later, Prospect's contemporary architecture spans the town center and includes the majority of the homes. If any of the early resentment stemming from the community's architectural evolution remains, it is not obvious. Today, Prospect residents and

Photo: Simmons Buntin

Whether traditional or modern, the homes at Prospect New Town usually feature broad front porches on tree-lined streets.

business owners take pride in their community's distinct design. "I've loved the architecture from Day One," says Nest Antiques, Garden & Home owner Renee Kimes, who had to reluctantly cancel a contract on a home in Prospect's first filing when she and her husband moved to Florida. Six years ago, they returned and purchased a resale Colorado farmhouse-style home designed by architect Christopher Melton. "I love the traditional designs. It took a little while for the contemporary homes to grow on me, but today I find Prospect's architectural mix and originality to be really exciting."

Though the town architect's review process may be questioned—a process that neighbors believe is "a little strict, but good," says Kimes—there's no denying that it has succeeded in creating a prominent vernacular that brings variety and notoriety to the community. To an ever-increasing degree, Prospect has become an inspiration for communities across the Front Range, influencing design in such pedestrian-oriented developments as Stapleton, the Holiday neighborhood of north Boulder and even

the zero lot-line homes of Lakewood's new downtown, Belmar.

Ironically, the debate of architectural style at Prospect would never have occurred if Wallace's original ambitions for the buildings had been met: early in the community design process, "time was spent studying an environmental architecture which could have affected the look of Prospect," says Duany, "but in the course of the terrible permitting experience, it fell by the wayside and was never resuscitated when the time came to build."

A Mix of Homes with "Activatable" Spaces

Prospect New Town features a rich mix of single-family detached, attached and live/work homes, all alley-loaded. The first phase of predominantly traditional houses is anchored by luxury townhomes of Italianate, Beaux Arts and Tudor styles around a triangular park. Across from the park is the Rib House, a brick barbeque restaurant with outdoor patio—Prospect's only commercial building not a part of the downtown, which itself is only a five-minute walk away.

Elsewhere, the contemporary architecture presents a colorful, almost industrial texture–an "elemental, purposeful feel that many of Prospect's houses evoke, with stripped down facades, bold color choices and dramatic roof forms and building volumes," says Bressi. Additionally, one required architectural element has "generated a layer of unexpected richness: building fronts must have porches, stoops, or balconies. Every house in Prospect seems to have its hand out, reaching to the street or the sky. Mediating between the house and street is a zone of activatable spaces–porches, steps, terraces, decks, dormers, towers," he says.

Prospect will consist of up to 610 predominantly custom housing units at buildout. The single-family homes range from 1,800 to over 5,000 square feet on lots that average 4,800 square feet, though two lots may be purchased together for larger homes. Some 65% of the houses include a 400- to 700-square-foot studio or carriage home above the garage, as well.

Initial prices ranged from $285,000 to $500,000, compatible with Boulder County's high-priced housing, and then peaked at more than $1 million before the economic downturn. As of December 2011, Prospect homes have a wider price range due to the Solar Village Prospect's smaller units. An 809-square-foot unit sold for $99,000 in October 2011, a 2,260-square-foot live/work unit near the town center lists for $285,000 and a 5,038-square-foot home built in 2005 recently sold for $550,000. The median sales price in November 2011 was $345,000 for all residential units. As of November 2011, there were 295 residential units at Prospect.

Despite the attention Prospect's contemporary architecture has brought to the neighborhood, Wallace believes the modernist homes "haven't quite hit the mark" for Longmont's real estate market. "The downside to contemporary," he says, "is that in doing whatever you want, the neighborhood becomes iconoclastic, which can hurt individual home sales." New Urbanist town planner Jeff Speck wonders whether Prospect's slow sales are a result of the project's suburban location. "I have always been curious about the potential misalignment between the self-image of the modernist homebuyer and the self-image of the person who makes the choice to live in a new subdivision, complete with its homeowners association and welcoming committees," he says. "In my experience, the majority of modernist buyers are chasing either the dream of urban pioneering or the dream of communing with nature. They tend to be somewhat iconoclastic and countercultural and not interested in either the conformity or the middle-of-the-road suburbanism implied by joining a new subdivision, even if it is a beautifully designed village. The modernist segment of the homebuyer market is small. The sub-segment of those modernists who also run against type by being 'joiners' seems too small to populate more than a few acres of real estate in any region."

Duany doesn't disagree with Speck's assessment, but wonders whether sales have suffered because of the modernist aesthetic or "from the sometimes impractical floor plans" the modernist designs can create. "The extent is impossible to determine," he concludes. For his part, Wallace believes that the houses' floor plans are the primary reason sales have been sluggish.

"I fear that the intentions behind our primary design experiment in Prospect–to provide variety–are obscured by the modern versus traditional debate," says Sofield. "Those intentions are threefold: to maximize any given site's potential and minimize its constraints, to appeal to the broadest cross-section of buyers and to enhance the development's sense of urbanity."

In order to meet city approval, Prospect was required to designate 10% of its housing as "affordable" to people who make 80% or

The live/work streetscapes at Prospect often feature traditional materials, including dark brick and exposed wood, with modernist, pedestrian-oriented architecture.

less of the Boulder County median income. Implementing the affordable housing mandate would have been tricky. "Nothing out here will be permanently affordable," admitted Wallace at the project's inception. The affordability requirement was met in the first filing through carriage houses; since then and until 2011, however, Longmont had changed the affordability rule so that residential units must be owner-occupied. Prospect was grandfathered into the original clause. "Otherwise," says Sofield, "meeting the affordability requirement, particularly for the single-family homes, would have been nearly impossible." In 2011, Longmont eliminated its affordability requirements altogether "since more than 30% of the homes on the market are now affordable by city definitions," says Wallace.

Prospect's approach to housing has always been one of flexibility. "If we find the townhouses are in more demand than single-family homes," said developer Bruns during the project's first phase, "we can regroup some single-family lots and make townhouses out of them. That's part of our neighborhood. We're going to go with what makes sense: what's in demand and works best for this community." One example is the Cottage Court, a set of four smaller homes that will share a common central courtyard and feature permeable paving and small, open yards. The four homes will be built on two small, joined lots and are expected to list at between $325,000 and $345,000.

Another project that demonstrates the flexibility of Prospect's land plan and regulations is a net-zero energy house currently nearing completion. Built on the development's southern edge, its primary axis is oriented east-west to optimize solar orientation. To achieve this–and gain larger side setbacks than are typical–its owner purchased two rectangular lots whose long dimension is oriented north-south, and the house straddles the former common lot line. The design team, led by Sofield, was reassembled from the group of students he taught at the University of Colorado, for its entry in the 2007 Solar Decathlon. The house's owner is a board member of the nonprofit Solar Electric Light Fund and the house will function as both her primary residence and a meeting space and

13

Prospect's downtown, as viewed from its town square: the mixed-use buildings include retail space at ground level and office and residences on the second and third levels.

demonstration facility for her organization.

From January through November 2011, Wallace could not sell any new lots because the local bank holding the loan on the project had folded. Wallace believed that the bank would be bailed out by another local financial institution, but by the time he discovered that wouldn't be the case, he was unable to transfer the financing to another lender. In January 2010, the FDIC took over the bank's debt and, toward the end of the year, bundled the Prospect loan with other debt, selling the package to another financial institution—even though Wallace had tried to work with the FDIC to release or transfer the loan so lot sales could begin again. In November 2011, the new lender confirmed its support for the project and Prospect once began selling lots and new houses.

Prospect's Downtown: Convenient and "Truly Unique"

Downtown Prospect is comprised of a series of two- and three-story buildings with street-level retail and second- and third-floor residences surrounding a town square. In reviewing the community for the Congress for the New Urbanism, designer Stephen Filmanowicz makes a note of "something for which Prospect deserves more attention–the easy and natural way that mixed uses continue and taper off as one moves from the formal town center to streets of more residential character, just as they would if one were moving from a busy street to a less-busy street in a long-established neighborhood."

Downtown buildings have been added slowly over the project's development, to allow for the accumulation of a critical mass of residents necessary to support the businesses. The first mixed-use commercial building was completed in 2000 and the newest was completed in 2009, with lots south of the town square planned for additional mixed-use and live/work buildings. The most recent addition is Ion Place, a three-story building designed by architect Kimble Hobbs and located to the east of the town square. On the street level, the building hosts a restaurant space and two retail spaces. On the second level, office/flex space is provided. On the third level, three luxury residences ranging from 2,400 to 3,000 square feet were built. The building is 100% wind-powered and LEED-certified.

Located across Ionosphere Street from Ion Place is Solar Village Prospect, a renewable energy-powered, mixed-use building with four retail and restaurant spaces on the first floor and 16 lofts, flats and two-story condos designed around a central courtyard. The architecturally distinct building–designed by Tavel Weise Architecture and Urban Design and named the 2006 Exemplary Solar Building of the Year–takes advantage of passive solar orientation and design. It includes concrete floors for thermal mass; a 21-panel solar-heated, in-floor radiant heat and domestic hot water system; solar photovoltaic panels mounted on awnings that also provide window shade; a high-efficiency central boiler; and wind power. Additionally, it features R-21 wall and R-90 roof efficiency ratings, low- or no-VOC interior finishes, non-toxic cellulose insulation, bamboo flooring and recycled carpet. The residential units range in size from 760 to 1,250 square feet, with between one and three bedrooms and one and two-and-a-half bathrooms. For the first year, residents also received free yoga classes at Solar Yoga, located in the building.

According to Solar Village LLC cofounder Mark Kostovny, "Unlike single-family home owners, many condo owners feel like there is nothing they can do to lower their utility costs while maintaining the comfort levels they want. . . . Solar Village Prospect was the first project of its kind in the Colorado region and its occupants have enjoyed some of the lowest bills ever seen."

Though a few downtown restaurants have closed, new establishments have replaced them and as of December 2011, despite the economic downturn, Prospect's commercial space is sold out. Of the 39 commercial spaces built so far, all but three are occupied. Restaurants include Two Dog Diner, Vic's Espresso, Big Daddy Bagels, Your Place or Vine wine bar and Comida Cantina, plus the Rib House, located two blocks from the town square. Downtown services and other businesses range from pilates and insurance to a barbershop, Tenacity Wine Shop, yoga boutique and several gift and craft shops, including Kimes' Nest Antiques. "We have a convenient and truly unique downtown," she says. "My business since opening four years ago has been excellent. But we need a few more restaurants for the downtown to really shine."

Prospect's business owners have joined forces thanks to support from the 3/50 Project, a national organization that promotes "saving the brick and mortars our nation is built on." They have created the DestinationProspect.com site, which promotes community businesses and provides a calendar of events.

In addition to the retail and service establishments, the community features several artists who work out of studios in their homes or in live/work units designed specifically to meet their artistic needs, including such entities as Spruce Jewelry, Susan Wechsler International Mosaics and Brenda Ferrimani Dream Art Studio. The artists have likewise joined together–as the Prospect Artists Association, which, among other activities, hosts tours of Prospect's studios.

Wallace believes that Prospect's downtown finally has enough business and energy to be sustainable. "I really feel that it's come together this summer," he said in September 2011. "There are enough residents and successful businesses to call this a downtown." There's no denying the energy of the town center. It's especially apparent on a mild Monday evening, when hundreds of residents gather together in the park to listen to a local band play while food trucks from Boulder and Longmont pull onto the grass and serve tacos and brick-oven pizza. This gathering is a tradition that began in the summer of 2011. In Longmont as in Boulder, food trucks are not allowed to sell food on city streets. Prospect's town square, however, is

Celebrating community: Prospect's Monday evening "Gourmet Food Trucks" gatherings, featuring a mix of food trucks, produce sellers, and live music, have been a big hit.

Photo: Simmons Buntin

private land, so a dozen or more trucks, plus one or two local farmers, set up an hour before sundown to serve up local fare. "We're their most successful venue," says Sofield, "and it's a great way to celebrate community."

From Food Trucks to Historic Preservation: Amenities and Community

Prospect offers a variety of amenities to go along with that community. Beyond the town square, with its new concrete stage for the Monday "Gourmet Food Trucks" gatherings and a weekend farmer's market, Prospect features a playground every bit as eclectic as the neighborhood's architecture, a community garden, a series of formal parks and smaller pocket parks, plazas, a network of secondary landscaped pedestrian paths and a swimming pool.

In 2003, Wallace worked with Historic Boulder, Inc., to relocate the Johnson's Corner building from the Longmont Main Street corner (where it was slated to be demolished) to be used as the pool clubhouse. The

two-story art deco gas station and lunch counter was built in 1937 and designed by acclaimed Denver architect Eugene Groves. It is renowned because it was the only establishment in Longmont to serve minorities at a time when "Whites Only" signs appeared regularly in store windows. It is also mentioned in Jack Kerouac's *On the Road.*

Though Historic Boulder contributed $150,000 toward relocation and Wallace planned to spend another $300,000 to renovate it, the building sits unrestored by the swimming pool, the result of a shady building mover. As he relocated the building to the neighborhood, the mover drove across all of the surrounding unbuilt lots before unloading the structure. Then he placed a lien on those lots, claiming he was due $50,000 more than the agreed price. By the time the dispute was settled, Wallace had used $150,000 of the funding originally slated for renovation to pay for litigation and settlement fees. Though it remains unused, the precast concrete building adds another compelling architectural element

Photo: Simmons Buntin

Prospect New Town is a community designed for residents of all ages.

to the community.

Architecture and design not only bring a distinct aesthetic to Prospect; they also bring residents together. At its inception, developer Bruns noted that Prospect's design "addresses the social issues that are totally lost in suburbia." Resident Karen Benker, who moved to Prospect in 2002 from suburban Denver, agrees. "The architecture is fun," she says in *The Denver Post*, "but to purchase a home here, people have to be community-oriented–they have to have a desire to get to know their neighbors." Given the wide variety of well attended community activities–wine tastings, book club, New Year's Eve dinner, ice cream socials, welcome committee and an active neighbors' email discussion list, to name just a few–neighbors are passionate about getting to know their neighbors, and about Prospect.

Conclusion: Redefining the Shapes and Textures of Community in Colorado

Prospect New Town's evolving character

continues to draw more and more people to the community–not just to visit, but to live and conduct business. With its cohesive town plan, Prospect's land use provides a strong and distinct street network. Add in the neighborhood's mature landscaping, a funky mix of building types and styles and colors, a small but thriving downtown, and residents who care deeply for their place, and it's not difficult to see that Prospect is both a result of, and a contributor to, what Sofield calls "the emerging sensibility of the place itself."

"This is like a great big classroom," said Wallace early in the project's life. A dozen years later, Prospect New Town continues to offer a hands-on course of how to redefine the shapes and textures of community for the Colorado Front Range, and beyond.

DEFINING SUCCESS
Q&A with Kiki Wallace, Developer, Prospect New Town

What was the largest obstacle to obtaining project approval or buy-in and how was it overcome?

The largest obstacle in obtaining approval for Prospect was the new city manager and the community development director who detested New Urbanism. Luckily, not understanding protocol, I built up support for the development by calling city council members directly and educating them about the New Urbanism before submitting the project for approval and also partnering with local developer, Dale Bruns, as a mentor who understood how to manage city staff opposition.

What is an unexpected delight or success from the project?

Being able to let my seven- and nine-year-olds go to the stores alone, and watch Prospect evolve into a real place with equal buy-in from all owners, renters and visitors. The social aspects really do work, which is always amazing to me as well as the residents.

What hasn't lived up to expectations or has required unanticipated change?

Most people demand compliance with the rules and regulations for their neighbors but then fight the requirements when applied

to them. Residents, for the most part, really love the homeowners association aspect, which I find baffling. They feel it gives them a level of protection from the general buying public by setting standards for maintenance and architectural compliance, thereby controlling or weeding out those pesky people who they perceive as a threat. I am horrified by the elite attitude that HOAs instill in residents and feel it is one of the most destructive quasi-judicial forms of government our society faces.

What continues to challenge or surprise you with the project?

I return to my concern over HOAs: I have in effect been forced to change my attitude from one of "I don't care what anyone does in the neighborhood with their own property once it is occupied," to "It is your neighborhood: let's freeze it in a time capsule." It makes me really appreciate that "the best master plan" is that we all eventually die.

How do you define and measure success?

I define success as each one of us improving the world we live in–and hopefully leaving it a little better off at our departure, with people rising above the fragments of society. Success can probably only truly be measured in the rearview mirror by other people.

NorthWest Crossing
Bend, Oregon
by Ken Pirie, AICP, LEED AP ND

Viewsheds are an important component of design at NorthWest Crossing.

Photo: NorthWest Crossing

The state of Oregon has received national attention for its progressive approach to land-use planning. Spurred by an engaged citizenry, this planning has contributed to some uniquely livable and compact cities and towns, with bustling streets and walkable neighborhoods interwoven with restored natural areas. Even in fast-growing suburban areas, places like Hillsboro's Orenco Station are much-studied and admired for their contributions to a new model of residential development that aims to create complete, walkable and connected new communities with a mix of uses, housing types, parks and schools.

While the personal commitment of many Oregonians to environmental protection has played an important role in promoting sensible urban planning, many would agree that the state government has also influenced this kind of development. Statewide land-use and transportation regulations and urban growth boundaries are official attempts to encourage higher densities close to revitalized urban centers, reduce state roadway construction costs and protect the valuable agricultural land and wild landscapes that make the state so distinctive.

Some private developers struggle with these mandates, while others embrace them to create unique new communities worthy of

The NorthWest Crossing former tree farm site, shown here prior to development, features a mix of constraints and opportunities around natural features.

attention. One such community is NorthWest Crossing in the central Oregon city of Bend.

Local History: Bend, Oregon

Bend is a rapidly growing former mill town of over 80,000 on the Deschutes River. Outdoor enthusiasts and retirees from across the country are attracted to its mild climate and high desert landscapes with top-quality skiing, hiking, golfing and fly fishing accessible in close proximity. Its recreational attractions and booming population have created opportunities in the housing market for both vacation homes and traditional single-family neighborhoods. The developers of NorthWest Crossing, Brooks Resources Corporation and Tennant Family LP, set out under the banner of a new company, West Bend Property Company LLC (WBPC), to accommodate a portion of the city's surging growth by planning a new neighborhood 1.5 miles from downtown Bend.

Brooks Resources is an outgrowth of Brooks-Scanlon, Inc., a large timber company

that once dominated the Bend region with five mills, the last of which closed in 1994. With significant timberland holdings in and around Bend, the company recognized the potential to enter into real estate development and found early success with the retirement and vacation community of Black Butte Ranch and other resort developments such as Mount Bachelor Village. In possession of almost 500 acres of relatively flat tree farm at the western edge of Bend, but within the city's state-mandated urban growth boundary, WBPC decided in 1999 to develop the site in an innovative, environmentally responsive way.

Growth and Controversy Set the Scene for NorthWest Crossing

Bend's explosive growth was not without its share of detractors. Many residents, alarmed at the rapid pace of the city's expansion in the late 1990s and increasing traffic congestion, pushed city planners and politicians to consider a moratorium on growth. Sensing that such a moratorium would challenge plans for their property, West Bend Property Company partners Mike Hollern, Kirk Schueler and Mike Tennant became facilitators of a rigorous public conversation by sponsoring charrettes to discuss controversial public projects (such as a new bridge crossing the Deschutes River). They hosted "Building a Better Bend" lectures featuring national smart growth personalities, assisted with the expansion of the High Desert Museum and located their offices close to the city's historic downtown in a renovated convent.

Forming a "consortium" with other westside developers, West Bend Property Company was able to ease concerns about growth on their property and associated impacts on infrastructure by agreeing to provide a coordinated network of well-landscaped streets and roundabouts, as well as schools, parks and utility lines. Using roundabouts, which were unprecedented in Bend (and Oregon, for that matter), avoided over-scaled five-lane, signalized intersections on new and retrofitted streets.

The consultant team for this project, hired after an invited design competition, was led by Portland's Walker Macy Landscape Architects, which had a relationship with Brooks Resources dating from the 1970 plan for Black Butte Ranch. Fletcher Farr Ayotte Architects assisted with building massing and commercial parking studies, while civil engineering was led by WH Pacific. Much of the team had collaborated on the earlier Orenco Station west of Portland and had thus already tested some of the New Urbanist design techniques that the client was envisioning for NorthWest Crossing.

Shaping the New Urbanist Design

NorthWest Crossing, like many New Urbanist developments across the U.S., employs design principles derived from beloved older neighborhoods. These include a grid of interconnected narrow streets, a mix of architectural styles and shops, and parks and schools within walking distance of most homes. The consultant team

JUST THE FACTS

- Located on the west side of Bend, Oregon.
- 486 acres total at buildout; 380 acres developed so far
- Average density: 5.2 du/acre (through present development)
- 1,200 homes at buildout, including single-family and multifamily; 735 homes built so far
- 41 acres of neighborhood and community parks plus 12 acres of natural open space
- 64 acres of school property
- 88 acres of mixed-employment and commercial area
- Awards include 2006 Most Successful Development in Oregon by *BUILD-ERnews*, 2007 National Association of Homebuilders Green Building Award, 2007 ULI Development of Excellence, 2008 PCBC Master-Planned Community of the Year and 2010 *Natural Home Magazine*'s Top Green Neighborhoods in the Nation
- Developed by West Bend Property Company
- Design team: Walker Macy Landscape Architects, Fletcher Farr Ayotte, Urbsworks and WH Pacific

was familiar with these elements but found that some education was needed to convince city planners and other regulators of the benefits of such ideas. The developers believed that adhering to these "new" design principles would result in safe, attractive, walkable, tree-lined streets and neighborhoods that would likely encourage greater social interaction and–even more importantly–would be a compelling marketing tool, attracting a range of residents, from young couples to retirees. City

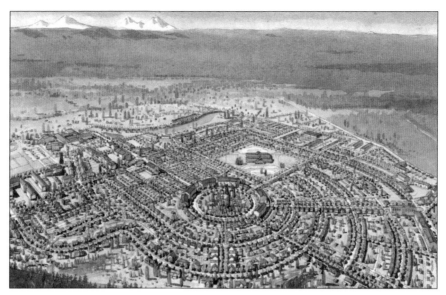

Graphic: Martin Kyle-Milward

An aerial rendering of NorthWest Crossing.

planners have confirmed NorthWest Crossing as a model for how they'd like to see the city grow by adopting many of its design provisions into the city's overall zoning code.

With the development team's desire to build a neighborhood that felt like a seamless extension of existing West Bend neighborhoods, which predominately feature a vernacular Craftsman style of home, the Portland firm of Urbsworks was commissioned to draft a Prototype Handbook for NorthWest Crossing. These "pattern books" are commonly used by New Urbanist town planners, inspired by the format of early 1900s catalogs of house types produced by companies like Sears Roebuck & Co. NorthWest Crossing's Handbook is intended to provide a lasting "form-based" land-use code and a basic architectural framework for the project. It includes detailed design guidelines for both builders and architects.

An associated new overlay zone for the City of Bend's zoning code was crafted to enact the Handbook's vision. The most significant deviations from the city's existing code center on street standards, auxiliary dwelling units,

commercial parking standards and specific overlay districts for mixed-use residential and live/work development. The changes made to the city code have been subsequently employed by other developments.

The Homes at NorthWest Crossing: A Homebuilders' Lottery

West Bend Property Company was established to develop a master-planned community, not to build homes. But it maintained control over the architectural feel of the project through a number of innovative mechanisms. The North-West Crossing Architectural Rules and Design Guidelines serve as the guiding documents for all construction in the community. Homebuilders interested in purchasing lots were pre-screened to ensure a high quality of work and financial stability, as well as connections to the local economy. Then, small numbers of lots were allocated via lottery to no more than 25 prequalified builders, and no builder had more than a handful of adjacent lots.

The result is a fascinating range of customized home designs on each block, with

A NorthWest Crossing single-family home streetscape featuring Cratsman-style architecture, new and mature trees, and mountain views.

builders competing with each other to produce superior homes that preserve mature trees. The streetscape is thus much more reminiscent of a traditional neighborhood than more homogeneous conventional subdivisions built by production builders.

"We started with NorthWest Crossing and completed one of the first homes in the development," says Greg Welch, president of Greg Welch Construction. "There are good quality builders who pay strict attention to detail and there has been some great competition among the builders to also create new ideas and an eclectic neighborhood. All in all, we are pleased to be a part of the Builders' Guild involved with NorthWest Crossing."

NorthWest Crossing was designed to include a broad range of lots and housing types and sizes. Housing options include single-family homes, duplexes, accessory dwellings, townhomes and condominiums, multi-family apartments, cottages and apartments above commercial/retail uses. This diversity was intended to encourage a community that reflects the demographic composition of the

area and that would also allow residents to continue to live in the neighborhood as their lifestyles and needs change. In terms of market absorption, NorthWest Crossing has matured in a period of unprecedented real estate demand in central Oregon. NorthWest Crossing even continued to sell homes during the recent crash in the real estate market, albeit at a slower pace than it did previously. According to WBPC, homebuyers anecdotally report that they are attracted to these homes because of the neighborhood amenities such as protected trees, walkable streets and high-quality construction.

To further ensure that NorthWest Crossing continues to be developed and maintained to the highest aesthetic standards, additional architectural guidelines have been established, based on the Prototype Handbook. The Declaration of Covenants, Conditions and Restrictions (CC&Rs), developed by WBPC, is intended to protect existing homeowners and supplement the Prototype Handbook's guidelines for new homes and other buildings within NorthWest Crossing. In the absence of

23

Photo: West Bend Property Company

NorthWest Crossing's architectural guidelines apply to both residential and commercial spaces, ensuring consistency in design across the community.

a homeowners association, an application and approval process directs new designs through the community's Architectural Review Committee.

The fact that NorthWest Crossing has no homeowners' association is also significant. The community's public spaces are all owned and maintained by the public. Consequently, there are no homeowners' association dues (although the retail districts have small associations to maintain decorative lighting). As a representative of Brooks Resources said, "NorthWest Crossing makes the statement that a second form of government (i.e., homeowners' association) does not have to be formed in order for residents to enjoy a higher standard of living."

A Design Rooted in Place

With a landscape architect as lead master planner, NorthWest Crossing was designed to respect the site's natural landscape and mountain views. Trees and rimrock topography were preserved wherever possible. Steep slopes were mapped and left as open land or conserved in easements on deep lots. An old pumice mine on the site will be transformed into a new central open space amenity in a future phase. The urban form of the land plan was also influenced both by connections to existing adjacent streets and solar orientation.

The plan is organized around a large central circular park (Compass Park), creating a distinctive heart to the community and establishing the urban form for streets and blocks. A detailed survey of the mature second-growth ponderosa pines on the site—an old tree farm—was integrated into the site planning process, with blocks, roads and lot lines laid out to preserve as many large specimens as possible. As a result, mature trees throughout the community lend the impression of a much older, more established neighborhood. Many of the trees are on private lots where new homes have not only been designed to minimize grading and thus root disturbance in the well-drained

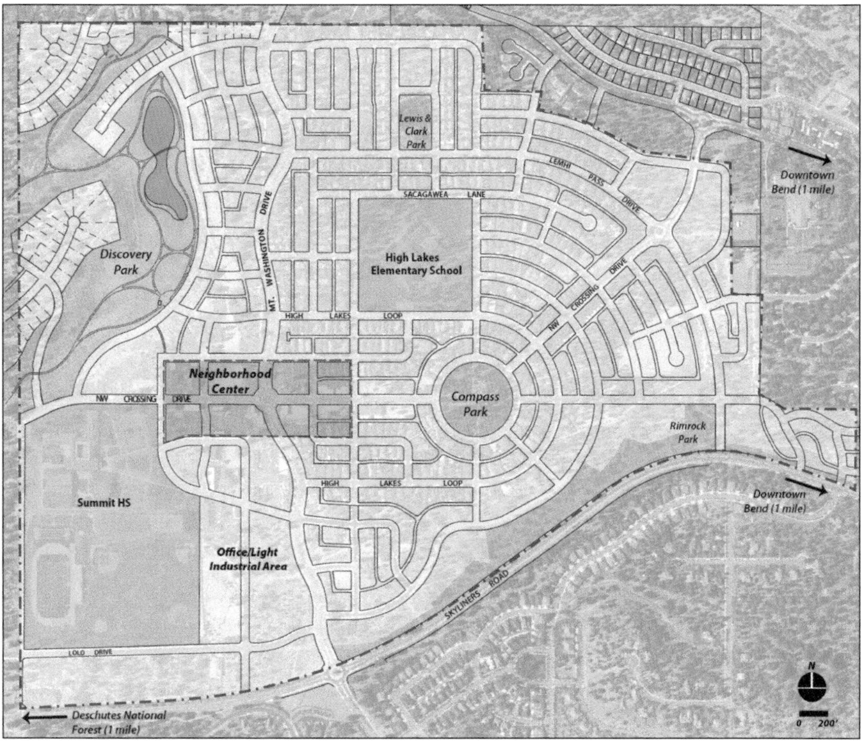

Graphic: Walker Macy

The NorthWest Crossing site plan.

volcanic soil, but also have often physically incorporated the trees into the design of eaves and porches.

NorthWest Crossing also added a community garden with 59 raised-bed plots near Discovery Park Lodge, a senior housing facility. The garden is open to community residents, businesses, and the public. Plots may be rented for $30 per season. Two plots are reserved for local restaurants. A compost system is in place, along with a picnic table and shade area for gardeners to gather. Educational opportunities are offered through the community's association with the Oregon State University Extension Service.

A Connected Community Meeting Everyday Needs

NorthWest Crossing is intended to meet many of its residents' daily business, personal and recreational needs without compelling them to travel outside of the community. Commercial buildings, schools and parks are designed to serve local residents and to draw users from the larger regional area. To encourage neighborhood-based school, a high school site was sold at a deep discount to the local district and an elementary school site was donated. The completed schools are located so that many children can walk from their homes on a complete network of sidewalks. Residents can also use playfields after school hours.

A grid street system at NorthWest Crossing provides good connectivity, while narrowed street sections, curb extensions, on-street parking bays and roundabouts slow vehicle speeds and accommodate pedestrians throughout the development. Unsightly but necessary

25

NorthWest Crossing's commercial areas provide easy access by car, bicycle, or foot.

Photo: West Bend Property Company

infrastructure facilities, such as transformers and utility boxes, are installed in alleys. An extensive network of trails and separated sidewalks connects schools, neighborhood parks, commercial facilities and job centers.

Mt. Washington Drive, which links NorthWest Crossing with the rest of Bend's west side, was designed with a series of roundabouts and medians and was intended to be a parkway fronted with homes. The concept of serving these "alley-loaded" homes with on-street visitor parking on the boulevard met with significant resistance from City of Bend Public Works staff, however. They saw the route as a significant arterial that, under conventional models of traffic engineering, is treated solely as a conduit for automobiles instead of an attractive, tree-lined and walkable thoroughfare. After their initial resistance, city staff members softened their position and allowed parking bays to be cut into the boulevard.

With a range of public parks and an extensive trail system, NorthWest Crossing is close to central Oregon's many outdoor recreational areas. Residents can bicycle or walk into downtown Bend and along the Deschutes River, on trails and dedicated lanes; or they can

head west into the still-wild public fringe of the city. Just five minutes away is Shevlin Park, a 500-acre, city-managed forest with old-growth pines along Tumalo Creek, which flows out of the Deschutes National Forest.

A Neighborhood Center

Wide sidewalks, park benches and attractive landscaping define NorthWest Crossing's neighborhood center, offering what will eventually be a blend of restaurants, retail, offices and second-story housing designed by a number of different architects. The neighborhood center is currently home to a café, wine bar, boutique, caterer, bank, two salons and three restaurants as well as the NorthWest Crossing Sales Center. The neighborhood center serves as the civic heart of the development as host to regular events such as spring and summer festivals, street festival, concerts, and farmers markets.

A unique live/work townhome project has been developed near the neighborhood center. The 7 townhomes consist of retail and commercial street-level spaces, with living space above. The location of the live-work units provides a transition from strictly commercial

Photo: Walker Macy

Townhomes at NorthWest Crossing provide a lower-priced option for families while maintaining the neighborhood's distinct Northwest design.

buildings into full residential areas. Each two-story townhome unit consists of 600 square feet of commercial space on the lower level, with 1,300-1,600 square feet of living space above. Use of the commercial space is restricted to services, such as a preschool, physician's office and massage therapist. Higher densities have also been inserted into the project in other, subtle forms such as duplexes and smaller cottage-like homes. A senior housing facility with 54 dwelling units was completed adjacent to the neighborhood center and a community park.

A second, larger commercial area–located adjacent to Mt. Washington Drive–is reserved for professional offices and clinics. A mixed-employment area is developing in a campus setting to serve research and development and light manufacturing businesses. It also provides employment opportunities for local residents.

Sustainability through the Earth Advantage Program

The community of NorthWest Crossing is designed to support sustainable development practices beyond the obvious benefits of a walkable community with plentiful open space. The cornerstone of NorthWest Crossing's environmentally friendly objectives is participation in the Earth Advantage program, operated by the Earth Advantage Institute. The program addresses building issues such as energy efficiency, recycling, building materials, landscaping, water and indoor air quality.

"We see the Earth Advantage program as a critical component in fulfilling our commitment to sustainable building practices," says WBPC General Manager David Ford. "While the majority of our existing homes are already Earth Advantage certified, we have now taken the next step by requiring adherence to these

NorthWest Crossing's town center hosts several events per year, including well-attended concerts.

Photo: Brooks Resources

important standards."

Homes must comply with the following guidelines:

- Resource-efficient building materials from framing to finish work, including the incorporation of recycled materials
- Indoor air quality through the use of less toxic construction materials and floor coverings, plus air filtration systems
- Environmentally responsible building practices with less toxic outdoor wood, water efficiency and proper disposal of construction materials
- Energy efficiency through improved duct sealing, high-efficiency windows and heating systems, efficient lighting and appliances and shade trees

As an additional sign of its commitment to sustainable building practices, the development team installed photovoltaic panels on the roof of the NorthWest Crossing Sales Center and on a large commercial building nearby.

"By taking the next step and requiring that all its homes adhere to Earth Advantage standards, NorthWest Crossing has shown its commitment to community growth that has less impact on the environment and important benefits for homeowners," says Duane Woik, new construction consultant for Earth Advantage. "We are glad to see a development take these steps toward environmental sustainability, as well as healthier indoor air, increased comfort and more value for home buyers."

Conclusion: A New Model for Sustainable Urban Growth

NorthWest Crossing provides a new model for sustainable urban growth in a rapidly growing region. The community is strikingly rooted in its landscape and urban context. Its early financial success and public popularity have inspired other builders and developers to mimic the New Urbanist design philosophy and city and regional planners are able to point to NorthWest Crossing as a concrete example of some of the smart growth design principles they espouse in their plans.

Homebuyers continue to be attracted to the community, even in the face of a difficult local real estate market, because it imparts a sense of permanence and quality. NorthWest Crossing also provides integrated amenities not found in other neighborhoods, such as schools, retail, parks and trails, as well as a sense of civic commitment to activities such as community gardens, a summer Saturday Farmers Market and music street festivals. The developers of NorthWest Crossing have succeeded in their determination to create a seamless extension of Bend, providing a new model for urban growth that rejects the standard, insular, placeless and "product-based" model that prevails too often in suburban growth.

DEFINING SUCCESS
Q&A with David Ford, General Manager, West Bend Property Company

What was the largest obstacle to obtaining project approval or buy-in and how was it overcome?

The biggest obstacle was securing the City of Bend's approval for a mixed-use development that the old development code did not allow. Significant time was invested in working with city planning staff and holding numerous open houses and public forums presenting a New Urbanist, smart growth, mixed-use development on Bend's west side to garner community support. Planning staff assisted in drafting a new section of the development code that would become the NorthWest Crossing Overlay Zone, a special planning district.

What is an unexpected delight or success from the project?

There are two. First, event marketing at NorthWest Crossing has pleasantly surprised us in terms of its ability to attract visitors and grow at a healthy rate year over year. Our goal with NorthWest Crossing is to provide a safe, healthy and enriching community in which to live, shop and recreate. One aspect to the success of reaching this goal has been the addition of our own neighborhood events and hosting citywide events that provide phenomenal exposure to the community. Criterium cycling events, concerts, movies in the park and street fairs have become highly anticipated events, with local businesses calling us to ask if they can participate and sponsor. The most recent event success has been the NorthWest Crossing Saturday Farmers Market. Marking year five in 2013, the market has grown from 20 vendors to over 50 and during the summer has become a favorite gathering place to visit friends and family, listen to live music and purchase fresh produce from farmers. The second delight is the NorthWest Crossing resident community garden. The garden has brought together a wide diversity of age groups within the community and has proven to be yet another example of true community spirit.

What hasn't lived up to expectations or has required unanticipated change?

The success of the NWX Business Association has not lived up to expectations. The developer is a participant in the association, but has decided not to take the lead role in managing this group. The association has had multiple leaders and turnover on its board and has struggled with its brand and an integrated marketing approach and message.

What continues to challenge or surprise you with the project?

The commercial aspect: the ability to recruit and retain local, successful businesses for the neighborhood center. While we certainly have our anchor tenants, the recent recession has wreaked havoc with lease rates and the sustainability of some businesses. We have also experienced a challenge in bridging Mt. Washington Drive, which bisects the property and creates east- and west-side businesses that don't yet have a cohesive feeling of community.

How do you define and measure success?

Retention of home values, continued home sales, continued lot sales, a healthy Builders' Guild and successful/profitable/sustainable businesses within our community. If our Builder Guild continues to buy lots, build homes and sell homes within a reasonable time frame, then I would say that is success! People want to live in NorthWest Crossing and they continue to visit, shop and buy real estate here, even despite the horrible recession and economic struggles we have faced in the last several years. Our events have grown every year and I would say that is a measure of our success in terms of attracting a growing audience and being a destination in Bend.

Lenox Village
Nashville, Tennessee
by Simmons B. Buntin

Photo: Shane Johnston

Lenox Village is Nashville's first traditional neighborhood development, changing the paradigm for planning mixed-use communities across the region.

Lenox Village, middle Tennessee's first full-scale neo-traditional neighborhood development, is nestled among wooded hills 13 miles south of downtown Nashville. The 208-acre development patterns itself after the traditional small Tennessee town, with a village commons, a variety of housing types in a predominantly Southern vernacular (ranging from condominiums to townhomes to distinct single-family homes) and a mixed-use "town center" bridging the primarily residential portion of the neighborhood with the commercial corridor along Nolensville Pike.

By turning an environmental constraint (a farm pond that had become habitat for the endangered Nashville crayfish) into an opportunity, and by subsequently restoring the pond to a natural stream with riparian habitat, Lenox Village developer Regent Development found an innovative solution to building a mixed-use neighborhood more responsibly on the land.

Traditional Design in a Suburban Setting

In 1998, Tennessee adopted smart growth legislation that required cities and counties to set 20-year coordinated urban growth boundaries. The Nashville Planning Department subsequently set a goal of reshaping regional planning policy to emphasize design and community participation in new development. The

31

JUST THE FACTS

- Located in southeast Nashville, Tennessee
- Nashville's first neo-traditional neighborhood development
- 208 acres
- Construction began in fall 2001; model homes opened in October 2002
- Town center construction began in 2005 and is being completed in phases–final buildout expected by 2016
- 1,200 single-family homes and townhomes, predominantly rear-loaded
- Town center features mixed-use buildings including a "lifestyle center," retail center, townhomes and condominiums
- 317 leased condominiums currently built, 184 in new building under construction and 220 more planned
- 75,000 square feet of retail, office and restaurant use, with another 9,000 to 15,000 square feet planned
- Covered parking structures and internal and retail-facing parking serve town center
- Eight live/work units located in heart of development
- Pre-existing big-box church
- Minimum of one acre of open space for every 30 single-family homes, including village green and other formal parks, pocket parks, 15-acre greenway with rehabilitated stream and undisturbed wooded hillsides
- Developed by Lenox Village, LLC
- Land plan and design overlay by Looney Ricks Kiss, Inc.
- Covenants, codes and restrictions by Doris S. Goldstein

smart growth framework for Lenox Village was thus established at both state and local levels.

Nevertheless, the community's neo-traditional design "was expensive, because we basically had to develop a code to enable the neo-traditional design and plan," says David McGowan, CEO of Regent Development. What resulted, with assistance from city planners, is the Lenox Village Urban Design Overlay (UDO), a form-based code that outlines everything from opportunities and constraints to the overall village vision; from the physical plan to the design review process.

In addition to the time required to develop the code, Regent Development struggled to secure financing early in the project, as no mixed-use project of this scale had been undertaken in the Nashville area. Gaining approval from the city's fire department for narrow streets with on-street parking, and obtaining public works buy-off on stream mitigation in lieu of traditional suburban retention areas, were also significant challenges–representative of those typically faced by the first neo-traditional developments.

The Nashville firm of Looney Ricks Kiss was hired to create the Lenox Village UDO, which was adopted by the City of Nashville in May 2001 and subsequently amended in July 2003. According to the UDO, Lenox Village is designed with "time-tested, traditional planning principles to provide a safe, integrated street network, neighborhood amenities and a sense of community." Village concepts include an interconnected street grid, alleys, pedestrian orientation, formal and informal public spaces, mixed-use village core, diverse residential building types and integrated housing typologies with compatible architectural design.

The goals of the UDO are to:
- Ensure the compatible integration of retail, office and institutional uses with residential uses
- Ensure the compatible integration of a variety of housing types, including

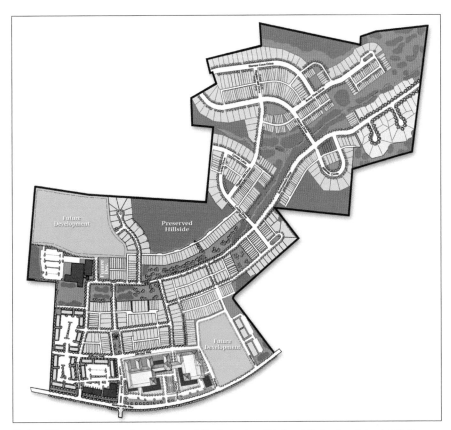

The Lenox Village site plan respects the curving, stream-fed landscape upon which the neighborhood was designed and built.

single-family homes, townhouses and multifamily, in order to accommodate the housing needs of a diverse population

- Maintain a scale and form of development that emphasizes sensitivity to the pedestrian environment
- Minimize the impact of automobiles into the setting through strategies such as shared parking, in which adjacent land uses having different peak-hour parking demands can share parking facilities
- Minimize the need for vehicles to travel on Nolensville Pike, or to travel significant distances on Nolensville Pike, by providing neighborhood commercial uses within close proximity to residents

- Achieve traffic calming benefits through an integrated street network providing options for traffic flow, the avoidance of excessively wide streets and the provision of on-street parking
- Provide for a variety of strategically-located and carefully-designed public and/or common spaces, including streets, greens, and informal open space
- Ensure the compatibility of buildings with respect to the specific character of their immediate context within the UDO boundary
- Encourage active ground floor uses, such as restaurants, shops and services, to animate the street within the town center

33

Photo: Simmons Buntin

Critical to Lenox Village was successful restoration of the onsite stream, which provides revitalized habitat for the endangered Nashville crayfish.

Lenox Village's Design Plan, a set of specific regulations and guidelines contained within the UDO, provides flexibility in the project's evolving design and uses, particularly in light of physical site constraints and the changing market. Variations in street and open space network design, individual block layout and dispersion of housing types are allowed, "so long that it meets the intent of the regulations and guidelines," says the Design Plan.

Lenox Village's Design Plan further ensures neo-traditional neighborhood design principles persist during design and development. For example, streets should terminate on axis with a primary building form, architectural feature, or open space at "T" intersections. On corner lots, architectural features should address both the front and side streets (using such elements as corner porches, side porches, and bay windows), and blank side walls should be avoided. The Design Plan also calls for key corner lots, axis terminations and other prominent residential parcels to be reserved for custom homes. The Plan also notes that

common pedestrian passages may be provided between parcels to allow exterior access from front to back of townhomes.

Open Space and Habitat Restoration

When considering the site, the design team realized that there are two major form-givers to the site: the wooded hillsides and the stream that feeds the pond. Lenox Village is tucked against the hillsides to the east, which buffer future development, provide wildlife habitat and create a sense of small town geography in the rolling Tennessee countryside.

The UDO notes how the stream bed, which is a tributary to Mill Creek, serves as a natural focal point within the site: "The stream provides a continuous public amenity with the potential to connect to the planned Mill Creek Greenway. Access and views down to this green spine become a major determinate of the street, lot and block orientation."

In removing the dammed, five-acre farm pond and rebuilding the stream to take advantage of and enhance the spine of the community, Regent Development was required to develop a habitat conservation plan describing the mitigation measures it would undertake to minimize the effects of the development on the Nashville crayfish. These endangered crayfish are limited to the Mill Creek watershed, taking cover under the limestone slabs, gravel and bedrock substrate of Mill Creek and its tributaries.

Once the habitat conservation plan was complete and a public involvement period ended, the U.S. Fish and Wildlife Service issued a federal incidental take permit, pursuant to the *Endangered Species Act*. To mitigate the impacts from draining the manmade farm pond, the developer agreed to install erosion control measures prior to draining the pond, to ensure minimal loss of sediment to the downstream channel. Regent Development also agreed to conduct a sweep of the pond prior to draining, to remove and relocate the Nashvill crayfish, and then conduct periodic sweeps through the full draining process. The developer reconstructed the stream channel by placing the channel in the pond bed, adding slabrocks to provide crayfish habitat and planting native vegetation in buffer zones along the stream bank. Finally, Regent Development strategically located retention basins (wet cells) throughout the property to collect runoff, allowing materials harmful to aquatic species to settle out before water is released to the stream.

Regent designated the reconstructed stream channel as greenspace in perpetuity, placing information signs along the channel. The developer also distributed informational flyers through the Lenox Village homeowners' association to residents. The flyers discussed the Nashville crayfish and ways residents can protect the species' habitat.

The 15-acre, stream-oriented greenway now serves as the predominant natural focal point of the community, as well as a means of stormwater management and flood control. In May 2010, for example, major flooding occurred across Nashville following extended heavy rains. Unlike other subdivisions, Lenox Village experienced no flooding because the greenway–which is designed to the 500-year flood threshold–absorbed all of the additional runoff.

In addition to natural open space such as preserved hillsides and mitigated streamway, Lenox Village incorporates a hierarchy of more formal public spaces. The Village Green is located near the town center and features a gazebo that has become one of the neighborhood's primary outdoor gathering places. The Green includes public art such as a bronze statue of a child climbing a water spigot, flower gardens and grass lawns. The Village Commons is set between Nolensville Pike and the commercial area. Like the Village Green, it is a formal park, but does not feature a gazebo or other community structure.

Neighborhood greens and other pocket parks are distributed throughout the neighborhood, often sited at the termini of streets, or along the streamway. These feature lawns, tot lots, playgrounds and formal seating areas. Lenox Village has a network of sidewalks and pedestrian paths throughout the neighborhood. The pathways also connect with adjacent neighborhoods. Additionally, the Lifestyle Center and other mixed-use buildings of the town center feature courtyards, gardens, verandas and small plazas.

A Small-Town Tennessee Vernacular Housing

Lenox Village has 1,200 units of single- and multifamily housing that initially ranged in price from $90,000 to more than $300,000. Homes include condominiums, townhomes, rear-loaded single-family homes, live/work units and front-loaded single-family homes, the latter located only on the neighborhood's periphery.

Townhomes and single-family homes are often sited around one of Lenox Village's many formal parks.

In fall 2011, one- and two-bedroom condominiums sold from $147,000, two- and three-bedroom townhomes sold from $159,900 to the $220,000s and single-family homes with up to four bedrooms sold from $240,000 to the $300,000s (resale). The UDO permits up to 900 attached and detached single-family residences, 500 multifamily residences and provides no limit for the number of live/work units—though only eight were constructed. There is no restriction on the mix of uses in the town center so long as design guidelines are met.

Condominiums and attached townhomes were big sellers early, since they were among the most affordable products of their type in the area. Multifamily housing is "intended to provide an opportunity for a more inclusive community." The desired goal is for renters to purchase property in the UDO over a period of time. McGowan and Sarah Loggins, manager of the Lenox Village Town Center Condominiums (leased condos in the Lifestyle Center), confirm that a number of renters have indeed upsized to townhomes and single-family homes in Lenox Village.

The economy weakened about the same time Regent Development began marketing its 273-unit, mixed-use Lifestyle Center in the town center, which held its grand opening in October 2009. The first residents moved in six months earlier since the residential portion of the building was completed before the street-level retail, restaurant, and office spaces. To accommodate the changing market—which saw a rapid decline in condo purchases—the developer decided to lease the condos. Rather than calling them apartments, however, Regent Development kept the term "condominiums" in order to market them as upscale. Accordingly, their amenities are among the finest in suburban Nashville and include assigned covered parking, private balconies, nine- and ten-foot ceilings, designer kitchens, courtyards and garden areas, business center and wifi-equipped cyber café, 24-hour fitness center, clubroom with catering kitchen, private movie theater and on-site temperature-controlled

Aerial view of Lenox Village's town center, including the mixed-use Lifestyle Center in the foreground.

storage space. In winter 2011-2012, the condos leased from $825/month for a 558-square-foot, one-bedroom studio to $2,100/month for a 1,800-square-foot, three-bedroom and three-bathroom unit, some $200 to $800 higher per month than other south Nashville luxury apartments, according to Apartment Home Living.

The Lifestyle Center is typically at 100% residency with a waiting list. This success encouraged the developer to bring another town center building online earlier than anticipated. According to McGowan, a 184-unit, all-residential building will anchor the southern corner of the town center—even though area developers have offered several times to purchase and build on that visible parcel. "Whether residential or commercial, we're picky about who we bring into Lenox Village," said McGowan in August 2011. Though he negotiated with a grocery store, chain fast food restaurants and a local YMCA to build in the town center, in the end they refused to meet Lenox Village's design guidelines, so

he declined. Instead, Regent Development is moving forward with the residential building, saving the parcel between the existing Lifestyle Center and the new residential building for a mixed use.

Though neither the Lifestyle Center nor the new residential building offer a pool, they do include water features–central gathering places where residents can gather even if they cannot swim. The new building will also include a dog park: Lenox Village has been voted Nashville's best pet-friendly neighborhood by *Nashville PAW* magazine several years running, after all. Like the Lifestyle Center, the new building's design will fit the village core, though with its massing, flat roof and façade, it may hold up as the town center's most urban design.

Detached single-family homes are predominantly two-story, most with six-foot-deep porches, high ceilings, tall windows and classic Tennessee small-town architecture. Many homes have sunrooms and lofts and feature either attached garages on narrow, landscaped

Townhomes and single-family homes are often raised above street level, providing privacy as well as an authentic, traditional streetscape.

Photo: Simmons Buntin

alleys or detached garages when located on the periphery. Foundations are raised 18 to 24 inches above sidewalk level to provide privacy, as front yards are shallow.

The UDO permits up to 25% of the homes and townhouses to have above-garage carriage units, limited to 600 square feet of conditioned space. These serve as offices, private guest quarters, exercise rooms and granny flats. About 10% of the homes were built with carriage units.

Home designs are regulated by the Village Design Codes and Regulating Plan, part of the UDO. The regulatory standards dictate such design parameters as front and side yard setbacks, minimum and maximum building height, minimum and maximum lot area, minimum lot depth, garage setback, driveway width, required length of street wall, minimum raised foundation, minimum first floor height and massing standards. In the town center, massing standards, window systems, public entrances, materials (primarily preventing vinyl siding) and glazing of façades at street level are all defined by building type: village

core, live/work and multifamily. Additionally, standards were included for parking (including shade trees and bicycle parking) and signs (setback, height and surface area). Finally, the UDO required that the developer form a design review committee to ensure consistent design beyond the parameters set forth in the UDO.

Design elements throughout the neighborhood include five-foot-wide sidewalks separated from narrow streets by landscaped strips, street trees and decorative lampposts. Streets and alleys are publicly maintained. Getting the city to agree to put Lenox Village's alleys in the public domain was no easy matter, according to McGowan. In the end, the development team convinced city planners that city-maintained alleys allowed for higher density—up to twice that of traditional, non-alley-loaded residential development. Higher density means more tax revenue based on the higher number of lots. Without city-funded alleys, McGowan said Lenox Village would not be able to support such a high density. From the developer's perspective, public streets and alleys also reduce

Street-level shops below leased condos in the Lifestyle Center.

Photo: Simmons Buntin

homeowners' association fees, since the HOA is not required to maintain them.

All homes were constructed by the developer's homebuilding division, Regent Homes. Homebuyers had the option of excluding garages, both in attached and detached single-family homes. The UDO only required that each home have two parking spaces. Though most single-family homes were built with two-car garages, about 40% of the attached townhomes have no garage—a measure that reduced the original cost of the townhome for the buyer.

An Arterial-Aligned Small Town Center

According to early Lenox Village marketing materials, "The Village Center is designed for a mix of activities that you would expect to find in a small town, so that its residents can perform many of their retail, commercial, civic and social activities in a convenient, accessible, central place." The mixed-use architecture likewise reflects that of a small Tennessee town, using authentic materials such as brick and stone on the façades and steps, and metal

roofing on the stoops and porches. The Design Plan also describes a vernacular style for shopfront signage.

The town center's design, as outlined in the UDO, "creates convenient automobile access for the entire community while allowing residents from the village and other adjacent neighborhoods to walk to neighborhood retail and services." Most of Lenox Village's residential areas are within a half-mile of the town center, which is adjacent to the neighborhood's primary entrance, on Nolensville Pike. More than 25,000 cars and regularly scheduled Nashville Metropolitan Transit Authority buses pass Lenox Village daily on the busy arterial that runs into Nashville from the southeast.

In addition to neighborhood retail and restaurants, the town center was designed to accommodate offices and multifamily housing. Taller and more compact multifamily condominiums are located adjacent to and above street-level retail, respecting the transect of the neighborhood's small-town scale. Attached townhomes bridge the northern half of the town center with the less-dense residential

39

The primary entrance to Lenox Village bridges Nolensville Pike's suburban architecture with the neo-traditional design of the rest of the neigbhorhood.

Photo: Simmons Buntin

areas of the neighborhood, while the main entrance provides direct access to the neighborhood's iconic Village Green and gazebo.

The town center is comprised of several mixed-use buildings constructed in phases beginning in 2005. The first phase–Village Shops–is a 7,906-square-foot retail strip that anchors the north edge of the town center and separates condominium and townhome buildings from Nolensville Pike. It bridges the more commonplace strip center designs found directly across Nolensville Pike with the neo-traditional vernacular of the neighborhood.

Lenox Village's first mixed-use building was the 8,437-square-foot Park View Building, completed in 2006. It includes 22 condos and a mix of businesses: investment and insurance firms, community cleaners, chiropractor, skin boutique, architectural services, wedding and events planning, massage and a bakery.

The third phase is the 12,655-square-foot, $7 million Regent Building, which anchors the north side of Lenox Village's main entrance with a distinctive clock tower. In addition to

retail, offices and underground parking, the building that features a large plaza and balconies "similar to the style of buildings found in Key West," says Regent Homes partner Rick Blackburn, includes 22 condos above street-level retail. Designed by the Nashville architectural firm of Kline, Sweeney and Associates, the building was completed in 2007. The Village Shops, Regent and Park View Buildings share a common, hidden parking lot with condominiums and townhomes.

Lenox Village's newest and largest mixed-use building is the $43 million Lenox Village Lifestyle Center, which offers 37,494 square feet of commercial in addition to 273 leased condos and 118 basement storage units. The four-story building fronts Nolensville Pike. A landscaped berm provides a visual barrier between the parking lot and the arterial in part because the Lifestyle Center is below grade. The berm also serves as a buffer to the noise created by traffic on the arterial. In addition to the street-level retail and restaurants, the building features a unique set of small suite spaces sharing a hallway and accessible from a single exterior door. The spaces are ideal for hair studios, designers and artisans and other small businesses that meet with one or two clients at a time. The Lifestyle Center is also home to a variety of restaurants, retail and offices.

Plans for the new, 184-unit all-residential building were submitted by Regent Development in August 2011 and the final phase of the town center is expected to be a mixed-use building that will include 220 condominiums and between 9,000 and 15,000 square feet of street-level retail. Like the condos in the Lifestyle Center, these units are likely to be leased but can be converted to purchasable units if the market changes. That building will be located between the current Lifestyle Center and the new residential building.

All streets within the town center are designed to encourage a pedestrian-oriented environment, with such features as wide sidewalks, outdoor dining patios, covered stoops and walkways, street furniture, shade trees and traditional streetlamps. Parking is internalized with the exception of a thin parking lot that fronts the Lifestyle Center. Additionally, the Lifestyle Center is built around a 500-car parking garage and five courtyards. Landscaped passages are provided between buildings to facilitate access from rear parking areas to the building fronts.

All of the residential units in the town center are EnergySmart—Regent's branding of the U.S. Environmental Protection Agency's Energy Star Home program, which certifies the units. The units meet or exceed Energy Star certification in four areas: energy efficiency, durability and sustainability, indoor environmental quality, and water efficiency. The resource efficiency applies to all buildings, residential and commercial, though certification and specific applications vary.

Additional design elements in the town center include covered parking, landscaped courtyards and garden areas, a regional architectural vernacular that includes the use of brick and wide porches on the first and second floors, open-air dining patios and public art.

Lenox Village's Hidden Gem: The Live/Work Shoppes on Sunnywood

Deep within the neighborhood–across from the creek and greenway and adjacent to townhomes that resemble traditional East Coast rowhomes–are the Shoppes on Sunnywood, a line of eight attached live/work units (5,500 square feet commercial in total). The architecture of the Shoppes is reminiscent of historic downtowns, as are some of the businesses, such as Mysteries & More Bookstore. Others are clearly modern-day: Dangerous Fret Guitars, Gen-X Studio, Niki G Fitness and the religious organizations One in Messiah Congregation and Visiting Orphans.

If the placement of the live/work units seems out of context, given their lack of visibility compared to town center businesses, that's because the city pushed for internal live/work placement more than the developer, according to McGowan. They don't have the traffic of other businesses in the neighborhood, which has resulted in slower sales and, in several cases, required the developer to further divide the buildings to separate commercial from residential, since the residential is in higher demand than the commercial in this location.

Getting Social: Lenox Village's Growing Events Scene

As the neighborhood has matured, it has hosted a growing number of local and regional events. The community's Cinco de Mayo in 2011, for example, drew between 600 and 800 neighbors. And while the South Nash Dash Community 5K was only started in 2009, it has already become a popular annual event. It begins each year in Lenox Village's wide greenway.

When control of the homeowners' association transferred from the developer to

View east from a bridge spanning the stream toward single-family homes and, on the left, the Shoppes on Sunnywood.

neighbors, much of the events management transferred with the organization. Homeowners continue to schedule activities. Additionally, Regent Development set up an advisory board of homeowners well before transitioning the HOA both to help with the transition and to ensure that homeowners had a clear communication channel with the developer as the community built out. Units in the Lifestyle Center do not fall under the HOA, and condominium owners and renters in the other portions of the town center are members of the Town Center Association, which is a part of the master association. The Lifestyle Center manager also facilitates events, such as the ChocolateFest that occurs on Valentine's Day.

In the summer of 2009, the Lenox Village Farmer's Market was created. During the summer, it is held on the Village Green and has been very successful, according to Lenox Village social director Kathy Niznik. In the cooler months, unlike other farmer's markets, the Lenox Village Farmer's Market moves indoors. "We hadn't planned on it," said Niznik in

2009. "We just decided since there was the space [in the town center], we might as well add it." Though the summer market is limited to food, the winter market features a mix of food vendors, crafters and artists.

A Successful New Suburban Community

Lenox Village has garnered praise since the beginning. In January 2004, for example, the Home Builders Association of Middle Tennessee awarded the master-planned community its Smart Growth Award. In 2002, the development won the AIA Merit Award for overall design from the Middle Tennessee Chapter of the American Institute of Architects.

Home sales, condominium leasing and retail leasing have been brisk–even in the economic downturn–because the homes are affordable and the neighborhood's design, amenities and accessibility offer an alternative to the typical suburban development of the area.

On average, new homes sold at a rate of

One of many gatherings at Lenox Village: Cinco De Mayo on the Village Green.

over 250 per year from 2002 through 2009. Today, condominiums in the project's Lifestyle Center lease quickly and businesses in the community's town center have thrived. The range of popular restaurants, particularly, has "made Lenox Village a regional destination," says McGowan.

"The idea that homes should be designed only for a family with two kids, a dog and an SUV only represents 30% of the market," McGowan said early in the project's development. "Lenox Village provides quality, affordable housing choices for people of all income levels and ages, as well as an important village retail center."

Nashville's mayor at the time, Bill Purcell, saw an even larger significance. Accepting the Lenox Village Smart Growth Award in 2004, he exclaimed, "Today, I receive this award for what it means to this neighborhood, Lenox Village and all that it stands for. You have many thanks for what you have done but more importantly the model that this provides for what we can do in this city and ultimately as a

model for the country."

Lenox Village in the Regional Context

The metropolitan Nashville region, like many burgeoning regions across the country, continues to sprawl. While Tennessee has landmark smart growth legislation and has found success with some mixed-use, pedestrian-oriented projects like Lenox Village, the challenge remains to encourage more Tennesseans to embrace smart growth.

In June 2004 the metropolitan governance organization, Nashville Metro, was awarded a grant from the Environmental Protection Agency to receive technical assistance from the Smart Growth Leadership Institute, a Washington, D.C.-based organization that works with municipalities and regional organizations to update existing subdivision and zoning standards. Their goal was to make the new standards "compatible and conducive to smart growth." A team of three professional planners was assigned to help the region work

Photo: Kirsty Barkley

Not all events are formal: hula hooping on the Village Green.

through outdated codes to create policy and regulation frameworks, review processes and design standards.

Lenox Village serves as a model for the new standards because, as much as it is a successful community for the developer and its residents, it is also a showcase for the entire metropolitan region. The project defined a new zoning district that makes it easier for developers to create neo-traditional neighborhoods in Nashville and across the region.

"Our goal is to provide housing, transportation and development choices for different needs and life stages," said Metro Planning Department director Rick Bernhardt. "To do so fairly and equitably, we must level the regulatory playing field and make it just as easy to develop a community with a mixture of retail, restaurants, townhomes and single-family homes as it is to build the conventional, single-use subdivision."

A standardized zoning category would help alleviate the costs and time involved in developing neo-traditional communities. McGowan notes that the planning and design process for Lenox Village cost about 20-25% more than a standard subdivision, and the process took much longer.

Said McGowan in 2004, "I highly recommend the city look into creating a zoning category called a TN (Traditional Neighborhood) or TND (Traditional Neighborhood Design) zone that someone can adopt and that would allow them to work on a property." Since that time, the City of Nashville has adopted two significant documents that bring the planning process closer to McGowan's goal: Specific Plan Zoning District, established in October 2005, and the Community Character Manual, adopted in August 2008 and amended to include neo-traditional-oriented Alternative Zoning Districts in May 2011.

The Specific Plan District allows for comprehensive project-based zoning with a "site-specific plan [that] shall establish specific limitations and requirements . . . so as to respect the unique character and/or charm of abutting neighborhoods and larger community in which the property is located." The Community Character Manual serves as a guiding document on land-use planning using the transect model. The Alternative Zoning District can work in concert with the manual and has the specific goal of creating "walkable neighborhoods through the use of appropriate building placement and bulk standards as an alternative to a zoning district that requires a site plan." Combined, these policies should enable Nashville planners, designers and developers to create more livable, mixed-use communities like Lenox Village.

Lenox Village also serves as a broader model. Published in November 2010, *Healing the Pikes* is a document that uses Nolensville Pike as a case study for reintegrating Nashville's historic pikes–the city's main thoroughfares–into the mixed-use urban fabric, making them "great streets" once again. In examining suburban centers, the authors state, "Lenox Village presents a hopeful step towards higher density residential communities, with some small retail and commercial development. Its success should serve as the framework for future suburban developments."

Conclusion: A Model for Suburban Neo-Traditional Neighborhood Developments

The success of Lenox Village demonstrates that challenges of policy, place and procedure can be overcome when developing greenfield mixed-use communities. By working patiently with city departments that both favored and resisted the development, Regent Development created a new land-use code that promotes walkability, diversity and affordability. By working with state and federal governments, the developer turned an environmental risk–the farm pond and endangered Nashville crayfish population–into an amenity that gives shape and context to the development. And by demonstrating flexibility in a changing market–both in convincing lenders that mixed-use could work and shifting from purchased to leased condominiums in the town center–the developer created an economically viable built environment where people want to be. As it moves into its second decade, Lenox Village continues to serve as a model for suburban neo-traditional neighborhood developments.

45

DEFINING SUCCESS
Q&A with David McGowan, President and CEO, Lenox Village, LLC

What was the largest obstacle to obtaining project approval or buy-in and how was it overcome?

Our biggest challenge came from Nashville's public works and fire departments. Public works wanted all of the streets and alleys at Lenox Village to be private, which was not our intent. We worked with planning staff to show the increase in tax base of the project and so the value of having public streets and alleys. To satisfy the fire department's concerns over narrow streets and on-street parking, our land planners set up traffic cones in parking lots to show how our street design would work.

What is an unexpected delight or success from the project?

In a word: absorption. We sold 250 units per year and re-sales even in the economic downturn. Apartments are 100% occupied and retail is currently 92% leased.

What hasn't lived up to expectations or has required unanticipated change?

Lenox Village residents complained about finding on-street parking. We have added parking restrictions in some areas and are requiring residents to park in garages or in parking areas located off alleys.

What continues to challenge or surprise you with the project?

We are delighted by the continued strong demand for housing and retail and continue to be amazed at how popular Lenox Village is. Additionally, residents have demonstrated a real happiness with the neighborhood.

How do you define and measure success?

Our goal at Lenox Village was to develop a diverse community that would have multiple housing types, with multiple price points and a mix of office and retail—all to support the region's diverse population. The fact that city leaders and planners from across the country tour Lenox Village to study our diverse land plan and buildings and that cities are changing zoning and codes to encourage developments like Lenox Village, means we've achieved success from a national perspective. More directly, Lenox Village is one of the most sought-after communities in Nashville, whether to live or operate a business.

Infill and Greyfield

Photo: Simmons Buntin

Rockville Town Square has become Rockville, Maryland's vibrant city center where only a failing mall existed before.

Rocks have the oldest knowledge on Earth, rivers have the oldest names and determine where the cities shall be built and what shall be their shape.

Alison Hawthorne Deming, *Genius Loci*

What should the shape of our cities be when we discover that their forms and functions will not, in the end, serve us as they did the first time around? Do we rebuild from scratch, or are there innovative ways to adapt to changing social, environmental, and economic circumstances? It may be that our metropolitan areas must be redeveloped place by place, as the three case studies of this section attest. To re-create dynamic places, however, takes dynamic leadership–as well as a participatory process that recognizes adjoining neighbors are just as impacted by rebirth as the communities themselves.

The rebirth of suburban Rockville, Maryland–north of Washington, D.C.–began with the death of a shopping mall, followed by the commencement of an ambitious town center master planning process. Twelve years after the mall's demolition, a vibrant new city center called Rockville Town Square rose in its place. The Square is composed of high-density residences above street-level retail, a state-of-the-art library, and an arts and business innovation center, all surrounding a lively public plaza with nearby metro rail access. In inner-city Atlanta, a 28-acre concrete recycling facility sat idle before a private firm with a focus on green development acquired the land and set forth to build Glenwood Park: a neighborhood of distinct urban homes, a pedestrian-scaled, mixed-use commercial core and a restored connection to the landscape manifested through an innovative stormwater management amenity. And in redeveloping what at its opening was the largest shopping mall between Chicago and California, the first-ring Denver suburb of Lakewood, Colorado, sought a local development team that could help create a downtown where none had existed before. Today Belmar is a thriving 22-block district featuring a range of residences, office and retail establishments and a central plaza and urban green–plus a 1.75 megawatt solar array.

These infill and greyfield redevelopments reflect the intricate nature of creating new places from old: the essential public/private partnerships, innovative public financing, need for flexibility in commercial and residential buildout over time and crafting of streetscapes and central gathering spaces. They show us, too, that the renewed shape of the city is as much a factor of sound planning and design as it is of simple geography. In redeveloping place, that renewal truly determines how cities shall be built–and built again.

Rockville Town Square
Rockville, Maryland
by Simmons B. Buntin

Featuring a dynamic library, residences above street-level retail, and a busy town square, Rockville Town Square has been called "the best New Urbanist center."

L ocated in the Washington, D.C., inner suburb of Rockville, Maryland, Rockville Town Square is a 12.5-acre, transit-oriented redevelopment that replaces a failed shopping mall with a vibrant civic, retail and residential core.

Part of a larger public-private town center redevelopment that encompasses the nearby Rockville Metro Plaza (with its Metro Red Line access), Rockville Town Square features a broad town plaza, state-of-the-art library, arts and business innovation center and pedestrian-oriented shops and restaurants with condominiums and apartments above. The redevelopment incorporates a variety of facades and other architectural elements; a six-story clock tower; an inviting streetscape of wide sidewalks, street furniture and trees; parking garages utilizing an advanced parking guidance system; and close proximity to the Montgomery County Courthouse Historic District and Rockville's central neighborhoods.

Rockville Town Square aims to complement the existing architecture and street patterns in the redeveloping town center area, expanding Maryland Avenue to create a "main street" adjacent to the public plaza. Additionally, the plaza serves as a focal point and gathering place, hosting a variety of outdoor events, from weekly farmers markets to the annual Rockville Uncorked wine and music festival.

Despite opening in the summer of 2007–when national economic decline was

JUST THE FACTS

- Located 15 miles north of Washington, D.C.
- Project grand opening May 2007; public dedication and retail grand opening July 2007
- 12.5 acres; full town center redevelopment is 60 acres
- Six-block urban infill featuring 28,000-square-foot public plaza with pavilion and water feature
- 102,000-square-foot county library and five-story VisArts arts and business innovation center
- 644 residential units (152 condos and 492 apartments, ranging in size from 553 to 2,225 square feet); 96 units "moderately priced"
- 181,000 square feet of retail, restaurants and grocery store
- Three public/private parking garages
- Direct access to Rockville Metro Plaza (separate project) and Metrorail, plus nearby access to Amtrak / Maryland Area Regional Commuter Train
- Development cost: $352 million ($264 million private and $88 million public funding)
- Developed by RD Rockville, LLC, a joint venture of Ross Development & Investment and the DANAC Corporation
- Public partners include City of Rockville and Montgomery County (public funding also includes State of Maryland and federal government)
- Retail development by Federal Realty Investment Trust
- Architecture: WDG Architects (full project) and Grimm + Parker (library only)
- General contractor: Whiting-Turner Contracting Company
- Awards include Best Mixed-Use Project and Best Smart Growth Master Plan (Maryland / DC Chapter of National Association of Industrial and Office Properties), Best Implemented Project (National Capital Area Chapter of American Planning Association), Best Public / Private Partnership and Best New Urbanism (*Multifamily Housing News*), Best Mixed-Use Development Finalist (National Association of Homebuilders), 2008 Charter Award (Congress for New Urbanism) and 2008 Best Community Impact Finalist (*Washington Business Journal*)

looming—and despite the closing of some Town Square retail since then, Rockville Town Square is a success: residential occupancy remains high and shops and restaurants are largely doing well. "We've been lucky to never have lingering vacancies in Town Square," says Cindy Cotte Griffiths of *Rockville Central.* "Even in this struggling economy, Federal Realty Investment Trust (Rockville Town Square's retail developer) brings new businesses into the mix in quick order."

In addition to the mix of shops and restaurants, the Rockville Memorial Library, Metropolitan Center for Visual Arts, Rockville Innovation Center and public plaza with its myriad events draw Rockville residents as well as visitors from across the metro area.

"The goal . . . is to create a heart and center for Rockville that wasn't there," said Rockville chief of redevelopment David Levy at the time of the project's dedication in July 2007. "It's a space where people can go and sit outside on a steamy mid-Atlantic summer evening and hang out."

History and Planning: From Mall to Town Center

Rockville Town Square is the latest and most comprehensive redevelopment of downtown Rockville, an area that has struggled to find success and identity for the last 50 years. In 1962, the city received federal funding to undertake "urban renewal" on a 46-acre portion of the city's commercial core, resulting in the demolition of much of the city's historic urban fabric. Over the next 20 years, Rockville constructed multistory apartments, county buildings, high-rise office buildings, and the 55-store Rockville Mall.

The mall opened in 1972 on 13 acres, but seemed destined to fail from the beginning. Though it was designed to house two anchors, only one could be contracted and that store–Lansburgh's–closed after just one year. Though it was replaced by another local department store and eventually a furniture clearance center, the mall continued to struggle. By 1981, three years after the mall was renamed the Commons at Courthouse Square, 35 storefronts were vacant. According to Alan David Doane of Deadmalls.com, the Rockville Mall's demise was the result of many factors, from inaccessible location to a reputation of crime and poor maintenance. For example, "[s]hoppers who did find the entrance to the mall's parking garage . . . found the garage dark, intimidating, and confusing, and the garage gained a reputation as friendly criminal element," he writes. In noting that a police substation was later added to the dying mall, he writes that "the unfortunate police officers assigned to this location suffered from the mall's horrible maintenance, publicizing that live roaches regularly blew out of vents into the substation."

In 1983, $50 million was invested by a local firm to redevelop the mall and adjacent area as Rockville Metro Center. A large United Artist theater complex, a billiards parlor, and restaurants were added, bridging access from Metro's Rockville Red Line transit station to the mall. Though the theater has been a success, the mall itself, anchoring the western portion of the Metro Center, could not recover and was demolished in 1995, following a campaign by Rockville mayor and (later) Montgomery County executive Doug Duncan, who successfully argued that the mall was inhibiting downtown redevelopment.

Before the mall was demolished, the city officially condemned the structure and relocated a number of businesses, reaching settlement agreements with individual property owners to move the redevelopment process along. Though the city's actions were legally challenged, Rockville's right to condemn the properties was upheld in court because "the project incorporates true public uses, including four municipal parking facilities, a public square and a new regional library–fulfilling the requirements of Maryland's relatively liberal eminent domain statute," writes commercial real estate legal expert Pamela V. Rothenberg in the *Journal of Property Management*.

The city spent nearly $8 million to assist condemned businesses in moving elsewhere, with the goal of having many of the businesses return to Rockville Town Square once complete. Several did. Other challenges faced the city, as well. A polluted former gas station on the site needed remediation so the property could be designated as "clean," while the city also worked with the U.S. Army Corps of Engineers to redirect an existing streambed. Removal and reinstallation of utility lines and work on the stream and other portions of the site necessitated the removal of several hundred thousand cubic yards of soil, which was then used as backfill during construction.

The Rockville Town Square development was enabled through the city's adoption of the Town Center Master Plan in 2001. The master

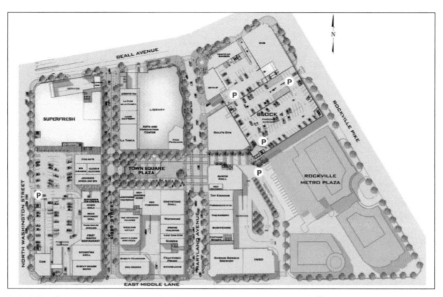

Rockville Town Square reconnects the street grid while providing direct access to Washington, D.C.'s Metro red line.

Graphic: RD Rockville, LLC

planning process was led by city planning staff in conjunction with planning consultants Development Concepts, Inc. and infrastructure developers HNTB. But visioning for a redeveloped Rockville town center began well before, with the initial work by Duncan. A *Potomac Almanac* article published in conjunction with the Town Square's dedication notes that "[b]efore construction even started on the town square, debates on what to do with Rockville's town center had been raging for decades, even preceding the building of the Rockville Mall."

The Town Center Master Plan was created during a nine-month process comprised of stakeholder interviews, Town Center Action Team meetings, feedback from the Greater Rockville Partnership (now Rockville Economic Development, Inc.), public surveys and a large open house held in September 2000. The open house incorporated four interactive stations to facilitate public discussion and solicit feedback:

- Existing Conditions and Planned Developments

- Development Framework
- Transportation and Circulation
- Urban Design Elements

At the stations, attendees prioritized previously prepared goal statements. According to the results of the public feedback gathered during this process, the favored elements to include in the Town Center were mixed-use development, around-the-clock activity and a pedestrian-oriented character.

Following the September public meeting, the city formed a 24-member Master Plan Advisory Group, which was charged with interacting directly with the consultant planning team. The Advisory Group consisted of residents, developers, property owners, business leaders and representatives from public entities including the city, Montgomery County, Washington Metropolitan Area Transit Authority (Metro), Maryland State Highway Administration, Rockville Chamber of Commerce and the Greater Rockville Partnership.

The Advisory Group created an overarching goal and set of nine objectives articulated in the Town Center Master Plan:

Town Center Master Plan Goal
Create a daytime, evening and weekend activity center that is easily identifiable, pedestrian-oriented and incorporates a mix of uses and activities.

Objectives
- Provide an environment conducive to and supportive of living, working, shopping and entertainment
- Accommodate a variety of densities and scales of development that are sensitive to an urban neighborhood environment and the demands of the marketplace
- Enhance links to transportation options which improve their visibility and accessibility
- Provide improved connections from neighborhoods to the Town Center
- Minimize the intrusiveness of Rockville Pike and the Metro and CSX rail lines
- Make the Town Center a unique, high-amenity destination for local and regional customers
- Utilize urban design to establish zoning and density requirements that will assist in defining the Rockville Town Center
- Provide sufficient parking for new mixed-use development and visitors to the Town Center
- Address integrating new aesthetic public parking garages with linkages from road networks

The Town Center Master Plan included not only the site of Rockville Town Square, but also the adjacent 2.5-acre Rockville Metro Plaza owned by Foulger-Pratt (the eastern portion of the original Rockville Metro Center). The Town Center is the first phase of a larger Rockville town center redevelopment by the city. The Plaza is slated to hold 600,000 square feet of office place; so far, only one

of three approved office buildings has been constructed.

The Master Plan also includes an Action Plan that defines 13 tasks–from creating a tax-increment finance district to establishing a tracking system that monitors the area's mix of uses. The Master Plan provides for zoning changes and creates Design Guidelines for use in a new urban design overlay district. With sections detailing site layout, building scale and massing, fenestration, parking design and signage, the Design Guidelines hope to achieve seven objectives: 1) Celebrate Maryland Avenue as the Town Center centerpiece through the use of outstanding and creative design solutions; 2) Celebrate Washington Street north of Jefferson Street as a high-quality, mixed-use street that serves as an appropriate transition to the residential neighborhoods; 3) Bring buildings up to the street edge and reinforce a sense of urban enclosure by placing parking behind buildings; 4) Encourage high-quality materials in all aspects of site and building development; 5) Incorporate open space (landscaping and/or plazas) into private building plans; 6) Create streetscapes and public spaces that feel comfortable to pedestrians by encouraging inclusion of open space and/or green spaces; 7) Utilize traditional storefront design techniques wherever possible; maximize opportunities for street activity by incorporating open and inviting ground floors.

Financing: Tapping Local, State, and Federal Resources
After the Master Plan was approved in October 2001, city staff worked with county, state and federal agencies to obtain financial commitments for the Town Center's first phase–Rockville Town Square. In total, $352 million was spent in the development of Rockville Town Square over the life of the project: $264 million in private funding and $88 million in public funding, including $60 million total from the city (with $40 million designated for

Photo: Simmons Buntin

The town square is an active space inside and out in all seasons.

streets, sidewalks and public parking garages). The county funded the library, at a cost of $26.3 million, and contributed $12 million over six years toward project infrastructure costs. Maryland state government contributed several million more dollars for infrastructure and a public parking garage, and the federal government provided funding for pedestrian improvements.

With initial public funding commitments in place, a preliminary development plan based on the Master Plan's Design Guidelines was created. The plan specified elements such as library, residential, retail and open space locations. It also led to a design competition in June 2002 that was sponsored by the city and Federal Realty–which owned and operated Rockville Mall and partnered with the city on town center redevelopment. After considering about a half-dozen submissions from national development firms, the city and Federal Realty selected as their private development partner RD Rockville, a collaboration of Ross Development & Investment and DANAC Corporation of Bethesda, Maryland. A general development agreement was signed by the city, county, RD Rockville and Federal Realty in January 2003, and construction began the following year.

Developers pursued an equity partner in 2003, but RD Rockville ended up taking on "pure debt–consisting of two first mortgages (because the deal was so large) and a mezzanine loan–with . . . five percent of the equity as cash upfront," according to the Urban Land Institute. In all, private loans of $34 million, $103.2 million and $73.6 million were secured by RD Rockville before and during construction.

Between 2002 and 2004, project planners held more than 40 public meetings. "This persistent effort to educate the community–as well as strong support from the mayor and council–created public support for the project, which many citizens originally opposed," reports the Urban Land Institute. The Town Square's architectural design was created by WDG Architecture, with the exception of the library and Arts and Innovation Center. Construction of Rockville Town Square spanned two and a half years. The project's grand opening was held in May 2007, followed by a public dedication and retail grand opening in July, when the redevelopment project was praised by Maryland's governor "as a way to revive the aging suburb," write Katherine Shaver and Miranda S. Spivack in *The Washington Post*.

Public Events Make the Town Square Lively

At the heart of Rockville Town Square is a 28,000-square-foot public plaza. The plaza, modeled after the central piazzas of walkable Italian cities, features a pavilion that can serve as a bandstand and lighted stage, a water feature with interactive fountain, sculptures and other public art, a grassy area with rock garden and trees and wide patios that front the surrounding multistory buildings and pedestrian-oriented streets.

The plaza is bordered on the north by the regional library and ground-level shops and restaurants; on the south by ground-level shops, restaurants and multistory residential; on the west by Gibbs Street; and on the east by the iconic six-story clock tower and Maryland Avenue, which serves as a kind of "main street" through the project. Shade trees and other plantings, benches and decorative railings and streetlights line the plaza and streets. In the winter–funding permitting–the plaza hosts an ice rink, as well.

The plaza is designed to encourage seating and gatherings, formal and otherwise and, like other successful New Urban developments, to foster chance encounters. "I love the Town Square because I can't walk more than a couple feet without seeing someone I know from doing business," says Robin Wiener, according to a 2010 *Reuters* article profiling the project. Wiener is president of Get Real Consulting, a business located within the town center. The article also notes how "[t]eenagers use Facebook to signal spur-of-the-moment breakdance sessions on the town square's bandstand because . . . it's really the only place they can 'hang out and break.'"

One of the reasons Rockville Town Square is considered a success is because of the city's concerted efforts to bring in regular events and make the project an integrated part of the city. "This is not just any old shopping center," said Levy at the grand opening. "This is downtown Rockville. It has a history and a past. This is not going to be just a generic place. There will be signature art, historical

Rockville Town Square's regional library is a "visual showstopper."

aspects and many other events that make it more than just another development."

Those events include a variety of regular activities, such as First Friday deck parties atop the Arts and Business Innovation Center, summer concerts on the square, Wednesday and Saturday farmers markets, the Hometown Holidays festival, Memorial Day parade, Mommy & Me and Daddies Too gatherings on the square, and Pride in the Sky atop the Innovation Center.

One of the more intriguing events is Rockville Uncorked, the annual festival of wine and music held at Rockville Town Square. A dozen Maryland wineries participate in the late summer event, which in addition to wine tasting also features three stages of local and regional live music, a wine and cooking demonstration stage and other live performances.

For large events such as Rockville Uncorked, the public pedestrian space of the plaza can be expanded by closing off Gibbs Street and Maryland Avenue, which were specifically designed for periodic closures in support of such gatherings.

Library and Arts and Innovation Center

If the public plaza is Rockville Town Square's heart, then its brain is the 102,000-square-foot, $26.3 million regional library, which opened in November 2006. As *The Washington Post* notes, "The Rockville library has visual showstoppers," beginning with an exterior wall undulating along the curve of Maryland Avenue. The subtle wave of three-story glass commemorates a significant Rockville occurrence—the mapping of the human genome by Rockville-based biotech company CELERA—and serves as a reference to one-half of the double helix of human DNA. Landscaping along Maryland Avenue completes the other half of the double helix.

Rockville Memorial Library was designed by Grimm + Parker Architects, which wanted to give the building "an appropriate civic presence, as well as a unique physical expression that makes a memorable, inviting impression on visitors to the new Town Center," according to Montgomery County Public Libraries.

The library is also defined by two towers flanking prominent corners. The first anchors the intersection of Maryland Avenue and Beall Avenue, the road along the northern edge of Rockville Town Square. This tower marks the northern gateway to the project and is visible from Rockville Pike–significant because Rockville Town Square is otherwise invisible to motorists along the heavily traveled route. In fact, the Urban Land Institute reports that "it took a summer 2008 water main break that forced the closure of most of Montgomery County's restaurants–except those in Rockville, which has its own water system–to put Rockville Town Square on the map for many county residents. The project's restaurants were 'discovered' that weekend and people continue to return to them on a regular basis." With visibility from primary highways a challenge, the design of the library's northern tower is critical for enhancing the project's exposure.

The second library tower anchors the building to the plaza, near the library's main entrance; the ground level of the round tower is actually restaurant space. The library's entrance is a three-story, glass-roofed portico. The entrance hall features what Grimm + Parker lead architect Melanie Hennigan calls "a wonder wall"–a series of video display terminals with touch screens for accessing the library's electronic catalog. Beyond that, an open central rotunda features a half-spiral staircase sweeping to the second floor, past a terrazzo mosaic lit by 250 lights suspended from the atrium ceiling– the library's featured, interior public art, created by Maryland artist Heidi Lippman.

The library's collection includes 200,000 items in print and digital format, special collections such as business and government information, free wifi, a public meeting room and a world languages area (with a focus on Chinese, Korean, Spanish, Russian and Vietnamese), which is of particular interest in a region rich in international diversity.

The five-story building adjacent to the library hosts the 53,000-square-foot Rockville Arts and Innovation Center, designed by D'Agostino Izzo Quirk Architects. The Center is comprised of the Metropolitan Center for Visual Arts (VisArts) and the Rockville Innovation Center, as well as the Rooftop, a social gathering space and rooftop garden.

VisArts opened in 28,000 square feet of the Center in September 2007, after being housed in temporary space in nearby Gaithersburg while the Town Square was completed. Formerly called Rockville Arts Place, the organization was a permanent resident of the Rockville Mall prior to its demolition. Though a private organization, VisArts partners with the city to offer arts education, exhibitions, professional artist development and community outreach to the residents of Rockville, Montgomery County and beyond.

The Rockville Innovation Center opened in 25,000 square feet of the fourth and fifth floors of the Center in June 2007. It provides space for up to 30 start-up technology companies. Programming is provided by Montgomery County's Business Innovation Network. The Innovation Center serves domestic technology start-ups in the areas of healthcare, medicine and bioinformatics, as well as international technology companies interested in opening their first U.S. office. The facility provides lease flexibility to tenants, shared amenities such as reception and work and conference rooms and programs that teach business skills and offer support with licensing, intellectual property and financing. Companies usually spend 2-4 years in the Innovation Center before "graduating" and moving to local commercial office space, according to Rockville Economic Development, Inc., which manages the Innovation Center.

Street-Level Retail: A Mixed Success in Challenging Economic Times

Rockville Town Square's retail and restaurant spaces fill most of the street level of the project's four mid-rise buildings, including space

Photo: Simmons Buntin

The Maryland Avenue entrance to Rockville Town Square is anchored by Starbucks and Gordon Biersch, national chains that have not struggled as some local restaurants have.

in the library and Arts and Innovation Center. A total of approximately 180,000 square feet for shops and restaurants is available, including the recently leased 32,000-square-foot grocery space that anchors the northeast corner of the project.

After early negotiations with upscale grocer Harris Teeter fell through, developers negotiated with regional chain Superfresh for two years before signing a 20-year lease in 2007. But the contract was canceled in March 2010 and until September 2011 was the only retail space that had not been filled. In December 2010, Federal Realty "shared with the city that they are very close to a lease agreement with a grocery store," reports Cindy Cotte Griffiths of *Rockville Central*. The grocery store, Dawson's Market, is the outgrowth of a single Ellwood Thompson's market located in Richmond, Virginia. The natural foods grocer advertises a simple mission: "To help people discover and celebrate a healthy relationship with food." To fulfill this mission, the store works with local farmers to supply meats and vegetables. Dawson's Market opened in late

September 2012. In addition to the grocery space, the building includes seating for 90 in the hopes that its café will "become a meeting place for Rockville," says Griffiths.

Federal Realty began marketing the retail spaces two years before construction was expected to conclude. Due to the site's location and the history of its own failed mall, however, Federal Realty was not able to attract large, national retailers. The result, reports the Urban Land Institute in a case study, is that the project "has more of an entertainment/service base than many town center mixed-used developments," and while Rockville Town Square has a core of mixed uses, it "probably will not fully mature until the area immediately surrounding it is built out with more office and retail space"—a defined goal of the city and Town Center Master Plan.

Starbucks Coffee was the first retail establishment to open, in 2007, at the southwest corner of Maryland Avenue—a primary entrance to the Town Square. Over the next several months, more than 40 additional shops and restaurants opened, with a mix of local and national dining, boutiques, retail and services. National and regional chains include Gordon Biersch Brewing Company (anchoring the corner opposite Starbucks), Gold's Gym, CVS Pharmacy (with its drive-thru in an adjacent parking garage), Five Guys Burgers and Fries and Capital One Bank. Local stores and services include Toy Kingdom and Jouvence Lifestyle Salon and Spa. The Waygoose Gallery of American Crafts, one of the shops located at Rockville Mall before its demolition, also moved in, though it closed its Rockville Town Square location in May 2011.

As businesses have closed, others have moved in. When locally-owned Greystone Grill shut its doors, Buffalo Wild Wings–a national chain–moved in. The Cingular/AT&T Wireless store was replaced by Sands Artwork Gallery and the original space of New Wave Discount Hair Supply–which moved into the space first occupied by The Papery–is now occupied by Color Me Mine ceramics painting.

Rockville Town Square business owners are concerned by this turnover, of course, but not overly so. "When you have a development like Town Square," says Austin Grill general manager and Rockville Town Square Merchants Association spokesperson Stephen Schadler, "you put in a mix of retail and restaurants that you think will be successful; however, you're never going to get that perfect fit the first time around. There's always going to be those businesses even in the best of economic times that are going to struggle and not make it one way or another. The hope is you bring in new merchants so that you can continue trying to get that right mix and give consumers what they're demanding."

Rockville mayor Susan R. Hoffmann, commenting in a June 2009 issue of *The Gazette*, agreed: "Based on what I know about the cycle of retail, this is a fairly common shakeout–two years in–that occurs even in the best of times."

One response to bolster business for locally owned retailers has been the city's implementation of a "buy local" campaign, initiated in late 2008. Toy Kingdom owner Carlos Aulestia is pleased with the program and his investment in it. "They are working hard to increase awareness," he says. "It provides us with good advertising benefits."

The Buy Rockville campaign is championed by the Rockville Chamber of Commerce and overseen by the Coalition to Preserve Rockville Neighborhood Businesses. According to Jeff Miller, president of the Coalition, "[f]or a relatively small contribution, a business can benefit from a $60,000 marketing campaign." The program is free to join, which gets businesses listed in its directory, but additional benefits such as enhanced pages on the program's website, participation in a customer loyalty program and promotion as sponsors at events such as the Rockville Restaurant Week that kicked off in October 2009 require a membership fee.

Town Center Action Team president Mark Pierzchala noted in an April 2009 Town Square Summit that while Rockville Town Square "is doing better than most people think," it had not yet fulfilled the vision of all members of the Action Team, a group formed to give community voice to the creation of Rockville's town center.

Activity is expected to increase soon, as Choice Hotels will move its corporate headquarters from Silver Spring, Maryland, to Rockville's town center, at Rockville Metro Plaza, in order to accommodate 75 more employees (for a total of 475) and a need for 130,000 square feet of office space. The move will take place in 2013 and is scheduled to include the construction of a Cambria Suites hotel across the street from the headquarters to accommodate an estimated 10,000 stays per year.

While the economy has posed challenges for some Rockville Town Square retailers, the design of the streets and building facades have fostered their success. The buildings incorporate a mix of rooflines, towers and turrets,

Retail shops, shown here next to a parking garage entrance, feature custom facades along tree-lined sidewalks.

prominent entryways, detailed brickwork and canopies and porticos that make the streets and business entries distinct and pedestrian-oriented. Restaurant patios extend onto wide sidewalks, fostering an active café and street scene much of the year.

Federal Realty paid a fixed price for the retail shells provided by RD Rockville, according to the Urban Land Institute, and then worked with retail tenants to design unique spaces to meet their specific needs. Federal Realty encourages its retail tenants to build out their own storefronts using a set of design guidelines, "to create their own identities, resulting in an eclectic design mix at the street level . . . [a] process that was intended to add to the illusion that the project grew incrementally over time," reports the Urban Land Institute. The result: nearly 40 Town Square facades incorporate different, customized mixes of finishes, from brick and stone to metal and siding.

Housing: Evolving to Meet the Market

As early as 2006, residential developer RD Rockville knew that the downturn in the economy could force it to change its strategy of selling all 644 residential units. Units range in size from 553-square-foot studios to 2,225-square-foot, three-bedroom + den penthouses originally priced from $300,000 to $900,000. "We've gone from a red-hot market to an ice-cold market," Scott Ross, president of Ross Development, told *The New York Times* in 2006. "Our game plan is to offer some of them for lease if the market continues to be slow."

Even though 30 units sold on the first day and 130 followed over the next two months, the market did indeed slow. In order to accommodate the market shift, however, RD Rockville decided to market only one of four residential buildings as condominiums—now called Palladian Condominiums, with 152 units—while selling the remaining 492 units to a company that could lease them as apartments. RD Rockville sold the remaining units, now called Fenestra Apartments, to CIM Group.

The condos are available for purchase and rent-to-own, which allows residents to apply 75 percent of the rent accumulated from the past

Photo: Simmons Buntin

Photo: Simmons Buntin

Residences located above Dawson's Market, with an older Rockville office building in the distance.

year toward a down payment on the purchase of the condo, without extra fees or an increase in monthly rent, according to the Palladian Marketing Center.

In addition to market-rate condos and apartments, Rockville Town Square has 94 units (15 percent of the total residential number) designated as "moderately priced" under the city's Moderately Priced Dwelling Unit Program. These units are therefore "affordable" to households earning under 60 percent of the area median income. Though they do not share all of the amenities of the other units–there are no granite countertops, stainless steel appliances, or hardwood flooring, for example–they otherwise are identical to the Palladian condos and Fenestra apartments.

All of the residential units are located above street-level retail and the buildings are adjacent to surface parking or parking garages.

A Cutting-Edge Parking Guidance System

Though not part of the city's original plans,

Rockville Town Square has implemented a $1.5 million parking guidance system, "one of the first applications of this technology outside an airport setting," according to the Urban Land Institute. The system announces parking space availability, both in number and locations, in the Town Square's three public garages and also includes payment kiosks.

Secure resident parking is separate from visitor parking. The city owns half of the parking spaces while RD Rockville owns the other half. In total, the Town Square includes approximately 2,000 parking spaces in garages, surface lots and on-street parking.

Though Town Square is just two blocks from the Rockville Metro station (at Rockville Metro Plaza) a February 2010 article in *The Washington Post* notes that "merchants said many customers drive there. Suburban shoppers accustomed to free parking have balked at paying for garage parking." Garage rates have since been reduced and, during the winter holiday season, eliminated entirely in the hopes of bringing in these suburban shoppers.

Additionally, merchants have handed out fliers at the Shady Grove and Rockville Metro stations, advertising $60-per-month commuter parking in town center garages. "The hope," the *Post* article concludes, "is that those commuters might shop or eat on their way to and from work, even if it means they contribute to traffic congestion."

Conclusion: Collaborative Redevelopment Effort Leads to the "Best New Urbanist Center"

Rockville Town Square is the first phase of what the city hopes will be an extensive redevelopment of its town center. As a significant first step—thanks to a comprehensive, stakeholder-involved planning process and a committed development team—the Town Square clearly has become a place in Rockville where people want to be.

Both residents and professional town planners agree: "I wanted a lifestyle where I didn't have to get in my car all the time, and something with a community feel," says Daniel Stauffer, a molecular biologist who moved from rural Virginia to Rockville Town Square for his job in Germantown. "I have a tailor, dry cleaner and breakfast place right outside my door."

Noted town planner and designer Andrés Duany is more direct, remarking several months after the project's grand opening that "[t]he best New Urbanist center, in my opinion, is the brand new Rockville Town Square. Very mature. Very credible as urbanism." Accordingly, the project won a prestigious Congress for New Urbanism Charter Award in 2008.

The Urban Land Institute reports that the project's positive impact has been economic, as well: "The area's property, sales and income taxes all have risen since Rockville Town Square was completed. As a result, the project's public sector costs will be pretty much recouped within a decade."

In striving to "create a daytime, evening and weekend activity center that is easily identifiable, pedestrian-oriented and incorporates a mix of uses and activities," as the "Town Center Master Plan" projected back in 2001, the city of Rockville and its partners have indeed achieved determined success.

DEFINING SUCCESS
Q&A with David Levy, Chief of Redevelopment, City of Rockville

What was the largest obstacle to obtaining project approval or buy-in and how was it overcome?

The largest obstacle to moving Rockville Town Square forward was to reach business agreements among key parties. Two agreements, negotiated over many months, established the foundation for the project. First, a Memorandum of Understanding between the City of Rockville and Montgomery County established the city's and the county's responsibilities in the project. The agreement established that the city would build roads, sidewalks, amenities, parking garages and an arts center; the county would build a new library and contribute financially to the city's responsibilities. Later, the county added a business incubator to its investments in Town Square.

The second key agreement was the General Development Agreement for the Redevelopment of the Rockville Town Square, which established responsibilities among the city and the two private sector partners, RD Rockville and Federal Realty Investment Trust. RD Rockville would be the master developer, building the residential units and the shell for the ground-floor retail; Federal Realty would agree to purchase the shells when built and then build out the rest of the retail. These agreements were detailed and difficult to achieve, and it took risk on both the public and private sides for them to occur. For Rockville, elected leaders needed to be ready to support selling bonds and spending public money to support the project. They did so, which made an enormous difference in public acceptance.

What is an unexpected delight or success from the project?

First, though the goal for Rockville was to create a heart and center for the city, it has achieved that purpose even beyond what we had all hoped. People from all over the city and beyond, come and "hang out." The mix of amenities is a key part of this success; but also the focus on design and amenities have created a look and feel that is attractive to people. Second, despite the recession and the threat of fiscal stress, Rockville's bond ratings have been upgraded to AAA since the completion of Town Square; and the project was cited as one of the reasons for the upgrade.

What hasn't lived up to expectations or has required unanticipated change?

The economic recession has unquestionably affected the financial performance of the project on both the public and private sides. Parking garage revenues to the city and retail sales have been particularly problematic and have needed various changes in strategy to make it through the difficult economic period. In particular, retail sales at this mixed-use project are not yet performing as well as some of Federal Realty's traditional suburban-style retail areas nearby. Both the city and Federal Realty remain optimistic that the improving economy will improve performance and that people will embrace this retail format over time.

What continues to challenge or surprise you with the project?

One of the continuing surprises of the project is how positively the public continues to think of Town Square; and how important the project is becoming in terms of redevelopment nearby. Town Square is really the Phase 1 implementation of the Rockville Town Center Master Plan, which was produced through an interactive community planning process in 2001. The city's investment in Town Square was designed not just to make this one project happen, but to simulate future Town Center phases without requiring the same level of public investment. Properties to the south, north and east all are ripe for redevelopment and some even have development approvals; but, again, the impact of the recession has muted those spinoff projects. Just recently, however, the first major spinoff was announced. Choice Hotels International decided to move its headquarters to a site adjacent to Town Square on the east, where a new office building will be built. A Choice headquarters hotel will also be built immediately to the south, along with new residential units and retail. The city's commitment to Town Square and to the continuing strengthening of the broader town center area is a primary reason.

How do you define and measure success?
For Rockville, success in Town Square and in the town center as a whole is defined both in terms of community pride and identity, as well as fiscal/financial health of the city. In the first area, Town Square has undoubtedly achieved the goals, by creating a center for the city. The fiscal and financial goals have been of moderate success in the short term. Property values have increased, thereby increasing revenues; and bond ratings have been upgraded, thereby lowering the cost of borrowing. However, the recession has made other measures of financial success slower to achieve. The city expects, however, that these measures will improve over time, both for the private owners and for the city. As a whole, the Rockville community continues to view Rockville Town Square as a major success both for having been achieved and for being such a great place to go and spend time.

Glenwood Park
Atlanta, Georgia
by Simmons B. Buntin

Brasfield Square anchors the commercial portion of Atlanta's award-winning Glenwood Park.

The award-winning, 28-acre Glenwood Park is a brownfield redevelopment that features a mix of well-designed homes and commercial and public spaces. The neighborhood is noted for its commitment to traditional neighborhood design, walkability, a mix of residential and commercial uses and environmental management practices. Glenwood Park is a certified EarthCraft Community for its focus on site selection, water management, planning and design, preservation landscaping, community involvement and green building.

The community is designed around a traditional main street environment–with on-street parallel parking–that culminates in a plaza (Brasfield Square) surrounded by three-and four-story buildings "framing a beautiful outdoor room," says Green Street Properties founder Charles Brewer. Alley-loaded,

single-family homes with views of the Atlanta skyline face tree-lined streets, public squares and pocket parks. Stoop-fronted townhomes and mixed-use buildings with residences above street-level retail provide a more urban (and relatively more affordable) context, while the large, oval Glenwood Park serves as a gathering place and environmentally benign water retention and filtration area.

"The most noteworthy achievement of Glenwood Park is the successful mixing of a full range of housing types and commercial buildings on beautiful streets," says Brewer. "The intricate nature of the mixing is in itself very important and is frequently an area where recent mixed-use development projects come up short. Another key is that the neighborhood reads as a collection of individual buildings, each of a manageable scale, rather than a 'project.'"

JUST THE FACTS

- 28-acre brownfield redevelopment located two miles east of downtown Atlanta
- 375 residences in a mix of condominiums, townhomes and single-family homes (including a 2005 *Southern Living* Idea House)
- 48,000 square feet of retail and 20,000 square feet of office space
- Emphasis on "making great streets where people will enjoy walking"
- Open space includes large public park with pond, two public squares, dog park, community garden and pocket parks
- Environmental features include energy-efficient buildings, onsite stormwater management and extensive waste recycling during construction
- Certified as EarthCraft Community
- Planning began in late 2001, infrastructure work began in early 2003, building construction began in spring 2004
- Commercial/mixed-use center completed in 2007, single-family homes completed by end of 2011; lots still available for townhomes or additional single-family homes
- Awards include 2003 Congress for New Urbanism Charter Award and 2006 Urban Land Institute Development of the Year
- Developed by Green Street Properties
- Planning led by Dover, Kohl & Partners and Tunnel-Spangler-Walsh & Associates

The keys to Glenwood Park's success, says Brewer, included the location of the site, positive relations with neighbors (who largely supported Glenwood Park's plan from the beginning), an insider-only financing strategy, a diverse team of accomplished partners and builders and architects, and a good working relationship with local permitting authorities, despite some challenges.

Site Characteristics and History: From Brownfield to Brownstone

Glenwood Park is located on a former Vulcan Materials Company industrial site that had most recently been used as a concrete recycling facility. A small amount of industrial land remains nearby, but the community is primarily surrounded by century-old, single-family neighborhoods, including Grant Park to the west and Ormewood Park and East Atlanta to the east. The northern boundary is an expressway, Interstate 20, running along an avenue on the western part of the site. To the south is a collector-level street and to the east is a single-family neighborhood called North Ormewood Park.

The site is located a mile in either direction of two Metropolitan Atlanta Rapid Transit Authority (MARTA) rail stops, and is served by an active bus route that leads downtown. Glenwood Park is also on the route of the BeltLine, a $2.8 billion network of public parks, trails and transit along a historic 22-mile railroad corridor circling downtown Atlanta and connecting 45 neighborhoods.

The surrounding neighborhoods suffered a sharp economic downturn in the 1960s, but have been on a gradual rebound since—at least until the economic downturn that began in 2007. Property values in these surrounding mixed-income and racially diverse neighborhoods have been escalating, though they are still far lower than those in northern parts of the city and its suburbs.

Novare Group, a successful Atlanta real estate developer, purchased the Vulcan site in 2000. Novare then created a mixed-use plan that featured a large office component sharing parking with condominiums and a grocery-anchored shopping center. The land was

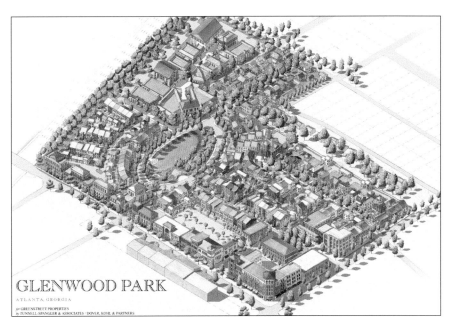

An early rendering of Glenwood Park, showcasing its rich urban texture.

rezoned to allow the initial mixed-use plan; yet given the broader economic downturn that began in late 2001, the specific plan no longer appeared to be feasible.

By that time, Katharine Kelley, Walter Brown and Charles Brewer had formed Green Street Properties—sharing a passion for cities, walkable neighborhoods and environmental protection. In fall 2001, Novare Group invited Green Street Properties to invest in the Glenwood Park project and take over the development. "From the get-go, principles of New Urbanism and green building were embedded in Glenwood Park," says Brown, Green Street Properties vice president of development and environmental affairs. "We envisioned a neighborhood that would appeal to people who want a quality of life that isn't just more suburban sprawl."

A New Urbanist Plan for the Heart of Atlanta

Green Street Properties' vision has driven the development of the site for over a decade:

Glenwood Park seeks to offer a compelling alternative for those who are dissatisfied with the choices provided by conventional development. Conventional development emphasizes the private realm, auto dependency, single use pods, privacy, exclusivity and bigger and bigger private houses. Glenwood Park emphasizes the public realm, walkability, mixed uses, community, diversity and quality over quantity.

In creating the plan for Glenwood Park, Green Street Properties focused on several core tenets, including creating a walkable community; emphasizing resource efficiency, environmental protection and restoration; creating a place for commerce; and creating a place to live, work, and gather.

"Glenwood Park will be designed to allow a great deal of flexibility in how the neighborhood evolves over time," says Brewer. "We greatly admire the flexibility of a town plan like Savannah's, which has gracefully accommodated a changing mix of uses over many decades. Furthermore, we think it is critical for any place that aspires to be truly loveable to allow for the unplanned to blossom."

Green Street Properties organized a design charrette in early December 2001, with the intention of developing the design vision for the development. Dover, Kohl & Partners of Miami led the charrette with assistance from Tunnel-Spangler-Walsh & Partners of Atlanta. Thirty people were invited to participate, representing local neighborhood groups, design professionals and friends and acquaintances that the design team believed would be helpful. The charrette was "a great success," according to Brewer, with many people making substantial contributions.

Over time, however, a number of changes to the plan were made. For example, the private school that was originally located in the northwest corner of the neighborhood was eventually eliminated from the plan due to concerns by school representatives over proximity to Interstate 20 and buildout costs. Additionally, buildings in a central block were reoriented to face east and west rather than north and south. Plans for the commercial center were likewise modified to accommodate additional building types and parking.

"We thought we had the neighborhood pretty thoroughly planned out up front," says Brewer. "But to our surprise each time a new area was ready for building, we found there was in fact considerable planning left to do to get it just right."

In the months following the design charrette, Dover, Kohl & Partners created the Glenwood Park Master Plan, Development Standards and Regulating Plan. The team also produced hand-drawn visualizations "to explain key project ideas [such as] the proposed form and massing," according to Dover, Kohl & Partners. "These types of detailed illustrations give a sense of the intended character of future development."

According to Brewer, neighbors have enthusiastically embraced the project, despite the fact that its density exceeds that of surrounding neighborhoods. In fact, developers believe the cordial relationship with neighbors has been one of the most gratifying outcomes of the development experience, for many reasons.

Neighbors had felt "under-retailed" and yearned for a retail center, said Brewer early in the project's development. Many neighbors preferred to shop at in-town, traditionally urban locations because they appreciate the very characteristics that the design team hoped to create in Glenwood Park. The site was also "such an eyesore before," according to Brewer, that the new neighborhood was a substantial improvement. Much of the anticipated additional vehicular traffic from Glenwood Park comes from the expressway. Since the community is adjacent to the exit, however, vehicles do not significantly impact neighbors before reaching Glenwood Park. Green Street Properties also reached out to neighbors for their input on planning and the neighbors were helpful, especially in their suggestions for the retail portion of the plan, says Brewer. Neighbors provided strong political support when needed, especially in the permitting process, which was critical for the project's success. Finally, it was evident since initial planning that Glenwood Park would have a positive impact on surrounding property values–and does, even given the economic downturn.

Permitting, Infrastructure, and the Unexpected Discoveries of an Industrial Site

Site engineering was completed and site development permits were acquired in 2002. Glenwood Park's zoning process went smoothly. The developer's advisor was Bill Kennedy, a retired and well-loved city zoning official. Bill

Glenwood Park successfully blends a fine-grained mix of retail, residences, and open space, making it one of Atlanta's most distinct new neighborhoods.

has since passed away, and Glenwood Park's main street, Bill Kennedy Way, is now named after him.

The design team pursued Planned Development Mixed Use (PD-MU) zoning, and with strong neighbor support received it without hassle. PD-MU zoning was added to the City of Atlanta zoning ordinance in 1980 to facilitate pedestrian- and transit-oriented development and redevelopment that supported services within close proximity to residences. The zoning includes specific guidelines for street and block locations and aggregate limits on development square footages, though it is flexible as to the types of buildings that go on each lot. This flexibility proved to be crucial as the plans were fine-tuned over time.

Glenwood Park experienced three major

challenges in its permitting process. The first centered on street widths and corner radii. Narrower streets and tighter corners were crucial to the plan's success. The developers had a series of lengthy and, at times, frustrating discussions with city officials to resolve city concerns that the streets were too narrow and corners too sharp for emergency vehicle access, says Brown. Resolution required elected officials to step in to promote a new city ordinance, allowing specific dimensions for qualifying traditional neighborhood developments.

The second challenge involved a drainage ditch that crossed a portion of the site. Prior to construction, the ditch entered the site in a storm sewer that emptied into a deeper ditch gouged into industrial fill. After a short distance, it then re-entered a storm sewer, flowing downstream to a combined sanitary/storm sewer treatment plant. At the lower end of the ditch was an outflow of raw sewage because of a broken sanitary sewer line. Developers wanted to fix the sewers and create a retention park that would collect stormwater from Glenwood Park in a pond, allowing the water to filter and be used for irrigation before slowly releasing downstream. It was a strong plan from an environmental perspective and all parties agreed.

Because of jurisdictional confusion and uncertainly regarding what was and was not "waters of the state," however, the design team had a difficult time receiving permission to alter the ditch. The issue, in fact, threatened the viability of the entire neighborhood plan for several months. After extended negotiations, however, the proposed changes to the ditch were approved and the project moved forward.

The third challenge involved the transfer of Bill Kennedy Way from the Georgia Department of Transportation (GDOT) to the City of Atlanta, which was essential to creating a main street environment that includes on-street parking and street trees, says Brewer. GDOT required a comprehensive permit that

would restrict driveway access if the road was to remain under the agency's jurisdiction. Jurisdictional transfer therefore became necessary. Both GDOT and the city agreed to the transfer–which Greenstreet Properties also supported–but it was still an unexpectedly lengthy process.

In January 2003, Glenwood Park held its groundbreaking ceremony and infrastructure construction began. The developers knew up front that the site had major geotechnical and infrastructure issues. The site was covered with 60,000 cubic yards of concrete, which required demolition but was salvaged for onsite fill. An additional 800,000 pounds of granite rubble blocks found onsite were salvaged and used to build the walls of the neighborhood's central park. Major sewer lines needed to be rebuilt. Many areas also required removal or relocation of improperly placed fill.

Most unusually, 40,000 cubic yards of wood chips were discovered underground– enough to cover a football field 36 feet deep. The wood chips were hauled away and used as fuel in an Alabama waste-to-energy power plant, generating enough electricity to power 1,355 homes for a year.

Even accounting for these issues, the infrastructure work at Glenwood Park took longer than anticipated. Various factors contributed to the delays, including wet weather at critical periods. One particularly vexing problem was the discovery of 13 previously unknown underground storage tanks. Each time a tank was found, work stopped and the tanks were tested. Appropriate cleanup and disposal were then required, though no tanks presented major contamination problems.

Project Financing and Environmental Design

Financing for the land development at Glenwood Park was provided by a small group of "insiders" allowing construction to begin in spring 2004. No bank debt was used. As a

The innovative stormwater retention pond at Glenwood Park also serves as a popular community amenity.

Photo: Simmons Buntin

result, the developer has been able to make decisions quickly without pressure from investors. "While we don't know what the process would have been like with other investors," says Brewer, "we suspect our financial independence at Glenwood Park has made our life much easier and is one of the things that has helped us stay true to our vision and avoid compromises that would have hurt the neighborhood."

Making Glenwood Park as "green" as possible was Green Street Properties' objective from the beginning. The dedication to environmental design is manifested most clearly through the fact that Glenwood Park is a brownfield redevelopment dedicated to urbanism. The project is relatively high density—even for a location near downtown Atlanta—providing the opportunity for residents to drive less both inside and outside of the development. By one early estimate, Glenwood Park would save 1.6 million miles of driving per year over what residents would have driven if they instead lived in a "typical" new Atlanta development, though today Brown suspects that most people

who work offsite probably do in fact commute by car. Glenwood Park has demonstrated a 15% reduction in vehicle trips compared to greenfield development, based on SmartTrack program modeling, "but it feels like more," he adds.

Though a reduction in vehicle trips may not meet the developers' expectations so far, another onsite design feature does. Stormwater that isn't infiltrated on a lot-by-lot basis is routed to a formal pond in the neighborhood's central park, where it has a chance to settle and filter before slowly releasing downstream. Water from the pond is then used for common space irrigation: 35,000 gallons per week are pulled from the pond, supplemented by well water, to irrigate drought-resistant street trees and landscaping in the common spaces, eliminating the need to use water from the City of Atlanta and saving more than 1.8 million gallons of potable water per year.

The developer and homeowners have planted nearly 1,000 trees on the site where, previously, no trees had existed. With other landscaping, the goal is to enhance the

Glenwood Park features a mix of housing, from single-family homes (foreground) to luxury townhomes (background) with a view of downtown Atlanta.

community's aesthetics while providing shading and reducing heat island effects. Residents also maintain a community garden on the northern edge of the community.

"Green Built" Residences Set the Standard for New Housing in Urban Atlanta

After surveying multiple firms, Green Street Properties selected Capstone Partners, Hedgewood Properties and Whitehall Homes as Glenwood Park's homebuilders. The builders used Glenwood Park's architectural code to create home designs while Green Street Properties retained design approval. "Our builders have really delivered for us," says Brewer.

Glenwood Park features a variety of single-family homes in an eclectic mix of Southern, Art Deco and Craftsman architecture with a green building emphasis. All homes meet Atlanta's EarthCraft House program standards. EarthCraft is a green builder certification program developed in 1999 by the Greater Atlanta Home Builders Association and the

Southface Energy Institute that certifies new homes, commercial buildings and communities throughout the Southeastern U.S. Certification addresses indoor air quality, energy efficiency, water efficiency, resource-efficient design, resource-efficient building materials, waste management and site planning. Glenwood Park is one of five projects that served as a pilot for inaugural EarthCraft Communities certification.

The community was also selected as the site of a 2005 *Southern Living* Idea House. Featured in the August 2005 issue of *Southern Living* magazine, the Whitehall Homes-built residence at Glenwood Park reflects "the development's emphasis on the environment, incorporating green-building techniques that reduce operating costs and add value to the home," says Brown. "The home is a showcase of environmental construction technology–and just drop-dead gorgeous–displaying a better way of building to the millions of *Southern Living* readers."

The full community's green building

features include:

- Construction waste recycling, reducing landfill waste by 80%
- Permeable pavement parking areas
- Water-efficient landscaping
- Rainwater harvesting and reclamation
- Graywater irrigation systems
- Recycled wood fiber exterior trim
- Porch decking made from reclaimed waste wood and recycled plastic
- Super-efficient insulation
- Tankless water heaters
- Programmable thermostats and lighting control system
- Energy Star lighting fixtures and appliances
- High-performance HVAC systems
- Energy recovery ventilators

Additional Idea House features include a solar photovoltaic system, reclaimed wood flooring, 100% recycled drywall, pre-finished and low-VOC flooring and bio-resistant paints, high-efficiency particulate air filters and ultraviolet air cleaner and a rainwater harvesting cistern combined with metal roof approved for rainwater collection.

The Idea House itself uses 38% less energy than a comparable home, with 15% generated from solar panels on the residence's roof. It also has "a higher standard of indoor air quality, comfort and durability due to the care taken during the home's construction process," according to Idea House literature. The 3,700-square-foot, Arts and Crafts-style house was the first Building America-rated zero-energy Idea House in America.

Moving Into a Neighborhood with a Lived-In Look, by Design

Glenwood Park's first residents moved into the neighborhood in October 2004 and the last of 99 single-family homes was completed in fall 2011.

According to Pam Sessions, principle of Hedgewood Properties, the homes at Glenwood Park "sold like crazy to start." As the economy has cooled, however, sales have slowed–not so much because of demand but because homebuyers are less likely to receive financing, particularly for the higher-priced single-family homes, which today sell between $400,000 and $1 million. Changes in the marketplace due to the housing crisis mean that high-end homebuilders must typically size houses smaller and lower their prices, says Sessions. Though the sizes of the final single-family homes completed in 2011 didn't fall considerably at Glenwood Park, their designs and time on market were impacted.

An article for *Georgia Trend* magazine, notes that "the neighborhood already has a lived-in-look, by design." Nowhere is that more clear and appealing than in the attached townhomes at Glenwood Park. In total, nearly 100 multistory townhomes are located in the development and range in style from brownstones and distinct live/work units near the town center to high-end residences near the community's large, elliptical park. As of fall 2011, the northern edge of the park remained unbuilt, but is slated for the development of townhomes, as is the eastern property along Bill Kennedy Way, with its easy access to Interstate 20.

One of the newest residential additions to the neighborhood is Glenwood Condominiums, a four-story building of nine "pool condos" ranging from 761 to 966 square feet each and priced from $124,900 to $159,900 (as of fall 2011). The condos comprise the top three floors of the architecturally distinctive building. The condominium building is adjacent to the Glenwood Park Pool, a 6-lane, junior Olympic-sized pool that can be used by members (who need not be Glenwood Park residents). Additionally, the building uses a geothermal energy system and was the first multifamily geothermal project in Georgia.

Another distinct addition is 454

Photo: Loren Heyns, Courtesy of Green Street Properties

Glenwood Park succeeds in part because of its close attention to landscaping and architectural detail.

Hamilton Street, a grouping of nine town-houses designed by Brunning & Stang that sits at Glenwood Park's highest point and provides unimpeded views of downtown Atlanta. The two- and three-story townhouses range from 1,700 to 2,700 square feet and, at initial offering, were priced from $429,900 to $679,900. They feature brick and stucco exteriors, roof-top terraces and other high-end amenities.

Mixed Uses and Retail: The Challenge of Right-Sizing Infill Commercial

Green Street Properties partnered with the Meddin Company, an Atlanta firm that specializes in developing street-facing retail, to develop the mixed-use and retail portions of the community that are located around Brasfield Square. Three different architects designed the buildings to ensure both compatibility and uniqueness, creating building types and façades that are "inspired by the best of Atlanta's great historic neighborhoods," say designers from Dover, Kohl & Partners.

Fifty condominiums initially ranging in prices from $170,000 to $300,000 were offered in four buildings surrounding the square. The one- and two-bedroom units feature bamboo floors, nine- and ten-foot ceilings, granite countertops and large windows. Like the single-family homes, they comply with the Earth-Craft House program. "The condominiums provide the opportunity to live in an exciting Main Street environment that overlooks retail stores and shops and a beautiful park reminiscent of the squares in Savannah," says Katherine Kelly, Green Street Properties president.

The only pre-existing building on the site was sold to Parkside Partners, which has successfully converted it into an office condominium. The building was "nearly windowless and remarkably ugly, though solid," says Brewer. "Parkside has done a great job renovating it and it is turning out to be an exceptionally beautiful addition to the neighborhood."

Glenwood Park's retail includes shops and restaurants that bring vitality to the streets, provide residents with walkable destinations

74

Brasfield Square, located at the heart of Glenwood Park's commercial area, is surrounded by live/work townhomes and street-level retail with offices and apartments above.

Photo: Simmons Buntin

and reduce the number of local daily trips. In addition to the popular Vickery's restaurant and lounge, however, there is only one retail tenant in Brasfield Square: Perk, a neighborhood coffeehouse. Original tenants Vino Libro, a wine bar and bookstore focusing on cooking, art and design and Babalu's, a Latin restaurant with international bar, have since closed. Though other restaurants such as the Shed at Glenwood, Matador Cantina and the Smoothie Shop and businesses such as the Music Class, Intown Pediatric & Adolescent Medicine, Snap Fitness, Give N Go Cleaners and Southern Smiles Family Dentistry are succeeding, Brown admits that Glenwood Park's retail, at 48,000 total square feet, was "somewhat more space than was required to activate the product." Brown notes that the community-serving businesses have been most successful, while services such as high-end hair salons that were more reliant on an outside clientele did not survive. "This is not Buckhead," he says, referring to Atlanta's glitzy neighborhood

north of downtown.

For local businesses, Sessions says that Glenwood Park needs the retailer's "fourth store"—a business that has at least three successful stores elsewhere and which can then take a chance on a new infill neighborhood. Brown, for his part, had originally hoped for a denser town center, with buildings of five instead of three stories and underground or double-deck, above-ground parking to assist retailers, but the costs were too high.

Eight live-work units were built on the east side of Brasfield Square, what Brown calls "top-dollar townhomes," though he notes that the units cannot have retail because of limited parking. Additionally, Brown believes that retail within the live/work units would "starve traditional retail." Considering the prevalence of retail space at Glenwood Park—as of November 2011, eight of 21 storefronts are vacant, accounting for 15,000 of 48,000 square feet—the move to restrict business uses in the live/work units was wise. Glenwood Park also

75

Perk, Glenwood Park's neighborhood coffeeshop, anchors the mixed-use building across from Brasfield Square.

includes 20,000 square feet of office space–including the live/work units and renovated Parkside building–otherwise located above street-level retail.

Brown concedes that the developers reduced visible retail parking "in order to accommodate Glenwood Park's delightfully de-emphasized surface parking," which actually may have kept some businesses from moving to the new community. Additionally, he says, the project's retail layout was created to serve the urban design of the project, and the developers assumed the attractiveness of the project and a strong economy would overcome the need to do more market research and "actuation marketing" to attract and hold tenants. Sessions agrees, noting that even though the project is completely distinct, "it was tied to formula more than intuition," which may have impacted its ability–beyond the challenges of a struggling economy–to fill the retail spaces. Simply put, commercial space at Glenwood Park is overbuilt, and so far Greenstreet Properties has not been able to fill the vacant spaces with the right mix of tenants that would be supported by residents and visitors alike.

Conclusion: Redevelopment that Marries Green Design with New Urbanism

Brewer, who now leads a sustainable development in Costa Rica, had high aspirations for Glenwood Park. He hoped to convince people that they "can once again create wonderful, walkable, loveable places," he says. "So many of us visit the wonderful old neighborhoods of our country, or the wonderful old towns and cities of Europe and come back home raving about how much we love them. But too many of us have allowed ourselves to believe that it is impossible to create that kind of place anymore. Well, it's not."

Glenwood Park's awards indicate that the aspirations of Green Street Properties are resonating with the planning and design community. They include a coveted Charter Award from the Congress for New Urbanism, a Development of the Year Award from the Urban Land Institute, EarthCraft House Development of the Year, Community of the Year from the Greater Atlanta Home Builders Association and Outstanding Community from the Georgia Urban Forest Council.

Resident and visitor participation and use of the public spaces also demonstrate the project's success. "People are using the spaces as envisioned and that's a delight," says Sessions. Festivals and neighbor events are held regularly, ranging from Hotoberfest Beer Festival to the EarthShare Party in the Park to the City of Atlanta's 2008 Earth Day Festival.

"Just decades ago, the site was an abandoned industrial brownfield," writes the Natural Resources Defense Council's Kaid Benfield. "Now it's one of the best places in the city to live and also one of the most environmentally sustainable in the country." That sustainability was Green Street Properties's objective from the start. By marrying green building with New Urbanist design, the developers have created an authentic, environmentally responsible inner-city neighborhood.

DEFINING SUCCESS
Q&A with Walter Brown, Senior Vice President, Development and Environmental Affairs, Green Street Properties

What was the largest obstacle to obtaining project approval or buy-in and how was it overcome?
We benefited from a broad base of support throughout the professional and private communities that propelled the approval process forward at a fairly rapid pace. There were a few obstacles regarding traffic and fire access issues that were the most difficult aspects of the project, which resulted in some minor modifications that are not really noticed today by residents and visitors to the neighborhood.

What is an unexpected delight or success from the project?
I think the whole team would agree that the ongoing, unsolicited positive feedback we receive from people of all walks of life who have come in contact with Glenwood Park is the most delightful and long-lasting success story.

What hasn't lived up to expectations or has required unanticipated change?
While we enjoyed the benefits of a strong economy to complete 85% of the project, we had always envisioned a mid-rise condo tower along I-20 at the northern edge of the development to provide great skyline views of Atlanta and to help block some minor noise impacts of being located adjacent to a major interstate. This has required some difficult choices in terms of re-programming this portion of the site.

What continues to challenge or surprise you with the project?
I think our biggest challenge is the loss of all the builders who helped us create Glenwood Park due to the economic downturn. In addition to Atlanta's loss of creative new urban practitioners, we could have really used their ongoing presence in recent years to answer construction-related questions by residents who no longer have their original builder to work with.

How do you measure success?
For us the greatest success has been the confidence and reputation we acquired building Glenwood Park—and the lasting model we have that helps demonstrate to our business partners, new clients, elected officials and regulators our strong commitment to a credible planning process and a quality product.

Belmar
Lakewood, Colorado
by Simmons B. Buntin

Photo: Continuum Partners LLC

Because of the dynamic mix of retail, residences, and open space such as Belmar Plaza, Lakewood, Colorado's Belmar has become the thriving downtown the suburb has never had.

Belmar is a 22-block redevelopment of Villa Italia, a massive, 1960s-era shopping mall in the Denver suburb of Lakewood. The mixed-use, pedestrian-oriented project, featuring an urban plaza and formal village green, is the culmination of more than four years of joint planning between Continuum Partners, LLC and the City of Lakewood. Though buildout is not anticipated until 2017, Belmar has featured a successful mix of retail, entertainment, residential and office uses since its opening in 2004. What makes Belmar distinct is both its ambition–creating a vibrant downtown for suburban Lakewood where none existed before–and its concern for authenticity. By incorporating historic elements of the Denver region's "American Mercantile" vernacular including pedestrian-scaled blocks

with buildings ranging from two to five stories, wide sidewalks featuring street furniture and artistic elements, locally-made blond brick and handcrafted lighting fixtures and welcoming public spaces, Belmar strives to create a sense of place at once unique to Lakewood and yet clearly a part of the urban context of the Colorado Front Range.

The city and Continuum worked closely with neighbors to envision the mall's redevelopment, resulting in Belmar's integration with adjoining neighborhoods and the large arterial roads that run along its northern and western edges. Just as important as the project's collaborative approach to planning is Belmar's focus on environmental and economic sustainability. The city estimates Belmar will add nearly $1 billion and over 7,000 permanent jobs to the

JUST THE FACTS

- Located ten minutes west of downtown Denver in the suburb of Lakewood, Colorado
- 104-acre, 22-block redevelopment of the 1.4-million-square-foot Villa Italia mall
- Creates a new, pedestrian-oriented downtown on a grid street system adjacent to Lakewood's civic center and Belmar Park
- Villa Italia mall closed in 2001, Belmar construction began in 2002, first phase opened in 2004; full buildout expected by 2017
- Comprised of subareas that span a mix of uses, from large retail along arterials, to mixed-use retail/entertainment core, to mid-density residential
- 833 residential units so far, including condominiums, apartments, townhouses, five live/work residences and ten zero lot-line single-family houses; 1,500+ units at buildout
- 848,000 square feet of retail including more than 70 shops, 15 restaurants and entertainment so far; 1.1 million square feet at buildout
- 278,000 square feet of office so far; up to 800,000 square feet at buildout
- 5,000 parking spaces in public garages, surface lots and on-street parking
- 10 acres of open space including 2.1-acre urban green and 1.1-acre central plaza
- 1.75 MW solar array on roof of three parking garages offsets 5% of total Belmar power consumption
- Other environmental features include brownfield remediation, 14 wind turbines that power parking lot lighting, LEED Silver certification and an expanded single-stream recycling program
- $850 million project developed through public/private partnership–buildings are privately owned; streets, sidewalks and parks are publicly owned
- Developer: Continuum Partners, LLC
- Partner: GF Property Group, since 2006
- Planning and urban design: Elkus Manfredi Architects, Ltd. and Civitas, Inc.
- Residential developers: McStain Neighborhoods, Trammell Crow Residential, Sunburst Design, LLC, KB Homes, Harvard Communities and Continuum Partners, LLC.
- Awards include Urban Land Institute Award for Excellence, International Economic Development Council Public/Private Partnership Award, 2005 Congress for the New Urbanism Charter Award, U.S. EPA Phoenix Award for Brownfield Remediation, U.S. EPA Smart Growth Award and American Public Works Association Award for Public Street System

local economy upon buildout. Additionally, several of the buildings are LEED Silver certified and a number of steps were taken during mall demolition and subsequent construction to ensure the project is as resource-efficient and environmentally friendly as possible. What results is a transit-accessible, mixed-use suburban core located only ten minutes from downtown Denver, yet just as walkable, textured and central to its community.

Project History: Replacing the Largest Mall Between Chicago and the California Coast

When the Villa Italia shopping mall opened to fanfare in 1966, it was the largest indoor

The Villa Italia mall during its prime drew visitors from as far away as Kansas and Wyoming.

shopping center between Chicago and the California coast. Surrounded by a wide skirt of surface parking, the 104-acre mall grew to be 1.5 million square feet and host 140 stores. It regularly attracted visitors from as far away as Kansas and Wyoming. It quickly came to be the area's commercial and social hub, and in 1969 the 13 communities surrounding Villa Italia incorporated as the City of Lakewood—the largest incorporation in American history at the time. Today, Lakewood is Colorado's fourth largest city, with a population of 144,000 residents over 42.88 square miles.

"For most intents and purposes, the mall (had) really been the downtown," said Lakewood city manager Mike Rock in 2002. Indeed, Villa Italia hosted more than stores: festivals, parties and other gatherings occurred regularly within the mall's climate-controlled walls. But by the mid-1990s, the mall was in decline—even as an additional level was added in 1988 to compete with newer, two-story malls. In 1996, mall owners proposed a $50

million renovation and expansion, but then backed away when two anchors refused to sign long-term commitments. Two years earlier, at Villa Italia's retail peak, annual tax revenue from the mall was $3.12 million. By 2001, tax revenue had declined by half and stores were failing: the first of four anchors, Dillard's, closed in 2000. In 2001 J.C. Penney and Montgomery Ward followed suit. According to DeadMalls.com's Andrew Button, "Gasping for life for the last years of its existence, most of Villa Italia became empty, as tenants left in force. The crowd in the latter 1990s changed from people who chose to shop and spend money to a crowd that loitered and ravaged the once glorious mall."

Lakewood had a vested interest in Villa Italia not just because of tax revenue and civic identity, but also because of its prominent location in the community. Beginning in the 1970s, city officials planned a civic center directly west of the mall. By 2000, the city had constructed a new city hall, library, law enforcement complex and performing arts center adjacent to the mall. "We didn't want the centerpiece of the community to be a failed mall," said Rock. But city officials also recognized that a large shopping mall wasn't a sustainable economic or civic engine moving forward. "When we saw the Villa declining, we just didn't want to do a 'me too' project where you go in and strip the mall out and replace it with big box discount stories," says then-mayor Steve Burkholder.

In 1998 Burkholder initiated discussions with Denver-based Continuum Partners, LLC, about the possibility of redeveloping the mall. "Our premise is that the things that hold the best value over time are mixed-use and things that are pedestrian-scale," said Continuum principal Tom Gougeon in 2002, "The project at Villa Italia was a natural for us."

In 1999 Continuum purchased the underlying land and improvement rights from the Bonfils-Stanton Foundation, which managed rights to the original 750-acre Belmar estate upon which Villa Italia was built. A year later, Continuum purchased the mall itself, through a complex lease structure. Many tenants resisted the acquisition, however. While the Foundation owned the land, a ground lease with 140 lease subinterests—each with veto power—was held by the real estate portfolio division of Equitable Life Assurance Society of America. Additionally, the Foundation and Equitable Life had been in litigation for several years. "We said, 'It's broken, it's dying, but it's not dead enough.' It's going to be messy. And someone is going to try to stop you. Someone always does," recalls Gougeon.

He was right: several of the mall's few remaining tenants resisted, requiring the city to exercise its powers of eminent domain to evict them, which Jefferson County Courts later upheld. "If the city hadn't been willing to use eminent domain, the mall would never be redeveloped in a timely way," said Rock, as reported in *Governing* in 2002. "Even one tenant can stand in the way."

With a projected cost of more than $850 million, Continuum tapped into a number of funding sources, creating "a classic public/private partnership" to ensure the project would move forward, says Burkholder. Continuum's internal equity came from Falcone family equity; Continuum founder and CEO Mark Falcone was able to use personal family funding to initiate the project. Continuum leveraged this equity to fund 100% of predevelopment costs of property acquisition, design and environmental remediation. Total public-purpose infrastructure costs were expected to reach $165 million, though current forecasts approach $188 million.

Approximately $79 million in public costs were funded through bonds, with the balance financed privately with a combination of debt and equity that will be reimbursed over time. In 2001, about the time the mall officially closed, the city enacted a 2.5% public improvement fee for retail transactions in the Belmar area to pay off the bonds. The sales tax remitted directly to Continuum. To address resident concerns about the additional tax burden, the city waived 1% of Lakewood's 3% sales tax—a reduction that will continue until the debt is paid off or for a maximum of 25 years. Additionally, the city rebated half of the construction use tax back to Continuum.

Additionally, in 2002 the U.S. Environmental Protection Agency's Brownfields Revolving Loan Funds program provided a $1.95 million loan for the removal of contaminated soil and in-situ groundwater remediation during and after mall demolition.

Public Participation

Before demolition and construction began, Lakewood and Continuum invited residents to help determine the future of Villa Italia. Mayor Burkholder set up an informational website and then initiated the 30-member Villa Advisory Committee, comprised of citizens, local

Located just ten minutes from downtown Denver, Lakewood was positioned to create a defining, mixed-use core in place of a large shopping mall.

business representatives, city staff, and other stakeholders in February 2000. Over a period of more than a year, the committee met regularly to create a vision that could be presented to the Lakewood Planning Commission and city council for approval. The city and Continuum representatives knew they had their work cut out for them: "Going into this, we didn't take it for granted that people would understand what was going on," says Gougeon. Indeed, at the first meeting, citizens favored low-density commercial development featuring plenty of parking–another mall, in effect. "A lot of people said, 'I went to my prom there. That's where I first saw the Easter Bunny and sat in Santa Claus's lap,'" said Burkholder in *Governing*. "There was a lot of nostalgia attached to that place." In response, committee members were provided cameras and instructed to photograph places that represent what they'd like the redevelopment to look like. As it turned out, the committee members' preferences were

quite different from the nostalgic notions they had articulated.

"Not one person took one picture of one building with only one floor," said Frank Gray, Lakewood director of community planning and development. Instead, they returned with photographs of pedestrian-oriented urban places: Denver's Lower Downtown and downtown Boulder and Colorado Springs, for example. "The photos showed flower-filled sidewalks, outdoor cafés, pedestrian malls, streets arranged on a grid system and multi-story buildings where people lived, worked and shopped," writes Christine Tatum in *The Denver Post*.

"Once they realized that density was not an evil thing–and that they actually liked it–our discussions took a whole new turn," says Gougeon. By the time the mall closed, the Villa Advisory Committee put its full weight behind a redevelopment that would combine office, retail, entertainment, housing and

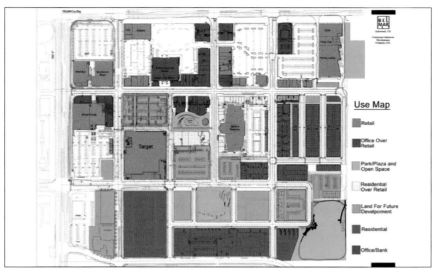

Belmar use map.

community uses. It supported a pedestrian-oriented downtown district reestablished on a street grid with "important public spaces and mixed-use buildings and subdistricts," notes a December 2001 staff report to the Lakewood Planning Commission.

With the developer and community vision in place, the city could focus on rezoning the property. Though the existing zoning did not allow for a mixed-use development, the property was part of the West Alameda Avenue Corridor Urban Redevelopment Area, which was adopted in 1998 and amended by the Lakewood Reinvestment Authority and city council in 2000 to include Villa Italia. With its amendment, Lakewood created the West Alameda Avenue Corridor Urban Redevelopment Plan, the property's urban renewal plan.

The Plan allowed Lakewood to rezone the site to Planned Development (PD), which, according to Planning Commission staff, identifies specifically how the property is to be redeveloped while allowing reasonable flexibility during future phases of development. The PD not only identifies what uses will be permitted on the property, it provides for a

specific review and approval process for future development. It is intended to assist the city and developer with a smooth review process in the future to encourage well thought-out and sustainable redevelopment of the site, while ensuring that the interests of all parties are adequately represented.

In its recommendation for the rezoning, Planning Commission staff noted that the zoning would allow for a development "that will make a positive contribution to the area and the City as a whole. The redevelopment of the dead mall, the introduction of a street grid system that is pedestrian-friendly, the provision of public space and the proposed mix of uses which in turn promotes an active downtown area provides an opportunity to develop the property in a manner that will be a significant improvement and benefit to the Community and the neighborhood."

The rezoning was approved in December 2001. In 2006, GF Property Group joined Continuum as development partner "to bring more depth of capital to the project," says Continuum development director Roger Pecsok. "By bringing in GF Property Group, Belmar

Retail within Belmar varies greatly, and changes as it radiates from the urban core. Retail along Alaska Drive reflects a transitional suburban streetscape, yet still pedestrian-oriented.

was not only able to continue developing through the economic downturn and to maintain many of our smaller inline tenants, but also to bring in three new anchors: Target, Best Buy and Nordstrom Rack."

Design and Review

While PD zoning sets base land-use parameters, the Villa Italia Modification No. 3 Official Development Plan (ODP)–created by Civitas in conjunction with Elkus Manfredi Architects and approved in January 2002 (revised 2006)–establishes the provisions and criteria of the redevelopment. Specifically, the ODP identifies permitted land uses, transportation network, open space network, required setbacks, building separation and building height, parking ratios, proposed bike path connection and pedestrian connections. These requirements are further defined in the Belmar Design Standards and Guidelines, approved in March 2002 (revised 2005).

The ODP notes that "Belmar is intended to serve as the symbolic and functional downtown for the Lakewood community." It codifies the city's objectives for the redevelopment and confirms that the project will build out in phases.

According to the ODP, Belmar shares several goals with the pre-existing Alameda Avenue Overlay Zone District, which was created in 2000. The shared goals include creating a unique place within the metro area for working, shopping, living and recreation; balancing open space with development intensity; and maintaining the integrity and viability of the adjacent residential neighborhoods.

Two additional goals were added by the ODP: 1) Reinforce the civic, commercial, recreation and park uses west of Wadsworth Boulevard in Lakewood Commons and Belmar Park to create a larger downtown area for the city; and 2) Develop a mixed-use retail, entertainment, employment and residential center that is compact, walkable, efficiently served by transit and eminently attractive and livable.

Additionally, the ODP creates a series of subareas within the 22 urban blocks of

Teller Street, viewed here from Belmar's Urban Green, serves as the community's "main street."

Photo: Simmons Buntin

the plan. With the ODP's phased approach, Continuum has the flexibility to update the subareas as Belmar builds out, according Liz DiLorenzo, former development associate at Continuum. That flexibility is facilitated through the Belmar Design Standards and Guidelines, which set the framework for decision-making by the Architectural Control Committee (ACC) established as part of the ODP. The ACC is charged with reviewing and approving all development within Belmar, including site planning, architectural design, landscape design, lighting and sign/graphic design. Example design principles include:

- Orient buildings and entrances to the street and/or public open spaces in order to create a defined street space and strong visual character, provide human scale, focus activity toward the public realm, and to promote pedestrian activity, safety and comfort.
- Create buildings that, individually and/or collectively, provide human scale and interest through the use of varied forms, materials, details and/or colors.
- Use durable materials, particularly on the ground level façade of the building. Consider the use of stone, precast concrete, cast stone and/or brick materials as a continuation of the region's masonry traditions.
- Maximize the transparency of ground floor, street-facing commercial façades.

Individual subareas may also incorporate their own guidelines. At a minimum, these additional guidelines must regulate site plan and/or urban design; architecture; landscape architecture; public and private street design; encroachments into the public right of ways; publicly accessible parks, plazas and open spaces; and signage. "The guidelines ensure over time that as each increment of development occurs, as each building is added to the district, that those buildings are appropriate," said Gougeon at the February 2002 rezoning hearing. "The ODP and the design guidelines create a framework for focusing on what is most important, rather than any particular single style."

The ODP and Design Guidelines and Standards established a distinct plan and, to

Photo: Simmons Buntin

Belmar Plaza serves as the focal point of Belmar, surrounded by residences, restaurants, and Belmar's wonderful public art.

a degree, visual representation of Belmar's blocks and buildings. But "[t]he building part isn't tough," says former Continuum principal Will Fleissig. "The hard part is creating a civic realm. The streets, the streetscape and a pedestrian quality all must be incorporated to make us feel like this is a real place." By Belmar's grand opening on May 14, 2004–celebrated by 100,000 visitors over that first weekend–the civic realm had indeed been established with the project's first phase: a six-block area of retail, entertainment and residential uses centered around the central public plaza. Today, three-quarters of Belmar is complete.

Achieving Lasting Value: The Street and Cultural Life

Belmar's Design Standards and Guidelines state, "A high level of architectural, landscape and street and park design quality is expected in order to achieve a lasting value for the district." Thanks in part to the collaborative work of a number of architects and landscape architects, Belmar's greatest strength may

be its high design quality, particularly in the district's streetscapes. These spaces transition smoothly from subarea to subarea through the use of human-scaled and inviting façades, wide sidewalks and patio seating at restaurants and elements such as street furniture and public art. For example, fragments of poetry and other creative vignettes can be found throughout Belmar, set into sidewalks and building exteriors. "We wanted to create little 'ah-has' in unexpected places so that people can discover them as they walk through Belmar," says Eliza Prall, Belmar's former director of marketing and community development.

"A great deal of thought went into the relationship between the street and the sidewalk," adds Gougeon. "No detail was too small, from custom designed light fixtures to tree grates to manhole covers." In their book *Retrofitting Suburbia*, Ellen Dunham-Jones and June Williamson point to Belmar's custom-fabricated stainless steel cable over-the-road lighting system as "[o]ne memorable design feature that makes Belmar streets distinctive."

The lighting system, created and installed by a local firm, recalls the historic lighting fixtures of narrow European streets. "If you see a photo with that lighting system, people will say, 'Oh, that's Belmar, that's Lakewood,'" says Gougeon. Though Dunham-Jones and Williamson question whether the lighting system is "overly busy," they agree with the success of the district's public spaces: "The streetscape at Belmar is both welcoming and intelligently, thoroughly designed."

At the heart of Belmar is the 1.1-acre urban plaza, "designed to be the focal point and social epicenter of the development," says DiLorenzo. The plaza is surrounded by outdoor cafés, a 16-screen movie theater with its iconic Art Deco-style spire, the five-story Residences at Belmar and other mixed-use buildings on what may be considered to be Belmar's main street, South Teller. During the mild months of spring, summer and fall, the plaza features a flowing fountain, architectural elements such as large marble globes, outdoor lighting, lush plantings, plenty of shaded seating areas and the energetic activity of residents, shoppers and diners. From November through February, it is transformed into an ice skating rink and decorations change accordingly, including artificial evergreens made of brightly colored street signs and skis.

Continuum actively programs activities across Belmar. Regular events include the Here Comes the Sun Sidewalk Sale with family activities and live entertainment in May; the Market at Belmar, a European-inspired public market every Sunday from June through September; Music on the Plaza, featuring live acoustic and jazz ensembles every Friday evening from June through August; and Festival Italiano, a September celebration of Italian food and wine stemming in part from the site's Villa Italia heritage. The Festival brings together more than 70 food, wine and artisan vendors and attracts 80,000 to 100,000 people over two days.

Anchoring the plaza's northern edge is a 90,000-square-foot mixed-use building with ground-floor retail and restaurants. An event and meeting space that included a 9,000-square-foot ballroom, conference rooms and an outdoor terrace overlooking the plaza was once located on the second floor. Today, the space hosts the Paul Mitchell School for Cosmetology. At one time, the district also hosted the Lab at Belmar, an institution "dedicated to contemporary art and thought, combining elements of a museum, think tank and public forum," according to Lab literature. The 11,500-square-foot, two-story building designed by Los Angeles architect Hagy Belzberg hosted art exhibitions, weekly lectures and literary readings and adult education programs. The Lab opened in September 2006 with the assistance of Continuum and the Denver Art Museum's Adam Lerner, the inspiration behind Mixed Taste: Tag-Team Lectures on Unrelated Topics, the Lab's initial series. In May 2009, however, the Lab merged with the Museum of Contemporary Art Denver and moved to the museum's new location in downtown Denver. Now the space is filled by the Ohio Center for Broadcasting, which trains students for careers in radio, television and production. The Center's Belmar campus also hosts a music station, MileHighUnderground.com.

Located one block east of the plaza, Belmar's Block 7 Arts District is comprised of an art and design co-op that includes a row of studios and a central gallery. The studios fill the street-level spaces along Saulsbury Street, featuring floor-to-ceiling glass fronts that allow passers-by to view the design work in progress. The co-op is open all year and holds special events every other month.

A Wide Range of Retail and Office

Though Belmar was designed from the beginning to provide a sense of cultural and civic identity, it must also replace the tax revenue lost by the closing of Villa Italia. Continuum

Photo: Simmons Buntin

The Residences at Belmar Plaza, Belmar's tallest building, features a range of high-end residences adjacent to Belmar Plaza.

is doing that, ironically, by reducing the square footage of retail by nearly one-third–848,000 square feet today with a total of 1 million square feet planned at buildout. Belmar's retail landscape varies by subarea and ranges from street-level shops and restaurants on Teller Street and Alaska Drive to large big-box stores that predominantly border Alameda Avenue and Wadsworth Boulevard. Considering the quick transition from the major arterials to the urban core, Continuum's approach–fostered by the city's flexibility in accommodating revisions to the subareas–is working. "As the project has matured, we've been able to respond to changes in the marketplace because of the city's sophisticated approach to planning," says DiLorenzo. For example, the original plan proposed a 250-room hotel accessible from Wadsworth or Alameda. However, in its market analysis Continuum concluded the hotel would not succeed. Adding additional large retailers, particularly at the intersection of Alameda and Wadsworth, though, seemed promising.

Best Buy and Nordstrom Rack have since been built at the intersection, matching existing big-box stores that bridge Alameda and Alaska Drive, including Staples, DSW Shoe Warehouse, Party City and Hobby Lobby. While those stores predominantly face Alameda and are served by surface parking adjacent to the arterial, Dick's Sporting Goods takes a hybrid approach, with accessibility both from Alameda and the pedestrian-scaled Alaska Drive. From both Alameda and Wadsworth, in fact, it is not readily apparent that Belmar is anything other than a series of suburban power centers with enhanced architecture. That was particularly tricky in the beginning, as Belmar's vibrant core is not readily visible to the 150,000 cars that pass the intersection of Wadsworth and Alameda daily.

The need for chain stores in addition to local retailers is critical, however. "What we do is borrow the strength of those national retailers because we need them, because that's who dominates the U.S. retail world today," says Gougeon in *Retrofitting Suburbia.* "But we consciously make the decision that we're going to forgo some income and make a commitment to having a mix." According to Dunham-Jones and Williamson, Belmar's leasing group created a plan for "enlivening the mix" that targeted successful Denver-area businesses, encouraging them with enticing lease options to open an establishment in Belmar. Additionally, Continuum provided direct funding to further assist some local shops and restaurants.

"We wanted a good mix of national and local tenants, but typically the local tenants have little value attached to them; you need retailers with solid credit who can pay larger rents," said Gougeon in 2005. "I think we've managed to create a good mix that allowed us to get the project off the ground while keeping it interesting and giving the locals time to succeed." Today, Belmar features over 80 retail and entertainment establishments, including one of the nation's largest Whole Foods natural foods markets, the theater, an urban Target located above a parking structure and a below-ground Lucky Strike bowling alley. Independent retailers and services range from Blissful MedSpa to Wild at Heart Boutique. Fifteen restaurants, predominantly local, offer a wide range of cuisine, from Baker Street Pub & Grill's English tavern food to Wasabi Sushi Bar and the Oven Pizza & Vino. Belmar hosts a coffee shop—the Press Coffee Company—as well as a tea shop: Wystone's World Teas. As of November 2011, retail spaces at Belmar are 90% leased.

Office space—located primarily on the second floor of mixed-use buildings along Teller and Alaska—is 100% leased and accounts for nearly 278,000 square feet. At buildout, Belmar may include up to 800,000 square feet of Class A office space, and Continuum offers build-to-suit opportunities for major office or medical users. Existing office tenants include the Corporate Office Images Executive Suites, the Integer Group (one of the nation's leading marketing agencies), MCAD Technologies and a number of other financial and real estate services. Medical tenants include Belmar Ambulatory Surgical Center, Metropolitan Pathologists, Mile High Family Medicine and several dentists and other practitioners.

Distinct Urban Residences in a New Urban Location

The homes at Belmar are decidedly metropolitan and, along with the office units, have rented and sold well from the beginning. More than 830 residential units have been built so far and Continuum expects to offer at least 1,500 residential units at buildout, up from the ODP's projected 1,300. As of November 2011, the 478 existing apartments are 98% leased. Sixty homes including condominiums and duplexes were under construction in late 2011; 282 townhomes, condominiums and lofts along with nine zero lot-line homes have already been built.

"The housing has been very well received," said Gougeon in *New Towns* in 2005. "It's an urban choice—no clubhouse, no pool. The amenity is you get to live in this 'downtown' setting." Though many of the residential units are located toward the eastern and southern edges of the property in residential-only buildings—adjacent to older single-family neighborhoods yet still clearly urban—a number of for-sale and leased units are integrated into mixed-use buildings surrounding the plaza. These include the four-story 410 S. Teller St. building of 35 urban apartments over ground-floor retail, ranging from 660 to 1,533 square feet and one to three bedrooms. The three-story 470 S. Teller St. building includes eight townhome-style apartments above retail. Each two-story unit of 1,200 square feet features two bedrooms, walk-up access and outdoor decks. Both Teller St. buildings feature parking in an adjacent garage and higher-end amenities such as granite countertops and maple cabinets.

Located across from the Block 7 Arts District, one block east of the plaza, are the 66 units of the Gallery Residences, which include 63 single-story, one- to three-bedroom apartments and three two-story, two-bedroom townhome-style units. The apartments range from 646 to 1,288 square feet in four three-story buildings spanning one block. The 7133 W. Virginia Building is located south of the plaza and the Gallery Residences. It features 62 luxury apartments ranging from 598 to 1,435 square feet and one to three bedrooms. The building features walk-up access and a landscaped courtyard. At the southern edge of the property, just south of Belmar Square, are the Alexan Belmar Apartments, developed by Trammell Crow Residential. The series of four-story buildings offers 307 apartments with private parking in an adjacent garage. Unlike the "downtown" rentals, the Alexan features a clubhouse, fitness center, swimming pool, game room, business center, cyber café and multiple courtyards in a more traditional suburban apartment complex layout.

As with the rental units, Belmar offers a wide array of for-sale housing choices from local and national builders. While the market pushed prices up rapidly during the first three years of Belmar's buildout, home prices have leveled and in some cases dropped since 2008. The $25 million five-story Residences at Belmar Plaza building anchors the southern edge of the plaza and is the tallest building in Belmar. Its 62 "sophisticated" condominiums range from one to three bedrooms plus den and 950 to 2,888 square feet. The condos feature granite countertops, hardwood flooring, nine-foot ceilings, terraces and balconies, access-controlled underground parking and five custom-built penthouse residences. The Residences sold from $219,000 to $996,000.

A set of smaller residential buildings is located along Alaska Drive, where the street nears the eastern edge of Belmar. Alaska does not continue into the adjacent neighborhood due to an agreement with the neighbors, who were concerned about increased traffic. The Theatre Lofts offer 12 units of 1,020 square feet each above street-level retail in a three-story building. The second-floor units feature

500-square-foot terraces. They sold for an average of $245,000 in 2005. The three- and four-story contemporary Eastside Town Homes are Belmar's only live/work units, though four separate live/work units are now under construction one block west. The five Eastside units average more than 2,100 square feet, offer three bedrooms plus "flex space," and include two-car garages. The first building is located on the south side of Alaska Drive, while a second, eight-unit building is planned for the north side. The five units built in 2008 were priced beginning at about $450,000 but now sell for as low as $319,000.

The Lofts at Belmar Square are located on the southern edge of the square, adjacent to the Alexan Apartments and sharing a multistory parking garage. The 75-unit, four-story building was developed by Trammell Crow Residential and features 61 single-story condominiums and 14 two-story condos ranging from 920 to 1,371 square feet. The Lofts share public amenities such as the clubhouse and fitness center with the Alexan. One-bedroom lofts sold from $168,000 in 2009 and in late 2011 two-bedroom lofts sold from $219,900.

McStain Neighborhoods, a successful local homebuilder with a focus on sustainable design, constructed Belmar's 132 Urban Row Homes located near the eastern edge of the site. The three- and four-story townhomes feature three-, four- and five-bedroom layouts from 1,593 to 2,471 square feet in five floor plans. Each unit has an attached two-car garage accessible from an alley. The rowhomes were priced from about $360,000 when construction and sales began in 2005; in 2009, prices ranged from $160,000 to more than $400,000. While the downtown mixed-use buildings incorporate brick and masonry as their predominant "American Mercantile" façade, the Urban Row Homes feature exteriors composed primarily of wood cladding with steel ornamentation—different yet still within the regional vernacular.

Belmar's only single-family detached

A parking garage predominantly supporting big-box retail on Belmar's periphery features roof-mounted photovoltaics and ground-floor retail.

Photo: Simmons Buntin

homes are nine zero lot-line, contemporary urban cottages built by local homebuilder Harvard Communities. The two-story homes on narrow lots feature attached two-car garages, ten-foot ceilings, gourmet kitchens, private courtyards, full basements and "dramatic modern details throughout including interior trim, railings and fireplace designs," according to marketing materials. The homes of 2,900 square feet listed from $550,000 and up.

Finally, national builder KB Home began construction on its "Built to Order" paired homes, or duplexes, near Belmar Square in early 2011. The homes range from 1,366 to 1,682 square feet and two to four bedrooms and feature private side yards and attached garages in four designs. They sell from the high $200,000s.

Sustainability Efforts at Belmar: Significant and Successful

Continuum's commitment to sustainability throughout Belmar is clear. "We are dedicated to energy-use reduction and the responsible use of limited natural resources," says Mark Falcone.

Harvard Communities' Courtyard homes take advantage of state-of-the-art design and technology that result in 40% less energy use than a typical new home. Harvard's homes are registered in three energy efficiency and green building programs: Built Green Colorado, Energy Star and Environments for Living. They are constructed with recycled and, when possible, locally produced materials using low-VOC paints and finishes. They incorporate tight shell construction, high insulation values, low-e windows, high-efficiency furnaces and fresh air ventilation systems. McStain's Urban Row Homes likewise feature a focus on green building. They are Energy Star-certified and feature sealed-combustion furnaces and water heaters, closed cell foam and blown fiberglass, low-e windows, low-VOC paints and finishes, recycled materials and water-efficient appliances. Indeed, every residential unit at Belmar meets Energy Star or Colorado Green Built standards.

The commercial and mixed-use buildings at Belmar are also super-efficient. Belmar used the U.S. Green Building Council's LEED criteria to guide the design and development of many buildings, including those that house Whole Foods and Mile High Wine & Spirits, two advanced mixed-use buildings and other retail spaces, which are all LEED Silver certified. Additionally, a three-story mixed-use building of office space above retail was the first of its type in the nation to receive LEED Silver certification.

Sustainability initiatives began well before construction, however. Continuum spent more than $4 million to clean up water, soil and concrete contamination (including PCE, PCBs and hydrocarbons) caused by dry cleaning and car repair facilities at Villa Italia, qualifying the site for federal brownfield remediation funds. Demolition also mandated significant asbestos abatement, resulting in the removal and disposal of 14,000 square feet of cinder block coating, wall and ceiling plaster and various other fittings and coatings. To remedy contaminated groundwater, in-situ remediation was conducted. A series of wells used to inject nutrients and a carbon source to facilitate the biological breakdown of PCE was installed. Groundwater treatment has concluded but onsite monitoring still takes place.

Rather than ship the waste material from the demolition of the Villa Italia structure to a landfill, Continuum recycled or reused 88% of all materials (by weight) from the original site. Two million square feet of asphalt were milled into more than 40,000 tons of material used for temporary roadways and base under building slabs. More than 200,000 tons of concrete from the original mall slab were crushed and reused onsite. All steel, copper and aluminum was recycled and many surviving windows, doors and light fixtures were reused in Continuum's downtown Denver headquarters—as well as at Belmar's onsite sales and leasing office.

To continue its efforts in recycling, Continuum has worked with Waste Management to "implement an expanded single-stream recycling program for all residents as well as office and retail tenants," according to the Lakewood Department of Planning and Public Works. Additionally, Continuum was able to salvage and successfully transplant 130 mature trees.

Belmar's most visible sustainability initiative is the 2008 installation of 8,370 solar photovoltaic panels on the roofs of three parking garages. The 1.75 MW array generates 2.3 million kWh of electricity per year, enough to offset 5% of Belmar's total power consumption. The electricity is delivered directly into Xcel Energy's grid as part of the utility company's Energy Solar Rewards Program. In return, Xcel provides electricity to Belmar at a price slightly under market rate. "This is one of the most ambitious renewable energy projects initiated in Colorado to date," says John Hereford of Hereford Capital Advisors, a development partner in the project. It was also the largest parking structure-mounted solar array in the country. "Any time you are first around the track, things can be challenging. Many developers talk about green, but it takes a committed visionary like Continuum to make this type of project a reality," he concludes. Smaller solar cells also power park-and-display kiosks that serve 350 on-street parking spaces.

Another unique power-generating feature is Belmar's 14-turbine wind farm, which serves both as public art and a means to power lighting for a large parking lot. The turbines, which are located in the large surface lot adjacent to DSW Designer Shoe Warehouse, Party City and Hobby Lobby in the northeast corner of Belmar, can generate as much as 106,000 kWh per year. Though lighting requirements exist to ensure visitor and resident safety, outdoor lighting is designed in cooperation with the International Dark Skies Association "to preserve and protect the nighttime environment and reduce light pollution," according to a

Belmar's Block 7 features highly visible art studios and galleries. The colorful Gallery Residences are reflected in the windows.

Belmar factsheet.

Prior to the development of Belmar, no transit served the site's interior. Now, however, several Regional Transit District bus routes circulate through the site, providing many stops and further meeting the city's goals of creating a pedestrian-oriented, transit-accessible downtown.

In all, Belmar's efforts toward reducing its environmental footprint particularly in the area of energy use are significant and successful. "The Department of Energy estimates that 39% of the total U.S. energy resources are consumed by residential and commercial buildings," said Gougeon in a KGUN 9 News interview. "By incorporating green building principles into our buildings, developers, builders and facility managers can have a significant impact on reducing energy consumption." Lakewood mayor Bob Murphy agrees: "Being able to showcase the use of alternative energy in projects like Belmar is important as we continue working toward attracting jobs from the new energy sector to Lakewood."

Conclusion: A New City Center and a Distinct Success

In 2009, the Lakewood Reinvestment Authority commissioned a study, conducted by Development Research Partners, to assess the economic and fiscal impacts of Belmar from 2002 through 2008. The report states that Belmar has had a total positive economic impact of $207.2 million, including a fiscal impact to the city of $10.6 million. In 2008 alone, impacts totaled $49.5 million, with a net fiscal impact of nearly $2 million. The impacts are measured in five categories: construction activity, business operations, employee impact, resident impact and visitor impact. The impacts are both quantitative–Belmar employee earnings totaled nearly $322.5 million from 2004 to 2008, for example–and qualitative: since redevelopment began in 2002, assessed property values in the area have risen significantly. In Belmar alone, property values increased 392%

from 2002 to 2008. Additionally, in the six-year span, Belmar attractions and events have drawn some 613,000 visitors resulting in $3.1 million in taxable purchases. The report concludes, "A similar level of impact will likely occur annually, assuming no changes to the tax structure, market conditions and development patterns."

Economic viability is important but city leadership recognizes that payoff comes in more ways than just tax revenue–and that payoff is rarely immediate. "The pressure on elected officials is to get something done during their individual terms of office," said city manager Mike Rock in *Governing*. "The council has shown the courage to say this is an important project and will take a long time."

Even in a down economy, Belmar is a distinct success–it has reinvigorated Lakewood, creating a dynamic, mixed-use downtown that serves as a model for redeveloping suburban malls across the U.S.

DEFINING SUCCESS
Q&A with Mark Falcone, CEO and Founder, Continuum Partners

What was the largest obstacle to obtaining project approval or buy-in and how was it overcome?
Two issues stand out. The first was getting the community comfortable with tearing down their mall. Villa Italia occupied a big place in people's memories in Lakewood. They had their proms there, their first date and for many people it was where they had their first job. Imagining a community without the mall was a very real hurdle for Lakewood. The Mayor appointed a citizens group of about 30 people and we met once a month for a year and created a visioning process with them. One of the great breakthrough moments was when we handed people disposable cameras (they still had them in 2000) and tasked everyone with taking photos of places they thought would be appropriate for the new Villa Italia. It is remarkable how consistent the images were that people brought back. From that point forward it went easily.

The second major issue was getting the larger retailers comfortable with a more urban format in the Denver suburbs. This was very difficult. We did not get there with a few of them and had to open the project without the anchor retailers we would have liked. We eventually wore them down and in subsequent phases were able to add retailers like Whole Foods, Target and others who have added tremendous energy to the retail offering, but it hurt us trying to operate without them in the early years. Interestingly, the office and residential users never flinched at the plan.

What is an unexpected delight or success from the project?
The residential and office were successful much earlier than we had expected. We were very concerned we would not draw well there until we had a critical mass of retail in place. It turned out that it does not take much retail to offer those users a lot more amenity than is available to them in more conventional locations. The scale and place-making characteristics were immediately appealing and evident to the office users and residential buyers.

What hasn't lived up to expectations or has required unanticipated change?

The retail has not drawn from as large a radius area as we had originally anticipated. We sincerely believed that the quality of the environment would cause people to bypass other options to come here. The reality is that retail shoppers are motivated by the variety of the offering and the convenience of the trip. The high street experience in and of itself was not necessarily the major draw for the retail shopper. We have adjusted to account for that reality and now have better defined our target retail market.

What continues to challenge or surprise you with the project?

How complex it is to actually manage and coordinate so many different uses and activities in one place. We manage everything from the parking meters to someone's apartment. Most businesses work hard to eliminate complexity and this kind of environment manufactures complexity. That reduces efficiencies and makes everything you do a bit more expensive. The challenge is learning how to manage to a tolerable level of efficiency without dumbing the project down. We get better at that every day. I now sometimes look at an ambitious new mixed-use project and think to myself: They have no idea what they don't know yet.

How do you define and measure success?

I don't think we have gone 12 months without some construction on this site since we opened in 2004. Even through the downturn this place has continued to grow and add to itself. It literally gets better every month. That is the way a vital downtown works. The more stuff that gets built, the better the place becomes. I really think this place has developed a life of its own and generates its own demand and inertia now.

Downtown Redevelopment

One of the most notable downtown redevelopments of the last 50 years is that by Suisun City, California, which replaced a polluted harbor, derelict housing and decaying Main Street with a dynamic new civic center, public plaza, marina, mixed-use projects, and neo-traditional neighborhoods.

Ours has never been, really, just a country of easygoing transients. There has always been a counter-tradition of learning to make the best of exile, of building from recollections of what was prized and torn away.

Robert Adams, *Why People Photograph*

How much has been "prized and torn away" in American cities in the last 50 years? Plenty. Too much of what has been torn away was wonderful, from native ecosystems to historic neighborhoods. For the three case studies of this section, however, what has been torn away–though considered serviceable and necessary in their day–stood in the way of what are now vibrant districts, neighborhoods and regenerated landscapes. Dedicated planning, good urban design and hard work have made them intentional and integral parts of their respective downtowns.

In Portland, Oregon, the city restored access to the Willamette River by tearing down a six-lane freeway. What resulted is RiverPlace: a vibrant mix of urban housing, a marina, riverfront lodging and a broad park and café-lined esplanade, all stitched into the fabric of downtown. In Austin, Texas, principles of sustainability created the framework for redeveloping a derelict, six-block section of downtown: Second Street District. At the center of the resource-efficient mix of retail, lodging, a green city hall and high-rise living is art–literally and figuratively, for in Austin, art, music and culture create the tangible sense of place. Suisun City, California, reinvented itself by reclaiming its heavily polluted harbor and restoring its historic downtown. Two decades later, citizens celebrate the Suisun City Waterfront District: a dynamic, mixed-use harborside downtown featuring a new civic center, town plaza, marina, eclectic Main Street and restored access to the Suisun Marsh.

Each of these projects demonstrates the importance of visioning, public-private partnerships, public involvement and creative financing when redeveloping areas at the downtown scale–areas that subsequently serve as catalysts for further redevelopment. They also reveal that persistence may be the greatest attribute of all if we hope to create city centers that will be prized once again.

RiverPlace
Portland, Oregon
by Simmons B. Buntin

Portland, Oregon's RiverPlace restores access from downtown to the Willamette River, replacing a freeway and industrial site with an esplanade, parks, retail, housing, hotels, and a marina.

RiverPlace was made possible by the Portland City Council's landmark decision in 1976 to remove Harbor Drive, a six-lane freeway running along the west bank of the Willamette River. The freeway effectively cut off downtown Portland from two linear miles of riverfront access. In addition to freeway demolition, the ten-acre steam plant site that became RiverPlace required remediation to remove contamination and ensure that toxins would not leech into the river.

The first of two redevelopment stages occurred from 1980 to 1996, resulting in the construction of 10.5 acres of mixed-use multifamily housing above retail and restaurants, two energy-efficient office buildings, a fitness facility, a luxury hotel, a marina with floating restaurant, underground parking and an extensive waterfront park with an esplanade and large grassy area that hosts regional events. The second stage started in 1997, when the Portland Development Commission (PDC) began developing the remaining portion of the site based on the RiverPlace Development Strategy, completed in 1997, and the North Macadam Urban Renewal Area, established in 1999. Following a set of recommendations stemming from a strategy workshop that brought members of the Portland Development Commission together with development experts from other large, West Coast cities, the waterfront park was extended south of the esplanade, reaching Marquam Bridge, the area's southern edge. An extended-stay hotel was built in 2001 and three glass condominium towers incorporating ground-floor

JUST THE FACTS

- Located just east of downtown Portland, on the west bank of the Willamette River
- 73-acre site includes 16 acres of residential and commercial, developed in multiple phases from 1983 to present
- Land acquired by Portland Development Commission in 1978 following 1976 Portland City Council decision to remove six-lane expressway adjacent to the Willamette River
- Former 10-acre steam plant site required brownfield remediation, resulting in award-winning collaboration among city, state and U.S. Environmental Protection Agency
- 712 multifamily housing units (condos, townhomes and apartments) with more planned
- 300,000 square feet retail/restaurant currently built, with additional retail anticipated
- 105,000 square feet of office space in three office buildings
- 84-room boutique hotel and 258-room extended stay hotel
- Two waterfront parks and mile-long esplanade provide public riverfont access in downtown Portland
- 83-slip marina with fishing pier and floating restaurant
- 47,000-square-foot athletic club
- Transit access via bus and Portland Streetcar
- MAX light rail line and station will be complete in 2015
- Development team led by Portland Development Commission
- Additional developers include Cornerstone Columbia Development Company, Trammell Crow Residential, RiverPlace Partners LLC, RiverPlace Partners II
- Designers include The Bumgardner Architects, GGLO Architects, Robert S. Leeb Architects and Planners, Robert Perron Landscape Architects & Planners, Walker Macy, Ankrom Moisan Architects, and Zimmer Gunsul Frasca Partnerhip

retail, underground parking, and gardens were completed in 2007. The site is now served by the Portland Streetcar, while construction of a MAX light rail line through RiverPlace will be complete in 2015. The Portland Development Commission is exploring possibilities for developing the remaining two vacant parcels.

The Waterfront as Portland's Focal Point

In the mid-1850s, clipper ships made their way from the wide Columbia River north of Portland to the Willamette, transporting supplies for the burgeoning grain and lumber industries. As trade expanded, docks, bars and warehouses appeared along the river's banks and over the next 100 years, Portland grew into a thriving city. From downtown, however, public access to the Willamette became impaired by industrial development and freeways, including Harbor Drive.

The idea of replacing Harbor Drive with a waterfront park first surfaced with the 1972 Downtown Plan and the subsequent Downtown Waterfront Urban Renewal Plan of 1974, which was created to reconnect the waterfront and Portland's central city. In 1975 the Urban Renewal Plan was amended, extending the urban development boundary south to the area where RiverPlace is now located. A year later, the decision to demolish Harbor Drive was made and the South Waterfront Development

Six-lane Harbor Drive and Pacific Power & Light's steam plant on the site adjacent to the Willamette River that has become RiverPlace.

Area was created.

The focal point of the project, as for most of central Portland, is the Willamette River. Portland's Central City Plan Fundamental Design Guidelines call for integration with the river:

> The river is also a center for activity; important to Portland's overall economic health and livability. The river's importance is measured not just as a working river, but also in terms of its aesthetic, recreational and tourism potential.

The Guidelines further direct development to:

> Integrate the river as an important design consideration into the projects which are located along or near the edge of the Willamette River, through means such as the composition of architectural and landscape elements; location of windows, doors and attached outdoor areas; and offering accessways for the pedestrian to, along and from the water's edge.

Additionally, Portland's 1988 Central City Plan set forth seven goals to ensure appropriate and accessible development along the river:

1. Recapture the east bank of the Willamette Riverfront between the Marquam and Steel Bridges by expanding and enhancing the space available for non-vehicular uses.

2. Locate a wide range of affordable and attractive activities and attractors along the riverbank and create frequent pedestrian access to the water's edge.

3. Encourage a mixture of land uses along the river, while protecting opportunities for water-dependent uses, especially north of the Broadway Bridge.

4. Maintain and improve public views to and from the river.

5. Improve the Central City's bridges for pedestrians and bicyclists and enhance the bridges' roles as connection between the two sides of the Willamette.

6. Foster opportunities for touching and entering the Willamette River.

RiverPlace's open marina, seen hear with RiverPlace Hotel and downtown Portland in the distance, was an instant success.

Photo: Simmons Buntin

Initial RiverPlace Redevelopment: From Infrastructure to Open Space

In 1979, the Portland Development Commission–charged with moving urban renewal plans forward to help "change the face of the city [and make] it a better place to live"– acquired 73 acres of industrial and undeveloped waterfront land between the Marquam and Hawthorne Bridges. The site was highly visible. It was also Portland's last centrally located vacant land of significant size. Over the next five years, PDC invested more than $6 million in infrastructure development and improvements, including riverfront and park expansion, marina basin dredging, utility relocation, construction of streets and enhanced pedestrian access. At that time, the area was added to the Downtown Waterfront Urban Renewal Area.

In 1985, Pacific Power & Light closed its onsite steam plant and agreed to relocate its major electrical substation to the southwest corner of the development area, where it

remains today.

The Commission also constructed RiverPlace's primary open space features: a marina basin enclosed by a floating breakwater and fishing pier, a five-acre terraced meadow (a part of Governor Tom McCall Waterfront Park), a swimming beach and a half-mile riverfront esplanade. Financing for these improvements was secured through city-issued bonds.

Phases I and II: The Original RiverPlace

With infrastructure in place, the PDC could begin searching for a developer. In 1983, the Commission sponsored a nationwide design competition for a ten-acre parcel of the area, calling for a mix of residential, office and retail uses around the new esplanade. Three firms were chosen to compete for the right to develop the area. Seattle's Cornerstone Development Company (now Cornerstone Columbia Development Company) was ultimately selected. Cornerstone's proposal met the Commission's basic requirements for 500 units of housing, two restaurants and shops overlooking a privately operated marina. According to the Urban Land Institute (ULI), Cornerstone's extensive management experience developing mixed-use projects in downtown Seattle and Tacoma gave it the edge. Additionally, Cornerstone was 80% owned by Wayerhauser Real Estate Company, so the company exhibited little financial risk.

Before construction could begin, the project required Portland Design Commission review, based on more than 20 design guidelines. A ULI case study notes, however, that the review was "remarkably speedy," and the time from plan submission to final approval was just six weeks.

Two issues surfaced during the design of Phase I. First, developers faced a conflict between the downtown area's design guidelines and the South Waterfront Project Design Guidelines over covered moorage for the marina. PDC advocated for covered moorage that would protect expensive boats, while the city's Design Commission advocated for open moorage that would give the marina broader visual exposure and aesthetic appeal. The Design Commission won out.

Second, developers were concerned about the project's visibility from downtown office towers, bridges, and freeways, all of which look onto RiverPlace. The solution was to mandate rooftop variability: no flat roofs were permitted on buildings less than five stories high. "The mix of gabled and other sloping roof types underscores the project's residential character," notes the ULI case study.

The tight mix of uses at RiverPlace created additional design challenges, particularly for ensuring privacy and noise reduction among residences. The designers worked to place the residential units between office and retail uses while setting the hotel and athletic club on the project's periphery, adjacent to public streets and open spaces. Still, the first residents complained of nighttime noise–a

problem solved in large part by converting the three residential units above one of the restaurants to office space. Additionally, creating hidden but still accessible service functionality for trash, storage, and delivery access proved to be a challenge. The majority of service access was shifted to one street designed to have less pedestrian traffic.

Phase I of RiverPlace was completed in 1985. The city's share of Phase I funding was provided largely through tax-increment financing. The phase included 158 condominiums, the 74-room RiverPlace Alexis Hotel (now RiverPlace Hotel, owned by Larkspur Hotels), a public marina with 83 slips for large sailboats and light watercraft, boat sales and crew facilities, a floating restaurant, specialty shops along the esplanade and a fitness center sized to serve both RiverPlace and the surrounding community. All docking spaces, retail shops and restaurants were leased to full upon opening. The condos represented the first non-subsidized market rate housing in the downtown core since the 1960s.

The following year, the four-story, 40,000-square-foot RiverPlace Office Building was constructed, as were 32 condominiums with below-grade parking.

Wood-frame construction was prevalent in the first phase, continuing the "timbered vernacular tradition of residential building in the Northwest," according to the Urban Land Institute. "The handsome gray-shingled athletic clubhouse evokes the Shingle style pioneered by H.H. Richardson and reinterpreted in 19th-century Portland architecture." The hotel features one large and two smaller octagonal canopies rising at the roof, visible throughout RiverPlace and from the river. The U-shaped hotel "projects an imposing presence relative to the adjoining park," notes ULI. "Its expansive porches and double-hung windows harken back to the grand seaside resorts of the last century."

Other commercial buildings–street-level

Lush landscaping and gardens bridge RiverPlace Phases I and II, including these apartments above retail, with the second stage of the project.

Photo: Simmons Buntin

retail and offices—feature a mix of brick, concrete, glass, and steel representative of the buildings in downtown Portland and surrounding neighborhoods. They incorporate shallow arcades and lush landscaping, as well.

RiverPlace was initially marketed as a full urban neighborhood in a "low-rise, resort setting," says ULI. Initial interest was strong; marina slips and dry dock spaces leased quickly, and restaurants found success and consequently drove year-round activity. However, Phase I suffered from seasonal patronage of the retail shops, which required additional marketing efforts in the non-peak months of November through March. Many of the condos were leased with the option to buy, a successful approach considering RiverPlace was at first perceived as "frontier territory," notes ULI.

By the time development of RiverPlace Phase II began in the summer of 1988 under Cornerstone, the project was seen less as frontier and more as the city's engaging new gateway to the river. Phase II included a 300-space public parking garage with six street-level retail spaces beneath 108 middle-income

apartments. In 1990, when the garage opened, further modifications were made to allow additional automobile access to RiverPlace and the public garage.

In 1994 the PDC received the necessary approval of the Oregon Department of Environmental Quality that allowed it to market additional land to meet growing housing demand. The Commission approved Trammel Crow Residential's plan to build 182 townhomes, which were completed and opened in 1995. The townhomes—the first to be built in Portland's downtown core—were quickly leased. A number of low-income units, as required by Portland's Downtown Development Plan, were included among the townhomes. The condominium clusters followed the design vernacular established in the first phase, incorporating wood, peaked roofs, seaside colors, and gated courtyards with lush landscaping.

In 1994 Pacific Gas Transmission constructed a state-of-the-art, eight-story office building on the southern edge of RiverPlace, near the Marquam Bridge. The $16 million building—now called the 2100 River Parkway

Building, since Pacific Gas Transmission has relocated–incorporates a super-efficient building envelope and heating and cooling system, onsite water and waste reduction technologies and low-toxicity building materials. The building is currently owned by a California teacher's pension fund and is leased to David Evans and Associates, a national architecture, engineering and design firm.

In total, the first 10.5 developed acres of RiverPlace include 480 condominium, townhouse and apartment units at a density of 90 units per acre. Some 26,000 square feet of retail and 147,000 square feet of office space in two buildings exists in this first stage of RiverPlace. Almost 60% of the parking in this section of RiverPlace is underground and all residential parking is either underground or hidden behind vine-covered façades or retail storefronts.

Strategy and Development Since 1997: RiverPlace Extended

At the time the RiverPlace Development Strategy was completed in July 1997 by the PDC, four parcels remained and the waterfront park ended at the southern edge of the marina. The Strategy itself was created from a single working session that brought together local representatives and port development experts from such cities as Seattle and San Francisco. In the working sessions, participants defined the objectives for developing the remaining parcels at RiverPlace. They agreed that the RiverPlace Strategy should 1) identify, confirm and prioritize opportunities and constraints associated with achieving the city's goals and objectives; 2) create one ore more economically and architecturally viable scenarios; 3) create timeline and development sequencing scenarios to help identify phasing priorities; 4) identify building types and uses for each of the remaining four parcels; and 5) select a viable preferred scenario.

The objectives of the strategy workshop were underpinned by the goals of the South Waterfront Development Program:

- Promote business, economic growth, formation of capital and the creation and retention of jobs
- Encourage development of a full range of housing
- Ensure that a balance of passive and active parks and open space is provided
- Enhance RiverPlace as a livable, walkable, secure area which focuses on the river, yet captures the glitter and excitement of city living
- Recognize that parking is an important element in the transportation system which supports growth, ensuring that each district, including RiverPlace, has adequate parking to supply current need while acknowledging and encouraging present and future mass transit to improve air quality and traffic flow
- Develop or improve blighted (vacant) properties
- Clean, contain, remediate, or treat contaminated sites to adequately protect public health and the environment
- Develop properties applying designs, uses and phasing that encourage development of North Macadam and the completion of development at RiverPlace
- Achieve highest return on investment for the City of Portland
- Continue to confirm and enhance the character of RiverPlace

To facilitate these objectives, appropriately recognize RiverPlace's relationship with the North Macadam area, and emphasize unique redevelopment opportunities and design typologies established by RiverPlace, the southern portion of RiverPlace (excluding the esplanade and waterfront park) was transferred from the Downtown Waterfront Urban Renewal Area to the North Macadam Urban Renewal Area, which was established in August 1999.

The glass towers of The Strand look north across South Waterfront Park and onto the Willamette River.

The RiverPlace Development Strategy notes that the "greatest challenges will be overcoming noise and vibration of the I-5 freeway and the magnetic fields in proximity to the PP&L substation." To meet this unique set of circumstances, participants in the strategy workshop recommended against residential (which would be adversely impacted by the noise and vibration) and for a "long stay" hotel on the parcel closest to the interstate and directly across from the substation (Parcel 5). They also recommended that PDC release the parcel for immediate development. Four years

later, the 258-room, extended-stay Residence Inn by Marriott opened and, even in the economic downturn of the late 2000s, the hotel has been successful.

To date, however, no viable proposals have been received for the 2.1-acre Parcel 3, which with Parcel 5 forms a "critical gateway" to the South Waterfront District. While Parcels 3 and 8 have not yet been developed, the Commission is exploring possibilities and a variety of uses are allowed, according to PDC senior project manager Geraldene Moyle.

Parcel 6–in 1997 the most visible

undeveloped location in RiverPlace, particularly from the east bank of the Willamette River–has been developed as The Strand, a $110 million series of three glass and steel towers (two of 11 stories and one of 13 stories) containing 220 condominiums and ground-level live/work townhomes "scaled to match the existing neighborhood," according to the PDC.

The Strand, which dominates the River-Place skyline from its 2.7-acre site, also features a 7,500-square-foot waterfront restaurant, two boutique retail storefronts of 500 square feet each and 100 public underground parking stalls. The project was completed in 2007 and the condos–ranging from 650 to 3,500 square feet and initially priced from $200,000 to over $2 million–sold out completely. Current prices for resale units range from $450,000 to $1,150,000.

Award-Winning Brownfield Remediation

According to the Center for Brownfield Initiatives, the redevelopment "was a landmark project for the future of brownfields development efforts in Oregon long before the term 'brownfields' was in use." Throughout the development of RiverPlace, the PDC and developers had to contend with the cleanup of the Lincoln Steam Plant, a site contaminated with petroleum byproducts (PAH, or polynuclear aromatic hydrocarbons, which were discovered in subsurface soils and groundwater) from the plant's steam, oil and natural gas operations from the 1880s to 1985. Demolition of the plant in 1989 resulted in the discovery of asbestos-coated concrete, which also required remediation. Further risk assessment revealed high levels of lead in the soil, as well.

The Commission joined forces with the Oregon Department of Environmental Quality and RiverPlace developers to participate in the Voluntary Cleanup Program, requiring complex groundwater flow modeling, surface

capping of discrete site areas, abandonment of an onsite water intake structure and installation of a riverbank stabilization system. Additionally, developers are prohibited from onsite groundwater use and must participate in a surface cap maintenance program, well monitoring and "specialized piling methods and post-piling groundwater monitoring," reports the Center for Brownfields Initiatives.

Additionally, the sawdust generated from an onsite plywood mill–which originally fueled the steam plant–had accumulated to a depth of 40 feet on the river's edge and flood plain. The resulting poor soil quality required developers to drive pilings from 70 to 90 feet beneath the sawdust layers. The unstable soils also required the construction of the concrete platform that encloses the parking garage and serves as the base for the first phase of housing, according to the Urban Land Institute.

The innovative and collaborative efforts between PDC, the state Department of Environmental Quality and developers earned their successful brownfield remediation efforts a 2003 Phoenix Award from Region 10 of the U.S. Environmental Protection Agency. Though remediation was expensive, the USDA's National Resources Conservation Services provided a $350,000 grant for waterfront bank stabilization and repair.

Extending the Open Space: Waterfront Parks and Esplanade

While RiverPlace's mix of urban residential and retail provide an evolving, urban neighborhood in which to live, work and shop, the waterfront parks and esplanade create a regional draw. Providing some two miles of riverfront access to residents and visitors in a mix of uses and landscaping–marina, piers, a beach at low-water level, formal gardens, natural plantings, sculptures, ponds and more–the open spaces of the waterfront complete the area's original vision.

The 36-acre Governor Tom McCall

Photo: Walker Macy

RiverPlace's South Waterfront Park provides access to the Willamette River as well as to the original phases of the community, the marina, and Governor Tom McCall Waterfront Park to the north.

Waterfront Park, which extends into the north portion of the redevelopment, adjacent to the RiverPlace Hotel and the marina from the Steel Bridge, provides a "terrace bowl" or informal, grassy amphitheater for regional events, including the Waterfront Blues Festival, Oregon Brewers Festival and the Bite of Oregon Festival.

The newest addition is the South Waterfront Park, completed in October 1999 at a cost of $4.3 million under the guidance of Walker & Macy Landscape Architects (now Walker Macy). The park serves as an anchor for The Strand and RiverPlace's newest development

and also repaired erosion from a significant flood in 1996. The park terminates under the Marquam Bridge, but the PDC anticipates that it will eventually connect with a river greenway that will extend south of the bridge and into the South Waterfront neighborhood. The Commission notes that the park was created through a "very public" design process:

A public/private advisory council comprised of neighbors, property managers and representatives of public agencies collaborated with PDC to establish a set of long-term objectives, which shaped the design plans for the four-acre South

Waterfront Park. Key objectives were to enhance natural habitat areas, create safe spaces and maximize access to the river. The advisory council also wanted a design that blended the dense urban form of the city with the natural sinuous form of the river.

The park features a mix of formal and informal elements, ranging from a garden of native plants with a sunken terrace, pools of lily pads and a "stone-paved grove" to a low knoll near the Marquam Bridge that helps muffle noise while providing a viewpoint to the river. There is a sculpture installation, a tree-lined, 18-foot-wide esplanade and a wood-and-steel pier that extends from the esplanade over the river. In late summer and early fall–low water periods on the Willamette, which fluctuates 20 feet annually–the river edge becomes a natural silty beach, "one of the few areas of the park where visitors can reach out and touch the water," notes the PDC.

The park's esplanade connects with RiverPlace's original esplanade, which curves around the marina–hosting decorative and functional street furniture, patios that extend from cafés, sidewalk vendors, public artwork and plenty of pedestrians and cyclists–and extends to the terraced grassy bowl north of the RiverPlace Hotel. Sidewalks and paths connect the wide riverfront walkway to the urban blocks of RiverPlace.

Getting Around and Out of RiverPlace

Within RiverPlace, tree-lined sidewalks provide easy pedestrian access to all buildings and, at the southern edge of the project, join a new stop for the Portland Streetcar. The streetcar runs every 15 minutes on weekdays and connects RiverPlace to Portland State University and downtown Portland to the west and the emerging South Waterfront neighborhood and the Oregon Health and Science University's

new 16-story Building One to the south. The $15.8 million extension of the Portland Streetcar into RiverPlace was a high priority for the entire area. TriMet, which operates the streetcar and all public transportation for the Portland metro area, wrote that the "Portland Streetcar is seen as a key catalyst to the development of housing, neighborhood retail and office space with plans calling for 10,000 new jobs and 3,000 housing units."

In early 2010 the Portland Development Commission and City of Portland Bureau of Transportation were awarded Oregon's only TIGER (Transportation Investment Generating Economic Recovery) grant, providing $23 million in funding dedicated to the SW Moody Avenue reconstruction project that begins in RiverPlace and extends into the South Waterfront District and the Oregon Health and Science University's Life Science Complex. Moody Avenue is being reconstructed as a "green street, with facilities to manage stormwater and improve water quality and enhance our watershed health," says a press release issued by the mayor's office. The project is also seen as facilitating "long-term job creation by unlocking parcels, which are adjacent to the project, for future development." Construction began in fall 2010 and, when complete, the elevated roadway will include three traffic lanes, dual streetcar tracks, a two-way cycle-track, pedestrian lanes and "tuck-under parking" that will not disturb adjacent, capped contaminated areas.

Conclusion: Creating the Sustainable City

RiverPlace is an early and ongoing example of the City of Portland's sustainability principles, adopted in November 1994. With the goal of promoting "a sustainable future that meets today's needs without compromising the ability of future generations to meet their needs," the Sustainable City Principles state that the city accepts its responsibility to:

The esplanade at RiverPlace extends into the heart of the neighborhood, where street-level retail and restaurants serve residents and visitors alike.

- Support a stable, diverse and equitable economy
- Protect the quality of the air, water, land and other natural resources
- Conserve native vegetation, fish, wildlife habitat and other ecosystems
- Minimize human impacts on local and worldwide ecosystems

"RiverPlace is exemplary of desired Downtown Portland waterfront development and is nationally recognized for its successes," notes the RiverPlace Development Strategy. "RiverPlace has set new standards for mixed-use development that will inevitably contribute to the Central City's share of regional growth management goals."

Urban design critics such as Paul Sedway, a board member of San Francisco Planning + Urban Research Association, agree, but note that the project's success is a result of the larger public-private collaborations and financing facilitated by the Downtown Waterfront Urban Renewal Area. "The Downtown Waterfront Urban Renewal Area is one of Portland's most successful examples of urban renewal and tax-increment financing," he wrote in 2005. "Since the project area was delineated in 1974, the assessed land values in the area have increased at an average of about ten percent per year."

RiverPlace represents a decades-long effort to ensure the Willamette River is once again a vital and accessible feature of downtown Portland. Developed around the guidelines and long-term vision of Portland's Central City Plan, RiverPlace Development Strategy and the urban renewal areas–and with an insistence upon environmental remediation–RiverPlace is a vital waterfront redevelopment and an integral part of a city willing to collaborate with private developers to bring its vision of sustainability to the urban core.

DEFINING SUCCESS

Q&A with Patrick Quinton, Portland Development Commission Executive Director

What was the largest obstacle to obtaining project approval or buy-in, and how was it overcome?
The proximity of the project to the Willamette River added value to the property, making redevelopment more viable. At the same time that proximity resulted in the project's greatest constraints and challenges, due to concerns about contaminants migrating via groundwater into the Willamette and threatening endangered wildlife species in the area. PDC used its full range of urban revitalization tools to remediate the site, and its collaborative efforts with the Oregon Department of Environmental Quality have become a model for effectively addressing the environmental problems of unproductive land through redevelopment and reuse.

What is an unexpected delight or success from the project?
The success of the riverfront development encouraged the city to look further south and led to the creation of the South Waterfront Urban Renewal Area. Without RiverPlace we might not have seen that extension as viable. The evolution of South Waterfront from RiverPlace to the 130-acre riverfront institutional, research and commercialization component of the Innovation Quadrant was at least partially inspired by what came before it—the successful RiverPlace development. RiverPlace has become a connector between Portland State University and the Oregon Health & Science University/South Waterfront campus—which was not a focus of the project ten to 20 years ago.

What hasn't lived up to expectations or has required unanticipated change?
The unanticipated market slowdown has required a corresponding change in the completion schedule. Still, the slower development has allowed the south end of RiverPlace to integrate more organically with the remainder of South Waterfront, and we're now seeing significant interest in the two remaining parcels of RiverPlace. The delay has also contributed to a change in thinking about the development of those parcels, originally anticipated as residential but now likely to be mixed-use (hotel/office) in light of the evolving "bookend" development which has taken place in the South Waterfront area (with the RiverPlace/north end residential and the south end more commercial/office).

How do you define and measure success?
Incrementally—each step is its own win and inspires the next. Without RiverPlace we wouldn't have South Waterfront. We've moved from RiverPlace to South Waterfront to the integration of both areas into a more blended neighborhood, which has instigated growth and the strategic alignment of Portland State University's development plans with those of the city. People almost take the RiverPlace project for granted now—as though it's always been there as an extension of Waterfront Park. It's become the jewel of the city, with an active marina and staging site for the popular dragon boat races, the use of the esplanade for athletic pursuits, and the continued liveliness of the retail and residential components original to the project.

Second Street District
Austin, Texas
by Simmons B. Buntin

Second Street District in Austin, Texas has invigorated the downtown by providing a mixed-use retail spine, high-density housing, a new green city hall, and easy access to Town Lake.

Photo: Simmons Buntin

S econd Street District is a six-block infill and redevelopment project located north of Town Lake and along the southern edge of downtown Austin, Texas. The city's vision for the project is broad: "to enhance the identity and image of downtown Austin as a civic and cultural destination for residents, visitors and businesses while preserving and enlivening Austin's sense of place." More specifically, the Second Street District Streetscape Improvement Project (SSDSIP) calls for "the inclusion of a critical mass of retail (and other pedestrian-oriented uses) linked by a coherent and uniquely identified, pedestrian environment . . . linking two important civic destinations–the new City Hall and the Convention Center Complex–along what will become downtown's key shopping or 'pedestrian-dominant' spine: Second Street."

With an original goal of adding over 168,000 square feet of retail space mixed with office, hotel, civic and mostly high-end,

JUST THE FACTS

- Located in downtown Austin, Texas just north of Town Lake
- Six-block redevelopment (five blocks owned by City of Austin) initiated in 1999 and completed in 2011
- Mixed uses, including street-level retail beneath office, residential, lodging and performance space
- 609 new residential units (including 451 leased units) in mid- and high-rise buildings
- New 115,000-square-foot, LEED Gold-certified Austin City Hall and public plaza
- 106,000 square feet of retail
- 385,000 square feet of office space (not including City Hall)
- 251-room hotel above retail and below residential
- 1,500-seat performance venue (Moody Theater, new home of "Austin City Limits")
- Extensive streetscape planning and implementation through Austin's Great Streets program
- Wide esplanade along Town Lake
- $200,000 toward public art committed by private developers
- Developers include City of Austin, AMLI Residential Properties, Computer Sciences Corporation, UP Schneider and others
- Designers include ROMA Design Group, Black & Vernooy + Kinney Joint Venture, Copley Wolff Design Group and others

high-rise condo and apartment developments, the Second Street District is being positioned as Austin's new core downtown retail area, where no retail core existed before. Taking into account adjacent projects and the city's goal of making a contiguous, pedestrian-oriented connection between the Convention Center on the east and Lamar Boulevard on the west, the District's impacts and influence extend well beyond its official six-block footprint. The SSDSIP scope actually extends the Second Street District streetscape improvements four block lengths eastward, beyond the six-block district, from Colorado to Trinity, and includes two block lengths along Brazos and Colorado north and south of Second Street. The city had owned five of the six blocks long before project inception, enabling the city to implement its vision without "the haste that often arises from market forces," says Fred Evins, Austin's redevelopment project manager.

While the district's architecture has been defined as "eclectic modern urban style," it also has a distinctly Austin flavor, in part because of a series of sustainability goals outlined in guiding documents, including principles of urban forestry and the use of locally available materials in construction.

All six city blocks and streetscapes have been completed: Austin City Hall and its public plaza on Block 3; two six-story Computer Sciences Corporation (now Silicon Laboratories) office buildings with street-level retail on either side of City Hall on Blocks 2 and 4; the seven-story AMLI Downtown apartment building with street-level retail on Block 20; the 37-story W Hotel and Residences with street-level retail and the 2,900-seat Moody Theater on Block 2; and the 18-story AMLI on Second Street apartment high-rise with street-level retail on Block 22. In total, Second Street District is home to 609 multifamily residences; 106,700 square feet of retail comprising 18 restaurants, 25 stores, a four-screen independent movie theater, two spas and other services such as dry cleaner and dentist; 385,000 square feet of office space; Austin's City Hall and public plaza; a promenade along the south side of Cesar Chavez Street; and 2,677 underground,

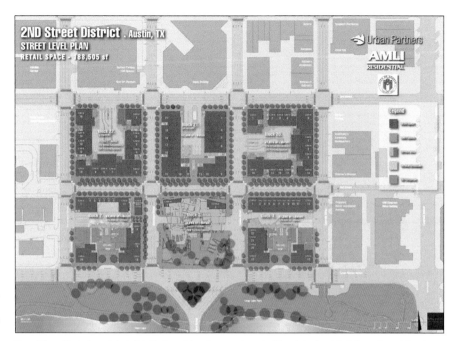

Second Street District is comprised of six blocks and the adjacent park north of Town Lake, though its influence is much broader.

Graphic: City of Austin, TX

structured and on-street parking spaces.

Project History: A Call to Action for a Vital Downtown

Second Street District grew out of city visioning and planning processes. Local and national experts, along with the public at large, first came together to craft a series of policies and plans addressing Austin's general livability, then turned their attention to its downtown design, and finally focused on Second Street District itself.

In 1989, Austin's Downtown Commission received approval from City Council to invite a Regional/Urban Design Assistance Team (R/UDAT) of the American Institute of Architects to Austin. Since 1967, the R/UDAT program has used volunteer technical experts, including architects and urban planners, to promote the importance of urban and regional planning, stimulate local public action and improve physical design in communities

throughout the nation.

In 1991, a three-day R/UDAT planning charrette was conducted with more than 800 Austinites who "assessed conditions and community interest in Downtown Austin and provided a framework for implementing actions to revitalize Austin's vital central core," says the R/UDAT. The resulting report, *R/UDAT*Austin*, spawned a set of implementation actions outlined in *R/UDAT Austin Implementation: A Call to Action*, published in May 1992.

Approved by the Austin City Council as a "guide for implementing downtown Austin revitalization," *A Call to Action* provided detailed recommendations in the areas of urban design, natural environment, community issues, cultural arts, transportation, economic development and creation of a downtown management organization.

The Downtown Austin Alliance, a partnership of individuals and businesses "devoted to promoting and maintaining a safe, clean, attractive, accessible and fun downtown environment," according to its literature, was subsequently born of the 1993 creation of a Downtown Austin Public Improvement District. Funding for the Alliance comes from a special assessment on privately owned large properties within the District. In 1996, the Alliance began a Great Streets program with the goal of improving "the quality of downtown streets and sidewalks, aiming ultimately to transform the public right-of-ways into great public spaces," says the Alliance. Later that year, Austin voters approved $5 million in bonds for the new Austin Great Streets Program.

In 1997, an Austin R/UDAT conference generated a short list of downtown revitalization projects and in 2000 the R/UDAT held another conference, at which then-mayor Kirk Watson discussed the emergence of Austin's downtown waterfront, including a new city hall, the new CSC buildings and their 3,500 employees, and the new retail core. "Austin gets an A for creating, in a very short time period, a Downtown Digital District with all the elements of a great downtown," he said

While the "Digital" portion of the District has not necessarily materialized, Austin's initiatives to redevelop downtown continued in two ways: 1) through the adoption of Downtown Austin Design Guidelines in May 2000 (and updated in January 2009), and 2) through the city's ongoing Great Streets Program.

Mayor Watson's comments were predicated on City Council's 1999 passage of a resolution "intended to ensure that the West (Second) Street area support pedestrian and retail-oriented businesses that could complement the proposed City Hall as a major public destination." Because of the resolution, the two planned, six-story CSC buildings were reconfigured to provide street-level retail. The city also retained AMLI Austin Retail, in collaboration with HSM Urban Partners, as its retail developer for Blocks 2 and 4. HSM Urban

Partners created a strategic retail program for the new Second Street Retail District through contracts with various project developers. In 2010, the city transitioned Second Street District's retail oversight and marketing from HSM to Plat.form, a "locally established and integrated firm that is more in touch with the Austin vibe," says Evins.

The city's Economic Growth and Redevelopment Services Office was at the forefront of the implementation efforts associated with the Council's 1999 resolution–and continues to provide city oversight through project completion and beyond.

In 1999, ROMA Design Group was hired by AMLI Residential to develop a retail and streetscape concept plan, which proposed converting Second Street to a two-lane (one lane each way) shopping street, with parallel parking located on the north side, adjacent to a 32-foot-wide sidewalk with a double-row of street trees. The resulting Austin Second Street Retail District – District Streetscape Plan was published in early 2000. That year, the city also commissioned Street Works to help create a vision for "main street retail" along Second Street, says Evins.

Great Streets Master Plan: Defining Streets as Places

After extending the District Streetscape Plan boundaries eastward to the Convention Center in July 2001, the "Second Street Retail District Plan" was subsequently incorporated into the "Downtown Austin Great Streets Master Plan", which was completed in December 2001 by urban design consultant Black & Vernooy + Kinney Joint Venture. ROMA Design Group's concept plan was further detailed and specific siting criteria within the public right of way, such as street and pedestrian lighting, were established.

The "Great Streets Master Plan" is based on the Downtown Austin Design Guidelines created by the Austin Design Commission and adopted the previous year (and revised in January 2009). Key areas addressed in the Guidelines include sense of history, unique character, authenticity, safety, diversity, humane character, density, economic vitality, and civic art.

Based on Second Street Retail District work, the design consultants suggested six guiding principles for the Great Streets Program, identified in the Master Plan itself:

Principle 1: Manage Congestion

Congestion is a fact of life in successful urban places. By definition, a place that supports a great concentration of economic and social activities within a pedestrian-scaled environment is going to be congested.

Principle 2: Balanced/Active Streets

Downtown streets must balance the needs of pedestrians, bicycles, transit and the automobile in creating an attractive and viable urban core. Downtown streets are for people first, commercial second, parking third and through-traffic fourth.

Principle 3: Streets as Places

The Great Streets Program envisions downtown as a vital focus of city life and as a primary destination. Our downtown streets are our most important and pervasive public space and common ground.

Principle 4: Interactive Streets

Urban Streets are the stages on which the public life of the community is acted out.

Principle 5: Pride of Place

Visible caring and upkeep are critical to the vitality of urban street life.

Principle 6: Public Art

Art in the public environment can help to establish a stronger sense of place and a continuity between the past, present and future.

Additionally, a number of Principles and Elements were included, ranging from pedestrian orientation to sidewalks, roadway lane width to bike lanes, street furniture to street trees and public art to enhanced key transit stops. Three street typologies were identified in the Master Plan, including the "Pedestrian Dominant Street." This typology referenced Second Street, ensuring the District would be pedestrian-oriented:

Pedestrian Dominant Streets generate high volumes of pedestrian traffic due to active retail uses at street level. City Council has demonstrated their commitment to creating Second Street as the new retail spine of downtown Austin. The north sidewalk . . . extends 32 feet wide, allowing for a double row of trees, sidewalk cafés, generous seating areas and impromptu street life. The vision of a premier retail district is particularly powerful when one imagines the sun-filled wide sidewalk stretching from Shoal Creek on the west to the door of the Austin Convention Center to the east.

Over the next three years, the city conducted engineering and archaeological and historical studies. The engineering study resulted in the creation of prototypical design solutions for handicap access and intersection geometry, resolved utility and tree conflicts and prepared plans for grading, drainage, utility relocation, traffic management, construction phasing and cost estimates. The archaeological and historical study explored the history of the corridor, which includes 19th- and 20th-century railroad and industrial uses, a red light district, underground vaults and a large Hispanic population until the 1920s.

Second Street District Streetscape Improvement Project

Austin's Great Streets Master Plan provides for cafes and retail to extend onto the broad, tree-lined sidewalk, creating a dynamic streetlife.

The "Pedestrian Dominant Street" typology of the "Great Streets Master Plan" was implemented through the Second Street District Streetscape Improvement Project, which began in July 2003 when the city selected a design team led by Copley Wolff Design Group of Boston. The project's Request for Design Consultant Qualifications clearly set forth the streetscapes' intent in five areas:

- Urban design, reinforcing the city's vision of a sense of place for the Second Street District
- Sustainability, in such areas as heat island effect, storm drainage and water quality, reclaimed water, renewable energy, light trespass, recyclables and public transit
- Context-sensitive design, so that the District integrates "the ideas and work of central Texas historians, artists and/or artisans to impart a distinct Austin sense of place and cultural identity through revealing its forms, meanings, values and history"
- Public involvement, led by the

Downtown Austin Alliance's District Stakeholder Group with city oversight, to "be informed by a high level of stakeholder input"
- District maintenance, calling for a strategy and mechanism for the ongoing management of maintenance and services

The project has been implemented in two phases: Phase 1 is roadway reconstruction from San Antonio Street to Colorado Street (within Second Street District) and Phase 2 is Great Streets sidewalks and roadway construction from Colorado Street to Trinity Street (extending beyond Second Street District).

The first phase resulted in reconfiguring Second Street from one-way, westbound traffic from Brazos Street east to its end at San Antonio Street, to two-way traffic from Brazos Street west to Colorado Street, spanning the major Congress Avenue/Second Street intersection. It was completed just prior to the opening of the new City Hall in November 2004, and provides vehicular access to, and visibility into,

As the District's retail and restaurant spine, Second Street features a double row of street trees, street furniture, and public art.

the southern portion of Second Street District, as well as Town Lake

Design work for the second phase was completed in 2005, providing for 32-foot-wide sidewalks and a double row of street trees on the north side of the street, providing broad space for sidewalk cafés adjacent to store fronts. Between the double row of trees, a path of large-size pavers, "used to enhance walk-ability and wheelchair user comfort, meanders like a dry stream bed, inviting a leisurely stroll through the retail district," according to city literature. Construction on the first block, from Colorado Street to Congress Avenue, was completed in 2011 and construction on the remaining two blocks began in 2012.

The District has also implemented the Great Streets lamppost, "uniquely designed for Austin's downtown [that] elegantly reduce[s] clutter in the streetscape by consolidating into one system roadway and pedestrian light-ing as well as traffic and pedestrian signals, street signs/wayfinding systems and special events banners," says Evins. The street's south

side includes similar streetscaping, but at an 18-foot width.

Improvements along Cesar Chavez Bou-levard from Brazos to San Antonio included widening the street and creating an esplanade with an alley of trees along the southern curb line, forming a transition from the Second Street District's built fabric to the grassy slope and riverside trail of Town Lake Park. Cesar Chavez was rebuilt first–transitioning from one- to two-way traffic in 2008. Second Street improvements were completed in 2009.

Streetscape, plaza and other public infra-structure maintenance around City Hall were funded by a tax-increment financing reinvest-ment zone that encompassed four blocks in the Second Street District.

The street and sidewalk improvements have made a significant difference in the vitality of the area, especially on 2nd Street between Colorado and Guadalupe. Effectively and artistically integrating the District's mix of retail, restaurant, office, and residential uses, the wide sidewalks create an inviting outdoor public space that is heavily utilized by pedestrians throughout the day—and particularly at lunch hour, in the evening, and on the weekend. Restaurants take advantage of the new public space through the use of outdoor patios, while shops often display merchandise outside, opening their doors to invite pedestrians in.

The Role of Public Art at Second Street

"Rivers, Streams and Springs" is the Second Street District streetscape project's theme and ties into the city's Art in Public Places program. Accordingly, where Second Street intersects the north/south streets, which are named for Texas rivers like the Brazos and Colorado, special paving treatments with medallions that interpret the social history and ecology of each river's watershed are being created and installed by local artists. Though art installations have been slow-going—"because of Americans with Disabilities Act accessibility requirements, implementing public art on sidewalks is challenging," says Evins—artwork has been installed at the intersection of Second Street and Colorado. Additional, sidewalk-based artwork will not be installed until after streetscape improvements along Second Street take place in 2012 and beyond.

A "Spring" sculptural zone, including a functioning drinking fountain, will additionally be located between San Jacinto Street and Brazos Street, while a larger-scale "Spring" is being implemented in partnership with Austin Water Utility, at the intersection with Congress Avenue. So far, one sculpture has been erected.

Two percent of the SSDSIP construction budget was set aside for the design and implementation of "context-appropriate" civic art. Other partners were pursued for additional water-related art projects along Second Street, and $200,000 in private developer funding has been obtained.

Implementing the Plans: Beyond the City's Vision

While the plans and projects establish a vision for the Second Street District, they do not set requirements for sustainability measures such as energy efficiency and renewable energy use or specific percentages for retail or residential uses. "Block-by-block, the city has negotiated with developers to include project elements that further the city's vision," says Evins.

As owners of five of six blocks, the City of Austin used an array of funding and other civic mechanisms to support development under the Great Streets Program and Streetscape Implementation Project guidelines. For example, the city was able to provide expedited permitting, development fee waivers, project-area design standards and funding for streetscaping, landscaping and parking on the two CSC (Silicon Labs) buildings on either side of City Hall completed in 2001 (Blocks 2 and 4). The city also constructed a connecting tunnel and funded improvements to city property and rights-of-way.

During negotiations with Computer Sciences Corporation on its development of Blocks 2 and 4, the city paid CSC $9.3 million towards the design, construction and subleasing of retail shell spaces on these blocks. AMLI Austin Retail, in collaboration with HSM Urban Partners, was selected as the retail developer and the retail sub-leases were then assigned to the developer, which was responsible for funding the development costs associated with leasing and finishing out the Block 2 and 4 retail spaces, according to Evins.

On Blocks 21 and 22, however, the developers were responsible for the construction, leasing and management of the retail spaces in their mixed-use projects. The city did agree to lease terms "that made AMLI's mixed-use development financially viable" on Block 22, says Evins. HSM Urban Partners was under contract to provide retail consulting services on Blocks 20, 21 and 22 (as well as Blocks 2

Photo: Simmons Buntin

AMLI Downtown was the first mixed-use residential building at Second Street District, and also provides the most affordable housing.

and 4) through 2010 to ensure a coherent retail mix and produce a viable destination retail center. Plat.form replaced HSM when the District received some criticism that the new retail echoed the retail of Dallas too much. As a local firm, Plat.form has a better sense of "how to preserve while transforming to keep Austin unique," says Evins. "We believe a strong, local retail presence is just as important as the streetscape improvements in making the District successful."

A Dynamic Mix of Urban Uses

Austin's goal for the Second Street District was 168,000 square feet of ground-level "destination" retail. Blocks 2 and 4–the retail uses in the CSC (Silicon Labs) buildings–also had a goal of 30% local business inclusion. Combined, the two six-story buildings have 350,000 square feet of office space, originally serving both CSC and Silicon Laboratories, which subsequently purchased CSC's interest in both buildings. The buildings contain

121

Photo: Simmons Buntin

The W Austin Hotel and Residences "has quickly become the city's place to see and be seen," writes the Austin American-Stateman.

700 parking spaces above 30,000 square feet of retail. Additionally, the city partnered with CSC to stabilize and sublease the historic, two-story Schneider Building, which was developed as Lambert's restaurant by UP Schneider, L.P.

Block 20, AMLI Downtown, features a 220-unit, seven-story apartment project above 43,000 square feet of retail and restaurants and 326 underground parking spaces. Apartments range from 700 square feet (renting at $1,500 per month in fall 2011) to 1,660 square feet (renting at over $2,500 per month). With the street's double row of trees, street furniture and outdoor patios–the redevelopment's first implementation of the Great Streets streetscape typology–the block provides a classic urban aesthetic and functionality. Street-level retail and restaurants provide an eclectic mix of destinations, from the popular Jo's Hot Coffee and Crú wine bar to milk + honey Spa and Design Within Reach modern furniture and accessories.

Stratus Properties, Inc., purchased Block 21 following a competitive proposal process managed by the city. Proceeds from the sale of the land have been reserved for Austin's new Central Library and three downtown trail and pedestrian improvement projects west of the District. Block 21 is home to W Hotel and Residences, a 37-story, $300 million project that includes 251 luxury hotel rooms (averaging $248 per night in 2012), 156 luxury condominiums, 35,000 square feet of office space, 29,000 square feet of ground floor retail and restaurant space and 490 underground parking spaces. It also houses the 1,500-seat Moody Theater, the new home of the popular *Austin City Limits* music series. The project is currently under LEED Gold certification review and the hotel features high-efficiency lighting and water fixtures (including dual-flush toilets), occupancy sensors, organic waste composting, recycling bins in all guest rooms and participation in a carbon-offset program. The Residences at W Austin opened in 2010 and range in size from one bedroom and 640 square feet to three bedroom + den and 4,255 square feet for a penthouse. Prices in fall 2011 ranged from $405,000 to over $3 million, averaging $1 million.

"It has been an amazing year for us," said Cindy Hill, director of W Austin sales and marketing, on the hotel's one-year birthday. "This market was thirsty for a hotel with the W's personality [and even] a person who lives here in Austin can come in and have a different experience every time." An *Austin American-Statesman* profile notes that "the trendy W . . . has quickly become the city's place to see and be seen, playing host to scads of big-name musicians, film and TV stars–and even President Barack Obama."

The Moody Theater, designed by BOKA

Powell and Rios Clementi Hale Studios, is located on the southwest corner of the block and hosts about 50 Austin City Limits Live concerts per year, plus another 100 concerts as well as a variety of conferences, presentations and gatherings. "We're doing quite a few high-profile events here," says theater private events manager Keri-Dawn Solner. "I really do see this venue becoming a national destination." The dramatic, state-of-the-art building, completed in 2010, brings an entirely new audience into Second Street District, says Evins. "It has filled in the missing space; completed the streetscape. The theater has taken the project to a whole new level."

Block 22 was also developed by AMLI Residential, which constructed an 18-story building of 231 rental residential units called AMLI on 2nd. Apartments are sized from 626 to 1,380 square feet and in fall 2011 rented from $1,600 to $3,000 per month. The project includes 12 affordable housing units (5% at 80% of mean income for 15 years) and was the first high-rise residential project to achieve a four-star rating under Austin Energy's Green Building Program. AMLI on 2nd hosts over 41,000 square feet of retail space and 421 parking spaces. Additionally, it preserved historic underground vaults discovered during site clearing in 2006.

Retail on Block 22 includes apparel, home furnishings, gifts and art and specialty stores such as Austin MacWorks, while restaurants offer sushi, tapas and Mexican cuisine. Most notable, perhaps, is Violet Crown Cinema, a four-screen arthouse cinema and restaurant that opened in April 2011. Considering that retail development on that portion of Second Street–which ends at San Antonio Street and the fenced portion of the city's former Green Water Treatment Plant–has been slow, the cinema was quite welcome. "Our block just doesn't see as many people as the other blocks," says tapas bar manager Lisa-Marie Pinder, according to an article in the

The Austin City Hall (shown with W Austin in distance) befits Austin's eclectic nature, sense of place and spirit of sustainability.

Austin American-Statesman. "When we moved here two years ago we doubled our size, but we haven't really doubled our business." Planning and construction of the cinema took two years, so it will make a go no matter how slow traffic is: "It was not inexpensive to build the Violet Crown," says owner Bill Banowsky, "and I intend to be here a long time."

Austin City Hall: Civic Sustainability at Its Most Local

The Austin City Hall (Block 3) is four stories and 115,000 square feet and features an iconic design by architect Antoine Predock. The LEED Gold-certified building, which received a 2008 Award of Excellence from the Green Roof Infrastructure Industry Association, among other awards, opened in November 2004 to wide acclaim. With the goal of being Austin's civic landmark for generations, the $56 million building is intended to befit Austin's eclectic nature, sense of place and spirit of sustainability.

The City Hall terraces down from Second Street toward Town Lake, "mediating between this busy city grid and the natural realm," describes the architect. The building is designed to reflect the warmth of Austin by incorporating native natural materials as well as a structure that angles away from adjacent streets, creating several "mini-plazas" around the building. Says Predock:

> Landscape dominates the project. A massive arc of Lueders limestone, emerging from bedrock at the lowest level of the parking garage, anchors the project to the site. Metamorphosing out of this wall is a limestone base that encloses the first two stories. A scrim-like copper skin, resting on the limestone base and capped with a folded copper roof, encloses the upper levels. As the arcing wall cuts through the building it creates an open four-story lobby transected by catwalk-like bridges at each level. A reflective copper ceiling over the lobby reflects light from a skylight into the space below. On the exterior, limestone, copper, glass, water and shade come together to create the city's "living room." Terraces spill out of

the building into the plaza in the same way the geologic forces in Austin's hill country produce the limestone overhangs known as balcones. These terraces, shaded with trees, are prime locations for viewing the activities on the plaza below and Lady Bird Lake beyond.

A large plaza with a limestone stage for performances and an amphitheater provides public meeting space at the base of City Hall. The large terrace hosts many public gatherings and demonstrations, and reflects Austin's openness to public feedback, in design and reality. When Street Works conducted its Second Street retail assessment in 2000, it noted "the value of having a civic center as part of the mix, contributing to the district's identity," says Evins. "To integrate City Hall with the retail district, we incorporated retail spaces in the corners of city hall."

Austin City Council's goal was to create a sustainable public building that would serve as an educational model for green building. Energy and environmental features include:

- High degree of recycled content in construction materials, including 99% of the reinforcing steel, 90% of the sheetrock, 82% of the copper material (66,000 square feet of copper is used in the building) and 45% of the concrete masonry
- Condensation from the air-conditioning system, at an average of 486 gallons per day, provides the water source for a multi-level waterfall and may also be used for irrigation
- More than 80% of the construction debris was recycled, primarily provided to artists and schools
- During excavation, workers hit a water source which had to be pumped to protect the foundation—that water was saved and is being used to irrigate the landscaping
- All landscaping is native to Texas and

large trees have been planted in the plaza to provide shading and reduce heat gain
- Photovoltaic cells on the building's awning above the stairs on the south-side plaza generate an average of 9 kW of electricity daily
- The building is part of Austin Energy's downtown district cooling system, a large thermal energy storage system that produces ice during the night when electricity is cheapest; the ice then creates chilled water used to cool buildings the next day
- Interior materials such as paints, carpets and adhesives have low or no volatile organic compounds, increasing indoor air quality
- Bicycle storage, showers and lockers encourage alternative transportation
- The building features intensive green roof areas

City Hall is not the only building tied into Austin Energy's district cooling system; most of the Second Street District blocks, at least the retail and commercial portions, also take advantage of the energy-efficient system.

The City Hall sits above 740 underground parking spaces and includes 3,700 square feet of restaurant space along Second Street "to help the retail district wrap around," says Evins. The space is currently occupied by Austin Java, an independent coffee shop.

Extending Second Street: The New Downtown Austin Plan

In 2011, Austin's City Council adopted a new Downtown Austin Plan that establishes action priorities through 2021, with outcomes that will last well beyond. The plan is based on the continuing growth of the downtown area since 2000, even through two economic downturns. In that time, 6,000 new residents, more than 6,000 new jobs, 1.7 million square feet of office space and 1,500 hotel rooms were added to

Second Street District and downtown Austin as viewed from Town Lake.

Photo: Simmons Buntin

downtown Austin. Second Street District is a significant part of downtown Austin's growth, and because of the District's success and the importance of extending Second Street–both physically and symbolically–the city is building on its public/private partnership development experience for other nearby projects.

Second Street District and the surrounding area are located within the new Downtown Plan's Core/Waterfront District. Through the district, the plan strives to:

- Enhance the Core as the premier employment, cultural and visitor center of the region
- Improve the quality of the pedestrian experience
- Make it easier to get to downtown and move around without a car
- Restore and activate the historic squares
- Ensure that the district is a welcoming and affordable place for all
- Preserve the historic building fabric

Directly east of Second Street District, two new, iconic mixed-use high-rises incorporate the Great Streets streetscape typologies and extend Second Street's dynamic urban context. The Ashton was developed by MetLife, Inc. and designed by HKS, Inc., of Dallas. The 36-story tower on Colorado and Second Street includes 258 luxury rental units and a five-level parking garage, ground-floor lobby (without retail) and a seventh-floor sky lounge and rooftop pool. The Austonian–located at the northwest corner of the Second Street/Congress Avenue intersection–is a mixed-use tower developed by Benchmark Land Development and designed by Ziegler Cooper Architects. The 700-foot building has 250 luxury condominiums above retail and restaurant space at the northwest corner of Congress Avenue and Second Street.

Other new projects adjacent to Second Street District include the revitalized, historic Republic Square (which hosts a weekly farmers market); a new federal courthouse; upgrades to the Third Street pedestrian bridge and Lance Armstrong Bikeway; renovations to the Austin Music Hall; and the stunning Ballet Austin Butler Dance Education Center at Third Street and San Antonio. A new 1,000-room Marriott and convention center is scheduled to be built on Second Street adjacent to the Austin Convention Center. The 44-story 360 Building, a 432-unit high-rise residential tower above 15,000 square feet of ground-floor retail and

Restaurants and cafés such as Jo's Hot Coffee line Second Street, providing further ambience to what has proven to be a wonderful streetscape.

restaurant space, overlooks Shoal Creek from Third Street and Nueces Street. The city will also extend Second Street west to the 1950s-era, Art Deco-designed Seaholm Power Plant and the surrounding 13 acres. The site is being redeveloped as a "high-quality, mixed-use cultural attraction," according to the city, that will include the newly approved 200,000-square-foot Austin Central Library plus more than two million square feet of mixed-use development.

Additionally, Evins notes that the city hopes to extend its fledgling streetcar line down Third Street from the Convention Center. The existing line runs from the Convention Center to northwest neighborhoods beyond the state capitol. A November 2012 ballot initiative was scheduled to approve the Third Street extension and provide the necessary $300 million funding.

Conclusion: A Promising Market for Urban Living

Given that city leaders hope to draw as many as 13,000 new residents to downtown Austin

in the next ten years and provided the growth of nearby hotels, conference centers and entertainment venues, the future for downtown retail and housing is promising. Indeed, "Second Street District has proven to the development community, as well as everyone else, that downtown retail can be viable in Austin," says Evins, "There is a market for urban living." Five-thousand residential units are in the works for downtown, including several mixed-use, high-rise projects that are poised to break ground "when the market is ready," according to Evins. These projects are a direct result of Second Street District's success.

While Austin experienced its share of challenges from the recent economic downtown, Second Street District has remained economically viable. In 2010, the six-block core area spun off $4.55 million in property taxes—a number that does not reflect the $300 million W Hotel and Residences, completed in late 2010. The project produced $2.29 million in sales taxes in 2010, as well. According to Rodney Gonzales of Austin's Economic

Growth and Redevelopment Services Office, "The success of the district, in spite of the recent economic downtown, has regenerated investment in residential and retail projects throughout downtown Austin."

Downtown Austin Alliance associate director Molly Alexander focuses on the project's retail mix, saying, "The increase of pedestrian activity on Second Street can be attributed to the number and mix of retail stores and restaurants that are located in the District." She recognizes that the City's Great Streets program has been essential, but contends the project's success is based upon its mixed uses:

> Creating the streetscapes was only one component of creating this destination. The most critical aspect to creating vitality and value is the mix of uses that occur at the street level. What the City of Austin and AMLI have done very well is to combine the best use of publically

invested dollars into a private-sector model that creates values at and above the street level. The mix of office workers, residents and hotel guests add to the vibrancy of the street, but at its core, it is the mix of uses that create the destination and brand that is Second Street. Long-term, the success of the District will rely heavily on the success of the retail and restaurant businesses.

Austin's Second Street District is a powerful example of how community vision and collaboration can help redefine place. By incorporating principles of sustainable design, building from the spirit of the place itself, taking an active role in project design and buildout and ensuring a rich mix of uses, the city has achieved its goal of creating a premier, mixed-use retail spine downtown

---

DEFINING SUCCESS
Q&A with Fred Evins,
Redevelopment Project Manager/Architect, City of Austin

What was the largest obstacle to obtaining project approval or buy-in and how was it overcome?
While the city's vision and plans for the Second Street District had good community support, the development industry was skeptical about the viability of reestablishing a downtown retail destination and expanding the market for downtown residential. This was overcome by the city's investment in downtown redevelopment, particularly the Second Street District and the financial success of pioneering private development projects. Once the strength of the downtown retail and residential markets was clearly demonstrated, interest began to build in the development community.

What is an unexpected delight or success from the project?
The Second Street District was always envisioned to contain a healthy mix of uses (retail, residential, office and civic). But the Block 21 development (Stratus' W Hotel and Residences) increased the vitality and vibrancy of the district even more than anticipated. In addition to introducing 24-hour hotel operations, the project included a 1,500-seat performance venue (Moody Theater) that hosts tapings of PBS's *Austin City Limits* music program and other performing artists. Block 21 has proven to be a tremendous activating influence and has introduced a whole new segment of the community to the district.

What hasn't lived up to expectations or has required unanticipated change?

Initial lease-up and finish-out of the Block 2 and Block 4 retail shells, which the city invested in, took longer to accomplish and cost more than was anticipated when the initial business pro forma was crafted. The pace of retail development was affected by the extended timeline on completing the Block 21 development and installing the second phase of Second Street streetscape improvements from Colorado Street to Congress Avenue. Some of the investment and payback provisions in the retail development agreement between the City and AMLI Austin Retail had to be modified accordingly.

What continues to challenge or surprise you with the project?

I have been very pleasantly surprised by how well the Second Street District has achieved the vision and urban planning objectives set out for it. We had great leadership and subject matter expertise and brave private development partners. But, you never know until a project is completed whether it will work as envisioned, particularly when the project involves the development and implementation of new design criteria and has myriad construction phases, investors and stakeholders.

How do you define and measure success?

Some of the metrics we use are increased property and sales tax revenues and increased residential stock downtown. We also look at the market demand for downtown properties and private investments that were stimulated by the success of redevelopment projects like the Second Street District. Additionally, we consider the public benefits achieved through our public/private projects (e.g., public art, enhanced streetscapes, affordable housing units, preservation, cultural uses and higher sustainable design objectives) to be a measure of our success.

Suisun City Waterfront District
Suisun City, California
by Simmons B. Buntin

Photo: Simmons Buntin

The redevelopment of downtown Suisun City, from its iconic civic center to restored harbor to Old Town, is a story of creativity, persistence, and planning for the unknown.

The redevelopment of downtown Suisun City, California, and its Waterfront District is a story of strong civic leadership and creativity in the face of considerable economic and environmental adversity. Before the city undertook redevelopment, a regional survey of livability ranked Suisun City last among San Francisco Bay-area communities. Its harbor, an extension of the country's most far-reaching inland estuary, was heavily polluted and adjacent land was dominated by prefabricated metal warehouses, vacant lots and decaying buildings.

Two decades later, Suisun City has overhauled itself, building new, neo-traditional residential and mixed-used neighborhoods while restoring its historic Old Town and Main Street. The city undertook extensive remediation to restore the Suisun Channel and raised an architecturally distinct city hall as the redevelopment's first new building. The Waterfront District also includes live/work units adjacent to the harbor, a marina, new office building and hotel and restoration of its circa-1910 train depot, hosting Solano County's only stop on the Capitol Corridor, the nation's third-busiest commuter rail line, connecting the Sacramento metro area with the Bay Area.

Despite these successes, Suisun City faces a challenging future, including weathering the continuing economic downturn in the near term, and responding to climate change and rising sea levels in the long term. And as with all California municipalities in 2012, Suisun City faces Governor Jerry Brown's elimination of its redevelopment agency and the sale

JUST THE FACTS

- Located just south of Fairfield, California, 41 miles northeast of Oakland and 44 miles southwest of Sacramento
- Redevelopment of 200-acre Old Town and area surrounding Suisun Channel initiated in 1982 and fully put into action in 1989
- Broader, transit-oriented planned development area of 448 acres
- Adjacent to 84,000-acre Suisun Marsh, the largest contiguous wetlands in the western U.S.
- Circa-1910 train depot with commuter rail (Capitol Corridor, jointly operated by Amtrak and the State of California) and bus station
- 150-berth marina with Harbormaster building and guest dock
- 28,000-square-foot public plaza and 5,000-foot-long waterfront promenade
- City hall as architectural icon in new Civic Center
- 700 single-family homes in neo-traditional neighborhoods, plus a series of historically preserved homes in Old Town
- 300 multifamily homes, including refurbished affordable housing
- 30 live/work units
- 47,000 square feet of office space
- 102-room hotel
- Series of mixed-use redevelopments along Main Street, including the addition of more than 300 parking spaces for a park-and-ride
- Public-private partnership enabled through Suisun City Redevelopment Agency
- New Urbanist design of original redevelopment area by Roma Design Group

of its assets to pay down state debt. This move, which was finalized in February 2012, effectively halts the city's ability to fund and lead future revitalization efforts.

Early Redevelopment Process

Suisun City is a California Gold Rush town, established in the 1850s as a shipping and trade port that connected the San Francisco Bay with the Sierra Nevada Mountains by rail and ship. It is located halfway between San Francisco and Sacramento, just south of the rapidly developing Interstate 80 corridor. Suisun City incorporated with a population of 200 in 1869. Though its population is only 28,000 today, it has grown from just 2,900 in 1970. Nearly all of that growth has occurred on the edges of the city, in a typical bedroom-community sprawl pattern: standardized, auto-oriented subdivisions with wide streets and cul-de-sacs, broken up by the occasional strip mall.

Until the 1960s, Suisun City served largely as an agricultural hub. When I-80 opened, however, commercial traffic was diverted to its neighbor to the north, Fairfield, resulting in "a period of disinvestment that crippled Suisun City's Old Town," according to the Bay Area Metropolitan Transportation Commission. By the 1980s, Old Town and the city core were in serious decline. Industrial oil facilities along the harbor polluted the ground and water, businesses failed along Main Street, the Crescent neighborhood required about half the city's police resources to fight drug dealers and high crime, and the city hall's once-temporary set of trailers had become its permanent home.

In 1982, with the city struggling to provide services, Suisun City's planning department brought together a group of concerned citizens, regional architects, planners and staff to develop a Downtown Specific Plan for revitalization of the city's Old Town and adjacent harbor. Though the group completed a plan for redeveloping portions of the downtown area, which was adopted in 1983, for years no

The Suisun City waterfront and Suisun Harbor in 1987, prior to redevelopment.

actions were taken and the city's economic, environmental and social landscape worsened.

By 1988, the situation was so bad that a *San Francisco Chronicle* survey of the quality of life in the Bay Area's 98 municipalities ranked Suisun City dead last. By then, however, a growing group of citizens and a frustrated city council led by Mayor Jim Spering decided that it was time again to develop a feasible redevelopment plan for bringing life back into Suisun City's Old Town and adjacent downtown areas.

Suisun City's redevelopment was defined by the five goals articulated in the 1990 Suisun City Downtown Specific Plan. The goals–developed by the mayor, city council, staff and a 13-member citizens committee–spurred a comprehensive turnabout in only seven years:

- Strengthen the economic viability of the Historic Old Town, Waterfront and adjacent areas and the city as a whole
- Preserve and enhance the historic character of the area
- Facilitate appropriate water-oriented and economic uses of the Suisun Channel and adjacent land areas
- Protect and enhance natural open space and recreational amenities of the Suisun Channel and adjoining areas
- Foster participation between the public and private sector in carrying out a program of revitalization for the Planning Area

Rather than developing a land-use plan and approval process for redevelopment projects as the first step, the city began by asking what the citizens wanted and then letting the Specific Plan follow. That process satisfied two criteria. First, it allowed the city to define what it wanted to accomplish up-front, based on citizen input, and then to design incentives and disincentives accordingly. Second, it allowed the city to let developers and business owners know what the city's plans were early on, so they could prepare for the coming disruptions and opportunities.

The first step for the city was to bring in assistance for redevelopment in the form of Camran Nojoomi, head of the city's redevelopment agency, and to contract with the San Francisco-based Roma Design Group, which developed conceptual plans and design guidelines based on staff and citizen input. Under Nojoomi, the city then reformed the redevelopment agency with autonomous administration and budget under California law by merging the functions of planning and housing. The reorganization allowed skilled staff to share expertise and avoided discrepancies often apparent when general plans and redevelopment plans are created and implemented under separate agencies. The redevelopment agency also defined redevelopment boundaries to include the entire city, rather than just the downtown itself, in order to "capture tax-increment financing from projects happening all over town," said Mayor Spering at the time. Though it was a bold move to include the entire city, there is no doubt that Suisun City needed revitalization across its incorporated area.

The city utilized staff expertise, input from the citizens committee and Roma Design Group's vision and skill set to revise the Downtown Specific Plan. These stakeholders narrowed their design focus to six locations: civic center (city hall, at the time in a set of trailers), Crescent neighborhood, waterfront (and a new town plaza), Main Street, Old Town and the train depot.

While the city initially hoped to obtain one developer to take on the hefty task of redeveloping the entire downtown, none was willing. So the city found itself in the precarious role of playing "public developer," as Nojoomi called it, and decided to undertake a series of steps to promote redevelopment on specific parcels. The amended Downtown Specific Plan was approved in 1990 and revised in 1999.

The Rules of Redevelopment: A Flexible Affair

In 1991, the city issued $58 million in tax-increment bonds to provide for design work, the purchase of dilapidated properties along the waterfront, new infrastructure including water and sewer pipes and streetscaping, façade improvement programs, construction of the new Harbor Plaza, dredging and restoration of Suisun Channel and wetlands in the adjacent Suisun Marsh, and other activities.

Many of the "traditional" redevelopment approaches were modified or developed anew as Suisun City's process moved forward. Creation of a redevelopment agency, for example, provided an opportunity for state-supported renewal of stressed places. Suisun City bent the rules in a strategic manner, however, by merging housing and planning within the redevelopment agency. The maneuver facilitated a more effective relationship between city staff, allowed the Downtown Specific Plan to be integrated with the city's General Plan, provided mechanisms for marketing the development, allowed for separate financing of redevelopment efforts and provided for effective public involvement. In addition to the citizens committee, participation was fostered through public hearings and city council meetings.

Another imaginative interpretation of California redevelopment law was the establishment of boundaries for the redevelopment district. Normally, boundaries are established only around the area that is to be redeveloped. The city's approach, however, allowed it to receive tax-increment financing to repay bonds from the entire city–particularly those residential and strip retail areas growing at its edges.

When Suisun City issued bonds in 1991, the lowest interest rate the city could acquire was 7.5%, even though the bonds were rated at A-. In 1993, however, the city refinanced at 5.75%, and obtained insurance for the bonds, enabling the city to borrow $10 million more than it did in 1991. Suisun City secured funding from other sources, as well. For example, state transportation funds were available to renovate the train depot, which now serves as a multimodal transportation hub. The city utilized a feasibility study and a $5.6 million loan from the California Department of Boating and Waterways to construct a 150-berth marina, completed in early 1994. Loan payments were deferred until 1998, the year that the marina was projected to be fully leased, allowing the redevelopment agency time to build a $2 million reserve fund for marina operations by the time payments began.

As part of the process for reviewing proposals to build Victorian Harbor, the new single-family development that replaced the crime-ridden Crescent neighborhood, the city worked through 50 developers before finding one (the O'Brien Group of San Mateo, California) that would comply with an acceptable number of the city's goals, which included pedestrian orientation, front porches, Victorian-style architecture, alleys with garages and narrow streets. Most developers proposed conventional suburban houses, refusing to give credit to the uniqueness of the neighborhood as a factor in marketing and sales. The O'Brien Group was well rewarded, though: the neo-traditional homes sold briskly, even in the state's stagnant economy of 1994.

During the early stages of redevelopment, the city was challenged by a lack of local examples to calculate lending criteria or risk. The harbor's industrial facilities were removed, opening access to the harbor and new commercial opportunities. However, developers still had no baseline on which to gauge the value of the parcels, using traditional measures such as land sale prices and lease rates. In order to lessen developer risks, the city took advantage of enterprise zone programs, including negotiable land acquisition terms for city-owned land, development and business license fee waivers, architectural design assistance, permit assistance and mixed-use flexibility.

Suisun City also partnered with the State of California and the federal government to clean up and dredge Suisun Channel, the waterway leading through the adjacent 84,000-acre Suisun Marsh. Nojoomi crafted an agreement with the U.S. Army Corps of Engineers to place dredge materials on an island just south of the Channel, creating new wildlife habitat without having to fully remove dredge materials. This successful approach has since become a model for effectively disposing of fill while creating new wetlands.

The Form of Redevelopment: Four Design Tools and a Study

Four design-focused tools have determined the form of Suisun City's redevelopment: the Downtown Specific Plan, Design Standards and Guidelines, enterprise zone programs and the Crescent neighborhood resident relocation program. Additionally, the Transit-Oriented Development Feasibility Study, completed in 2009, laid the foundation for future development in the broader, 488-acred planned area development that spans Suisun City's Old Town and Waterfront District and the vacant land directly north of it.

Suisun City's Amended Downtown Specific Plan of 1999 provides an introduction to the planning process and Specific Plan concept; discussion of existing uses and policies; goals and objectives; land-use regulations for residential and commercial districts, public facilities and open space, and parking; review of traffic and circulation; design standards and guidelines; and the means for Specific Plan administration.

The Downtown Specific Plan is the legal tool that ties the development process into the city's General Plan and zoning ordinances. The 1995 version provided a vision of the redeveloped downtown:

That Downtown Suisun City has the

Suisun City's Main Street serves as the main thoroughfare into Suisun City and has presented an opportunity for significant historic preservation.

opportunity to become a unique waterfront town that is pleasant to live in and at the same time serves as a regional destination. The Plan draws on an unusual mix of characteristics—a working Waterfront, an Historic Main Street, established neighborhoods, direct freeway access, an Amtrak/Intercity Rail Station, a rich natural environment and a location that is in the path of regional growth.

The Design Standards and Guidelines provide the basis for developers and reviewing agencies, including Suisun City's Architectural Review Board, Planning Commission, Redevelopment Agency and city council. The Guidelines ensure that any new development or façade renovation supports existing and desirable historic characteristics of Old Town. The Residential Guidelines attempt "to create a traditional townscape throughout the Downtown/Waterfront area which fosters community activities, social interaction and a strong cohesive image," while the Commercial Guidelines "are intended to preserve and enhance the

historic character of the Downtown commercial area and to ensure the new developments are compatible."

The enterprise zone incentive programs were established to facilitate business development along Main Street and the waterfront. Babs Delta Diner, the first business to move into the mixed-use area located along Kellogg Street, is a good example of the type of businesses the incentive programs sought to attract. Babs Curless owns the two-story, Victorian-style building, with the diner on the first floor and her residence on the second. Her move from another part of town to the redeveloping waterfront in 1995 was facilitated by the redevelopment agency's willingness to finance the purchase of the land, waive development and business license fees, provide free architectural design assistance and assist in preparing permit applications required for city and state agencies.

The resident relocation program may not initially sound like a design policy, but its purpose was to move residents out of the dilapidated Crescent neighborhood of fourplexes so that the Victorian Harbor neighborhood could be

Suisun City in 2010, with Old Town and Delta Cove left of the marina, the civic center, Harbor Park, and Victorian Harbor right, and the train depot, office buildings, and hotel at the far end. Fairfield lies just north of Highway 12, only a short distance from Suisun Harbor.

built. Four-hundred-seventy units were demolished in 1991 and 300 new Victorian-style single-family homes were built in their place (entry-level priced at $130,000 to $180,000). Relocation assistance was provided to Crescent residents, including four years of subsidized rent anywhere in northern California. Most of the residents took the assistance, while others simply moved away.

The Transit-Oriented Development Feasibility Study builds on the broad boundaries set in the 1999 Downtown Specific Plan, but was completed a decade later, after much of the city's waterfront redevelopment was complete. Its purpose is to analyze the 448-acre planned area development's economic base, growth projections, retail market and existing transit ridership and create a set of transit-oriented development scenarios. "Our goal," said community development director April Wooden in 2011, "is to build a transit village near the train station." She notes that the train depot is very successful, both because of the large park-and-ride across Main Street and because

of pedestrian commuters—those who live in or near the Waterfront District and walk to the depot to catch the train or bus to work.

The Feasibility Study offers six scenarios, ranging from infill spanning seven acres and adding 76 housing units, 24,900 square feet of commercial space and 144,200 square feet of office space to a scenario that expands beyond infill to include vacant property spanning 31.6 acres, 420 housing units, 128,500 square feet of office space and 61,000 square feet of new retail space. The study notes that "all of the development scenarios face considerable short-term market impediments...due to regional market conditions that limit the potential for housing, office and industrial development, as well as expanded supply of retail space in Suisun City." Yet the study explains that adoption of one of the scenarios is a strong possibility, pending the authority of the city's redevelopment agency to move forward on the project.

Defining Success through the Downtown Specific Plan

At 84,000 acres, the Suisun Marsh is the largest contiguous wetlands in the western U.S.

Photo: Simmons Buntin

There are a number of successes resulting from the 20 years of redevelopment of the Suisun City Waterfront District. These can be categorized through the Downtown Specific Plan's organizing elements:

The entire Downtown needs to be focused on the Suisun Channel which is its major and central feature.
By acquiring and removing abandoned industrial facilities along the Channel, the city provided public access to the water for the first time in 50 years. Through Roma Design Group's plan, the harbor–with its 150-berth marina and Harbormaster, Harbor Plaza and mix of supporting uses and civic structures–is clearly the central feature of the redevelopment and the community overall.

The northern end of the Channel must be expanded to accommodate a marina and create a stronger image of the Waterfront.
While the marina was not extended to the northern end of the harbor from its present location between Harbor Plaza and the Civic Center, the northern edge of the Channel has been redeveloped to include new public plazas, the 300-space park-and-ride and commercial buildings as part of One Harbor Center. The project features a three-story office building of 47,000 square feet and the 102-room Hampton Inn and Suites. Prior to redevelopment, 27 oil storage tanks and 160,000 cubic feet of contaminated soil were removed.

The Waterfront should maintain its extraordinary mix of natural wetlands and urban edge.
Redevelopment of the waterfront included a seawall and 5,000-foot-long promenade extending along the harbor. Natural wetlands were also preserved as the new Waterfront Park, located between the north end of the harbor and the Civic Center, the location of Suisun City's iconic city hall. Additionally, Suisun Marsh is permanently protected along both sides of the Channel.

Photo: Simmons Buntin

Delta Cove is a unique series of live/work structures along Suisun Harbor.

The commercial activities of the Downtown should be integrated with an expanded new marina at its northern end and a Town Square at its southern end.

While the physical locations have changed, the results are similar. The marina is located at the southern end of the Channel, while the 28,000-square-foot Harbor Plaza has been constructed between Main Street and the harbor on its west side. Commercial and mixed-use activities continue to be integrated and include waterfront live/work on Kellogg Street, the Harbor Square Courtyard and a renovated marina center. Infill, renovation and street and parking upgrades continue along Main Street, as well.

The existing Sheldon Oil site needs to be redeveloped as the center of the Downtown Commercial District and the Waterfront.

Industrial facilities were cleared from the site and soil contamination was removed. This is the One Harbor Center site, featuring an office building, hotel and parking shared with the train depot across Main Street.

The area to the east of the Channel offers an opportunity for the creation of several new low-density residential neighborhoods.

Victorian Harbor, a medium-density, single-family neighborhood, was completed in 1995 northeast of the Channel. It replaced the Crescent neighborhood. In order to further promote pedestrian orientation, the city revised this element in the 1999 Design Guidelines so that new residential plans for the Todd Park area east of city hall were pedestrian-oriented in design as well. The new neighborhood is called Harbor Park and includes 55 single-family homes of neo-traditional design built around a central green, replacing Todd Park. It was completed in 2003.

The west of the Channel offers an opportunity for a medium-density residential neighborhood.

A unique live/work neighborhood called Delta Cove was built west of the Channel and below Harbor Plaza. Twenty-six live/work units ranging from 1,800 to 3,000 square feet with commercial spaces up to 800 feet were built from 2002 to 2005. Half of the units face the waterfront promenade while half front Kellogg Street. Several of the units include first-floor studios, offices and other small business uses.

The Downtown needs a more cohesive system that allows for a greater distribution of traffic.
Street improvements and new streets are outlined in the Downtown Specific Plan and continue to be completed as parcels build out.

The Downtown needs a cohesive Open Space system that enhances the pedestrian experience of the townscape and the Waterfront.
The full range of Suisun City's redevelopment projects provide open space and pedestrian access. Victorian Harbor, Delta Cove and Harbor Park relegate garages to alleys and provide wide, landscaped streets and pathways for pedestrian access. A promenade runs along the Channel, linking the Civic Center on the east with One Harbor Center on the north with Harbor Plaza and mixed-used and residential development on the east. From there, sidewalks and trails lead into all portions of the Waterfront District, whether the natural open space of the marsh or the urban streets of Old Town. Pedestrian pathways were constructed along the Waterfront Park and sidewalk widening projects were completed along Main Street. Sidewalk widths range from ten to 12 feet on Main Street, five to 12 feet on Kellogg Street and 16 to 20 feet on the waterfront promenade and Harbor Plaza. Open space has also been provided in the form of pocket parks at Delta Cove, Harbor Park and Victorian Harbor—and larger parks exist at the Civic Center and between the Channel and One Harbor Center.

Additionally, in 2009 the city and county completed a continuous three-mile pathway through Suisun City dedicated to bicycles and pedestrians, providing access to the waterfront without having to cross Highway 12, which divides Suisun City from Fairfield. The path is part of the Solano Central County Bikeway,

the result of a regional partnership funded by the city and the Solano Transportation Authority, Bay Area Air Quality Management District, Caltrans, California State Parks and the Metropolitan Transportation Commission.

A 2006 pedestrian study by the Metropolitan Transportation Commission confirmed the Waterfront District's walkability, noting eight factors with significant impact:

- The waterfront promenade provides direct connectivity to major attractors, including the transportation center
- Wide sidewalks accommodate both pedestrians and recreational activities . . . and are well suited to handle large numbers of pedestrians during special events and festivals
- Low traffic speeds along downtown streets, along with good design, provide a level of pedestrian comfort
- The use of colored concrete softens the sun's glare and adds visual interest to the pedestrian environment
- Street tree planting and extensive landscaping provide a measure of separation from the roadway, enhancing the pedestrian environment along Main, Solano and Kellogg Streets
- Street trees also provide a vertical element to the streetscape to help slow vehicle speeds and provide shade for pedestrians in warmer months
- Ample pedestrian amenities–including seating, trash and recycling receptacles; and public restrooms–foster a positive pedestrian experience
- Ample parking allows visitors to get out and walk

The Suisun City Civic Center

The most significant symbol in redeveloping Suisun City's waterfront is its city hall, built on the eastern shore of Suisun Channel. "Before the city built its new Civic Center, as one of the first steps in Suisun City's revitalization, its

Suisun City's civic center provides an iconic building along the Suisun Channel and marina, an early and important symbol of the community's strength in redefining itself.

offices were located in a group of mobile trailers," said Mayor Spering. "We had the only city hall in California that was registered with the Department of Motor Vehicles."

Today, city hall and the Civic Center anchor the southeastern portion of the Waterfront District, nestled between the Channel and marina, the Solano Yacht Club, Harbor Park and natural wetlands. Though the Civic Center is not large, its three-story, silver-domed cupola atop an octagonal building provides a distinct image, particularly when reflected in Suisun Channel. The white building is shaped like a shallow V, with one-story wings that parallel the small park and adjacent channel. Its architecture is matched by the Harbor Master building across the channel, and through design elements found in buildings surrounding the Channel.

Harbor Plaza: A Center for People, Events and More

In order to provide public space and a community center, Suisun City built Harbor Plaza along Suisun Channel. The site was previously occupied by prefabricated metal warehouses and vacant lots but now adjoins a promenade along the harbor and a raised lawn at One Harbor Center. The plaza features landscaping, patterned walkways with colored concrete, lawns, a granite-and-bronze stage area and a gazebo.

Dozens of events are held on the plaza annually, including the May Boat Parade and blessing of the fleet, Mother's Day Artisan Faire, Shore Fest (featuring live music, arts and crafts vendors, local food and brews and jet ski racing), Friday Nights on the Waterfront (free live concerts), Saturday Night at the Movies, Sunday Waterfront Jazz Series, Independence Day Spectacular (including the region's largest fireworks display), Waterfront Festival, Halloween Parade, Old World Christmas Market, Snow Day on the Waterfront and Christmas at the Waterfront (featuring holiday vendors, food, live music, hay wagon rides, lighted boat parade, bonfire, outdoor synthetic ice skating rink, Christmas tree lighting and fireworks).

Victorian Harbor, shown here in 1996, replaced the crime-ridden Crescent neighborhood.

Suisun City's Neo-Traditional Neighborhood: Victorian Harbor and Harbor Park

The Victorian Harbor neighborhood replaced the run-down Crescent neighborhood, a mid-1970s development of fourplexes built on single-family lots. The city helped private developers fund the Crescent land purchase on the provision that the subdivision house low-income families. The city hoped the fourplex development would bring life into nearby Old Town. While 106 of the original units were salvaged and 52 rehabilitated during redevelopment, 470 Crescent units in all were demolished.

The neighborhood that replaced Crescent is a direct attempt to capture the turn-of-the-20th century flavor of Old Town. The single-family homes have front porches, Victorian-style architecture, lushly landscaped front yards, garages situated on landscaped alleys and small lots. The neighborhood incorporates pedestrian-friendly, traffic-calming elements such as roundabouts, narrow streets and cutout curbs for on-street parking. Sidewalks are separated from streets by grass strips with landscaping and traditional streetlamps. By the end of

1993, 94 homes were built and an additional 206 were added over the next two years.

The Waterfront District's other single-family subdivision is Harbor Park, located just east of city hall and completed in 2003. Fifty-five single-family homes face winding pedestrian paths; garages are relegated to alleys behind the homes. At the core of the neighborhood is a long, central green lined by benches and ornate streetlamps. Like Victorian Harbor, Harbor Park features traditional architectural styles, usable front porches and small lots.

Main Street Improvements and Historic Preservation

Main Street's improvement is actually a series of ongoing programs, directed by the redevelopment agency. The city's Historic Façade Improvement Program, for example, allowed businesses along Main Street to restore façades with the assistance of city funding. Infill projects that meet the city's design guidelines for historic structures have also been encouraged, and several buildings have been built along Main Street over the last 15 years due to the city's efforts.

The city has also fostered the conversion

of a number of buildings to uses–and even locations–that benefit the residents. In a successful effort to save the circa-1855 Lawlor House–once slated for torching as a fire department demonstration–the structure was trucked from its original location down Highway 12 and then floated by barge to an area just east of Main Street, adjacent to Harbor Plaza and the waterfront. It has been fully restored and now houses offices above the Lawler House Gallery, which exhibits work from two dozen artist members of the Fairfield Visual Arts Association. Other buildings have been similarly restored; the circa-1876 Bank of Suisun is now a coffee shop and the old Post Office for a time served as a microbrewery and pub.

A former grocery store east of Main Street now houses Solano Community College's drama department and theater, as well as the Harbor Theatrical Group. The building was converted into the 170-seat performing arts Harbor Theater, which includes classrooms, several small stages, the main stage and exterior sculptures.

Commercial and Mixed-Use Development on the Waterfront

In addition to the businesses and residences on Main Street and throughout Old Town, Suisun City has worked to create a unique and innovate mix of live/work buildings and commercial uses right on the waterfront. An informal restaurant district is being built along Kellogg Street, one block east of the marina and promenade. There, restaurants such as Bab's Delta Diner and Athenian Grill (both early participants in the redevelopment) are joined by such establishments as the Joy of Eating Café. In total, the redeveloped area near Harbor Plaza features a dozen restaurants and five retail pads which include such uses as a hair salon, apparel design, a consulting firm and a travel agency.

Suisun City's newest addition is Harbor Square Courtyard, a 40,000-square-foot building of retail, office and restaurants. The two-story, 3,600-square-foot courtyard is home to the region's largest freestanding outdoor fireplace. Businesses include a restaurant, lounge, coffee shop, sub shop, and financial offices.

The northern edge of the harbor is anchored by One Harbor Center, which so far is comprised of two buildings: a three-story, 47,000-square-foot, class A office building and the Hampton Inn and Suites Suisun City Waterfront.

While some retail outlets are struggling, the restaurants are doing well–they've become destinations for Suisun City and Fairfield residents, according to April Wooden. Most restaurants are independent, family-owned local businesses rather than chains. Though not by design, the mix of local restaurants lends even more to the Waterfront District's distinctive sense of place.

The hotel is also exceeding expectations, particularly during popular events on the plaza and programs associated with regional destinations like Travis Air Force Base. When constructing the hotel, the developer agreed not to incorporate a restaurant in order to funnel lodgers to the restaurants located along Main Street and the waterfront. In fact, Wooden reports that the hotel's manager visits each of the dozen local restaurants so he and his staff can provide honest recommendations to lodgers.

A Daunting Future: Climate Change and Rising Sea Levels

In 2006, California passed the Global Warming Solutions Act (Assembly Bill 32) and, two years later, the Sustainable Communities and Climate Protection Act (Senate Bill 375). Together, the acts address global warming and greenhouse gas emissions by requiring the reduction of greenhouse gas emissions to 1990 levels by 2020 and by linking transportation and housing planning to these goals–in large part through the development of regional

Sustainable Communities Strategies. In the nine-county San Francisco Bay Area, the Sustainable Communities Strategy is a joint effort of the Metropolitan Transportation Commission and the Association of Bay Area Governments (ABAG). Each jurisdiction, including Suisun City, plays a role in the development of the Strategy, which must be included as part of the Bay Area's 25-year Regional Transportation Plan.

The Sustainable Communities Strategy is scheduled to be adopted in 2013. According to planners, it will:

- Recognize and support compact walkable places where residents and workers have access to services and amenities to meet their day-to-day needs
- Reduce long commutes and decrease reliance on single-occupancy vehicles, increasing energy independence and decreasing the region's carbon consumption
- Support complete communities which remain livable and affordable for all segments of the population, maintaining the Bay Area as an attractive place to reside, start or continue a business and create jobs
- Support a sustainable transportation system and reduce the need for expensive highway and transit expansions, freeing up resources for other more productive public investments
- Provide increased accessibility and affordability to the most vulnerable populations
- Conserve water and decrease dependence on imported food stocks and their high transport costs

For the Bay Area, the Sustainable Communities Strategy is a response to the threat of more frequent extreme storms and rising sea levels that result in flooding, permanent seawater inundation, shoreline erosion and elevated groundwater levels and salinity.

According to the National Oceanic and Atmospheric Administration (NOAA), "Climate change will significantly alter the Bay, which is projected to rise 16 inches by mid-century and 55 inches by the end of the century." In the Bay Area, that puts $36 billion of shoreline development, 160,000 residents, 180,000 acres and 95% of tidal wetlands at risk of destruction from flooding by mid-century. For Suisun City–the Bay Area's deepest inland harbor–even a 16-inch sea level rise presents significant risk, says Wooden.

According to Suisun City associate planner John Kearns, the broad team creating the Bay Area's Sustainable Communities Strategy recently evaluated three scenarios:

1. Core Concentration Growth Scenario: Concentrates housing and job growth at selected Priority Development Areas in the Inner Bay Area along the region's core transit network.
2. Focused Growth Scenario: Recognizes the potential of Priority Development Areas and Growth Opportunity Areas across the region with an emphasis on housing and job growth along major transit corridors.
3. Outer Bay Area Growth Scenario: Addresses higher levels of growth in the Outer Bay Area (including Suisun City) and is closer to previous development trends than the other two scenarios.

In addition to the Sustainable Communities Strategy, initiatives such as the NOAA and San Francisco Bay Conservation and Development Commission (BCD) Adapting to Rising Tides project are working with Bay Area communities to begin planning for sea level rise. "The Bay Area is already working to reduce greenhouse gas emissions," say representatives of NOAA and BCDC, "but mitigation alone will not be adequate to address impending sea level rise and other climate change impacts. The Bay Area must consider adaptation actions that will reduce the vulnerability of the built and natural environment to the effects of climate change."

As a waterfront community, Suisun City is likely to be greatly impacted by climate change and rising sea levels. Though the impacts are not yet known, city planners do know they must play an active role in the Sustainable Community Strategy's creation.

The Future of Redevelopment at Suisun City–and across California

While climate change and rising sea levels present imminent challenges for Suisun City, legislation signed in summer 2011 by California Governor Jerry Brown to eliminate all redevelopment agencies–as a measure to generate an estimated $1.7 billion toward the state's $26.6 billion budget shortfall in fiscal year 2012–presented a more immediate problem for the city. Elimination of Suisun City's Redevelopment Agency, if the city cannot afford to pay its annual share, will result in a budget hole of 10% for Suisun City. "It also would end the single most important tool the city has used to transform itself into a high-quality community in which to live, raise a family and visit," says city manager Suzanne Bragdon.

Already Suisun City's budget is impacted by payments required by 2009 legislation. In 2010 Suisun City paid $5.7 million to the state, and in 2011 it paid $4.5 million. "Losing this money is challenging," says Bragdon. "The elimination of redevelopment by the governor is even worse. These actions by the state cripple our ability to build and expand our city's economy. By taking local funds, the state is not only harming us, but is likewise hindering the overall economic recovery of the state. Redevelopment is the state's economic development engine."

Though the League of California Cities and the California Redevelopment Association challenged the constitutionality of the legislation, the California Supreme Court upheld the dissolution of all of California's redevelopment agencies. Additionally, the court struck down a voluntary program to keep redevelopment agencies alive. Following from the decision, Suisun City's redevelopment agency was officially eliminated on February 1, 2012, resulting in a city budget cut of $1.4 million. Though a state-mandated Successor Agency has been created and charged with "carrying out the orderly wind-down" of the agency, the city may no longer undertake new redevelopment activities. Because the option to pay annually to retain the redevelopment agency was eliminated, the city's Successor Agency website notes that Suisun City stands to lose approximately $13 million in additional cash and assets. "This decision has severely limited future business development in a community like Suisun City," says Bragdon.

Conclusion: A Hard-Won Past, an Uncertain Future

Though the future is uncertain, the Suisun City Waterfront District demonstrates that creative, public-private approaches to redevelopment–through an official redevelopment agency and otherwise–can make a significant difference in the livability and economic and environmental success of a community. Calculated public involvement has greatly influenced physical design, resulting in a plan that restores the Suisun Harbor, further protects Suisun Marsh, creates a destination for residents and regional visitors, preserves and builds from historic Old Town, incorporates the train depot as a locus for transit-oriented development and brings business and residents back to the city core to live, dine, shop and play.

A new set of Suisun City guiding principles–adopted in 2010–may provide the best conclusion for how the waterfront redevelopment continues to be essential for the entire city:

Community Character
Suisun City will strive to enhance the City's authentic, local identity as a

Located next to the new Harbor Square Courtyard, the circa-1855 Lawlor House was saved from its one-time fate as a torching demonstration by a fire department.

vibrant waterfront community.

Destination Tourism and Entertainment

Suisun City will encourage the development of uses and protection of resources that attract visitors, enhancing the community as a tourism destination.

Downtown

Suisun City will continue to develop the downtown as a vibrant, pedestrian-scaled commercial and entertainment center that reflects our community's unique waterfront character.

Economic Vitality

Suisun City will strive for economic vitality, providing jobs, services, revenues and opportunities.

Infrastructure

Suisun City will provide quality community services and sound infrastructure.

Neighborhood Vitality

Suisun City will ensure that

neighborhoods maintain their character and vitality.

Public Safety and Emergency Preparedness

Suisun City will strive to protect the community and minimize vulnerability to disasters.

Quality of Community Life

Suisun City will foster an inclusive, multigenerational community that is economically and ethnically diverse.

Sustainability

Suisun City will practice economically, fiscally and environmentally responsible municipal decision-making to avoid shifting today's costs to future generations.

Transportation

Suisun City will provide choices for attractive, convenient transportation.

DEFINING SUCCESS
Q&A with April Wooden, Community Development Director, City of Suisun City

What was the largest obstacle to obtaining project approval or buy-in, and how was it overcome?
Skepticism. But nothing succeeds like success!

What is an unexpected delight or success from the project?
The rapid success of our waterfront Hampton Inn has been wonderful. In addition to serving its business and tourism customer base, the hotel has reached out to the families at Travis AFB that have loved ones serving overseas. The hotel generously provides a location for those families to get together weekly for a potluck and to enjoy the hotel pool.

What hasn't lived up to expectations or has required unanticipated change?
Development of retail has been much more difficult than anticipated. The number of restaurant/entertainment venues continues to increase, but we need complementary retail.

What continues to challenge or surprise you with the project?
The current economy has slowed development. With excellent sites available, it can be discouraging to see things move slowly. However, a recent success story is the establishment of a new commercial kitchen in the downtown. The facility provides cooking facilities, as well as a small retail space, for small, growing food businesses. One of the businesses has a product that will be provided to the Oscar night presenters.

How do you define and measure success?
The Suisun City Waterfront District development has improved everyday life for our residents. Crime is down, affordable housing has been built, the community is out walking, fishing, biking, kite flying and attending community events on the plaza, such as our 4th of July extravaganza and our Christmas at the Waterfront, during which Santa arrives on his sleigh-boat, escorted by a lighted boat parade.

Green Development

Whether new development or redevelopment, brownfield or greenfield, projects like Victoria, British Columbia's Dockside Green show that advanced green development is both possible and profitable.

This is a fundamental view of the world. It says that when you build a thing, you cannot merely build that thing in isolation, but must also repair the world around it, and within it, so that the larger world at one place becomes more coherent, and more whole; and the thing which you make takes its place in the web of nature, as you make it.

Christopher Alexander, *A Pattern Language*

A place that becomes more coherent and more whole, repairing the world around as well as within might come in many shapes—a bustling waterfront, for example, or a small farm-centered town or neighborhood of indigenous homes and native gardens. What the three case studies in this section reveal is that creating successful, sustainable communities is not a goal to be achieved but a process to be followed and then revised: an essential pursuit if we hope to build places that will last, on landscapes that will last even longer.

What the developers hope will last in Victoria, British Columbia, is a commitment to creating the world's greenest development–with steep penalties if the developers fail. The small brownfield redevelopment of Dockside Green is the first LEED for Neighborhood Development Platinum-certified community. It features a core of super-efficient residential and commercial buildings, a biomass energy plant and an advanced wastewater treatment plant in a distinct maritime setting. Water provides the shape and vitality for a farm-based suburban Chicago community in Grayslake, Illinois, as well: Prairie Crossing. A 668-acre, master-planned conservation development, the project features a transit-oriented town center, energy-efficient homes of a Midwestern vernacular and an organic farm, all among regenerated native prairie and wetlands. It's not water but rather an intimate relationship with the Sonoran desert that defines the resource-efficient community of Civano in Tucson, Arizona. With a mixed-use neighborhood center, a diversity of traditional and modern architectural styles designed for a desert climate and the "Greenest Grade School in America," the suburban neighborhood tracks its environmental stewardship through a set of quantifiable sustainability goals.

Though the ecological focus of these projects adds another layer to the planning process, the case studies demonstrate that municipal involvement and support are critical, as is a dedicated development team and a willingness to test new approaches and technologies, to fail and then try again. In doing so, the projects take their place in the web of nature–and keep striving.

Dockside Green
Victoria, British Colombia
by Ken Pirie, AICP, LEED AP ND

Dockside Green in Victoria, British Columbia, is a brownfield redevelopment that received the world's first LEED for Neighborhood Development Platinum certification.

JUST THE FACTS

- Located in downtown Victoria, British Columbia
- 15-acre redevelopment area
- Three neighborhoods (Dockside Wharf, Dockside Commons, Dockside Village), intended to be built over 12 phases
- Dockside Village will feature the most urban density, directly across a bridge from downtown
- Total of 1.3 million gross square feet (73% of which is residential) in 26 buildings
- Two mixed-use (office and retail) buildings to date, attracting green businesses
- Projected total of 2,500 residents
- Biomass energy plant has the ability to achieve a reduction in greenhouse gas emissions of up to 3,460 metric tons per year
- Residential units built 50% more efficient than code
- Synergy was the highest-scoring LEED
- project in the world at the time of certification (63 points)
- Project is aiming to provide at least 10% in affordable housing units
- Projected to save up to 70,000 gallons of public water annually, a reduction of 65% over similar conventional projects
- Dockside Green received the first LEED for Neighborhood Development (ND) Platinum stage two designation
- Membrane bioreactor package wastewater treatment plant: treated water looped back into buildings to flush toilets and irrigate landscaping
- Developer: Vancity
- Master Planners: Busby Perkins+Will
- Awards include 2006 Smart Growth of British Columbia Award for Process/Proposal, 2005 Canadian Urban Institute Best Overall Project and 2007 BC Hydro Power Smart Excellence Award for Innovation in Sustainable Building

Dockside Green, located near downtown Victoria, British Columbia, presents a breathtaking model of urban regeneration through brownfield reuse, green design and community building. Designers, planners and builders are noting the unprecedented innovation that Dockside Green represents and realizing its applicability to urban revitalization in their own communities. The development shows that LEED Platinum-level green building at a neighborhood scale can be contemporary and profitable, and attractive to those seeking an urban, energy-efficient lifestyle.

Site Development Process and Setting

Victoria, the capital of British Columbia, sits at the southern end of Vancouver Island overlooking the Straits of Juan de Fuca and Washington State's Olympic National Park to the south. The city, carved out of ancient cedar forest in only the past 150 years, has an agreeable maritime climate, benefiting from a rain shadow produced by the coastal mountains, which results in half the rainfall of Vancouver. With minimal temperature extremes and associated mechanical heating and cooling, such a climate is clearly an advantage for green building.

The city is prosperous, thanks to economic benefits generated by the provincial government, the presence of Canada's Pacific fleet, and University of Victoria-related employment. It has a reputation, perhaps undeservedly, for being staid and conservative, due to its strong British roots and large population of retirees.

But with an increasing reputation as a quieter, more livable and drier version of Vancouver, the city is attracting a wider range of younger professionals and families. While the greater metropolitan area of 330,000 sprawls over a series of inlets and rocky hills, the Capital Regional District has protected large expanses of wooded open space and beaches and established an impressive trail network.

With its location adjacent to the primary shipping lane to Seattle and Vancouver, it's initially surprising that Victoria does not have a larger shipping industry. But because Victoria is on an island, its lack of direct railroad links to the continent has prevented the construction of large container or bulk terminals. Other maritime activities are plentiful, however. The sinuous Victoria Harbour, which winds its way deep into the capital, once provided a sheltered haven for the First Nations Songhees tribe until the federal government acquired the land.

The protected Upper Harbour was once the home of Canada's Pacific whaling and sealing fleet and associated shipbuilding activities. Intensive log exports from the island's once majestic old-growth forests were processed in over 50 mills along the shores of Upper Harbour (also known as the Gorge Waterway). Later, warships were dismantled at a large facility and an oil refinery, shingle and asphalt plant were constructed.

All of this intensive industry left a severely contaminated shoreline and a collection of old vacant warehouses. The island's economic reliance on dwindling natural resources and Vancouver's emergence as the dominant regional node led local authorities to pin their hopes on tourism, marketing a genteel visitor experience centered on the adjacent Inner Harbour's Parliament Buildings, Royal British Columbia Museum, Empress Hotel and Beacon Hill Park. Disused docks were converted to marinas and waterfront walkways. Former industrial areas nearby were slated for mixed-use redevelopment.

An underutilized, 15-acre area with four parcels on the west bank of the Upper Harbour, part of which was once a landfill, was an unofficial dumping ground for construction waste, oil barrels and paint. The City of Victoria purchased the parcels, which it named "Dockside Lands," from the province in 1989 for $1. The sloping parcels sat one block off the water's edge, separated from the Harbour by the relics of Point Hope Shipyard.

The city commissioned a more detailed environmental assessment as part of the preparation of a business case for the property. It concluded in 2002 that development was possible, with some public financial support, favorable land pricing and rezoning to allow greater density (the existing zoning was light industrial with a floor-to-area ratio of 1:1 and the project is currently at a 2:1 ratio). Utilities already existed on the site, with capacity for new development. A new six-story office project called Upper Harbour Place was constructed adjacent to the site in 2002, proving the marketability of the land.

The city then prepared a detailed Development Concept, which it completed in May 2004 following extensive public visioning and workshops. The resulting document outlined vision and planning principles for a "new urbanism type of community," with a mix of uses, "people-friendly streets," and "high-quality public spaces . . . blended in overall harmony with the unique character of the location."

Even at that point in the process, however, international standards of sustainability and green building had yet to be fully fleshed out. The Development Concept only required new buildings to be built to LEED Silver certification. Perhaps more importantly, the concept directed future development teams to be selected according to strict "triple bottom line" standards, requiring that teams consider social, economic and environmental factors in all their actions. The Concept also encouraged developers to offer lower bids for the land

The Dockside Green site plan demonstrates the site's size constraints but also, with its access to the harbor, its opportunities.

in exchange for promises of innovation in sustainability.

Request for Proposals: Relying on a "Big Vision"

The city subsequently issued a request for proposals in September 2004 to remediate and develop 11.6 acres of the site. The RFP, sent to pre-qualified developers, required a detailed plan in response, including considerations of urban design, massing, circulation and "public realm" (parks and streets). The 40-day competition, which included a public presentation, was won by Dockside Green LP–a partnership between Vancouver City Savings (the majority shareholder with 75% stake) and Windmill Developments, which was partly owned by Joe Van Belleghem, who brought experience with other recent green development projects, including Canada's first LEED Gold building. Van Belleghem was the driver behind the project's green innovation. Most of the capital (75%) was provided by Canada's largest credit union, Vancity, which became a co-developer of the project in a partnership called Dockside Green Limited. Vancity has since bought Windmill's 25% and Van Belleghem has moved onto other projects.

According to project architect Jim Huffman from Busby Perkins+Will (selected to design Dockside Green based on its experience on preceding LEED Platinum-rated projects in Calgary and Ottawa), it was Van Belleghem's resolve on a "big vision" that inspired the project. If it had been merely greenwashing, many of the innovative features may not have survived early cost-cutting measures.

Master planning proceeded over the next year. Busby Perkins+Will (BPW) prepared the master plan for the development team, with Terence Williams Architect, Inc. (which subsequently merged with BPW). A wide range of consultant engineers and specialists in green design, including PWL Landscape Architects, were also part of the team. According to Jim Huffman of BPW, the project employed an integrated design approach that convened all consultants as well as development and finance staff for intensive meetings from the project's outset.

Under the September 2005 Master Development Agreement with the City of Victoria, Dockside Green Limited purchased the property for $8.5 million and agreed to develop it

Dockside Green utilizes a mix of natural materials, including wood siding, with glass and steel to fit into Victoria's urban, waterfront setting.

according to an approved site master plan and design guidelines with an extensive list of amenities, including public spaces and public art, interpretive signage describing the site's history and natural features, shoreline enhancement and trail improvements. Dockside Green Limited also agreed to contribute money towards a dedicated City of Victoria staff member to shepherd development review, and contributed $400,000 toward a new Sustainability Centre at Dockside. A key contribution to the project's success was the city's willingness to allow the developers to defer payment for the land, which freed up additional cash for quick construction of the project's infrastructure. Financing was relatively straightforward, however, since the majority stakeholder, Vancity, is a financial institution.

The city agreed to initiate zoning changes and amend the Community Plan and land-use designations. The city also created an interdisciplinary project team, bringing together city planners, engineers and finance specialists and including representatives of the local Victoria West Community Association and local First Nations indigenous peoples.

The Project, the Buildings, and the Neighborhoods

Dockside Green is intended to be built over ten phases in three neighborhoods, with a total of 1.3 million gross square feet (73% of which is residential) in 26 buildings, housing 2,500 residents. Dockside Wharf is the initial neighborhood, with two primarily residential projects and two commercial buildings. The first phase of the Wharf, a LEED Platinum condominium project named Synergy, sold 85% of its 96 units in three hours, with the first residents moving in May 2008.

These early buildings at Dockside Wharf express a warm, resolutely modernist language, comparable to new developments in Germany, Holland, or Scandinavia (such as Hammarby Sjöstad, in Stockholm). Jim Huffman of BPW said that the project was partially inspired by BedZed, a 99-unit residential development near London, which attempted to use only

Synergy, a LEED Platinum-certified building of 96 condominiums, sold 85% of its units in three hours.

energy generated onsite (although a planned biomass heat generator didn't work out) and features a striking contemporary design with bold color accents and sculptural roof vents. Huffman recalled that the developers were not as interested in a design that looked "odd," as they were in proving that green design could compete with conventional projects and perhaps eventually become standard practice.

Synergy's street façades feature columns of dark brick punctuated with recessed windows and balconies shaded with bold blue awnings. The eastern façades of Synergy feature much more glazing, with views eastward to downtown maximized by to a two-story grade difference. A vertical band of uniform planter boxes extends the streetscape and stormwater plantings to the façades. Upper floors on the towers step back to provide wrap-around windows and decks for penthouses. Two towers of eight and five stories above 94 spaces of underground parking are separated by a wood-clad townhouse block with three-story units raised off the street with front gardens. Rooftop patios seem quite exposed to views from surrounding towers, but the decks are screened with wood

slats. Entries to the towers are recessed (almost as arcades) behind columns on broad corner plazas and faced with recycled wood paneling. Lumber for construction of this phase included old growth reclaimed from forests flooded for BC's Lois Lake Reservoir in the 1940s.

Directly east of the first residential tower, a small commercial building, Inspiration, features a mix of commercial uses, including Fol Epi, an organic bakery, Caffè Fantastico, an organic fair trade coffee shop and two floors of office space, (ironically) leased to the BC Oil and Gas Commission, the regulator of petrochemical extraction activities in the province. Three small, roof-mounted propeller wind turbines partially power the elevator and common area. There are also solar panels above each window on the south side.

Inspiration achieved the world's highest rating ever–53 of 61 points–for LEED for Core and Shell and has a distinctive design, with a wood-panelled southern façade and bands of operable windows shaded against summer sun. The western side of the building features more robust aluminum sheeting, perhaps paying homage to the industrial materials of the

Most paved surfaces at Dockside Green are permeable surfaces to filter stormwater.

nearby shipyard sheds. The bakery's circular brick oven has been constructed to protrude outside the building, providing an interesting detail to terminate views on the central greenway and allow for simpler venting and reuse of oven exhaust.

The next phase, named Balance, features 171 condos in two nine- and ten-story towers built above 165 underground parking spaces. The Balance tower blocks are squatter versions of the well-glazed towers bristling with balconies that crowd Vancouver's waterfront.

Dockside Green's membane bioreactor package wastewater treatment plant treats all onsite sewage, bathwater and dishwater.

Photo: Ken Pirie

In keeping with Vancouver's precedent, the towers sit atop a two-story podium of townhouses that activate the street with individual entries and semi-private terraces. Between the two towers, a pocket park features a green wall and artistic stormwater planters.

Prosperity, the second commercial building, is a three-story office and retail structure along Harbour Road and the Galloping Goose Regional Trail. Surrounded by porous surface parking, the building with a distinctive sawtooth roofline echoing early industrial buildings faces Point Hope Shipyard with a retail streetscape, the first of a long row of several mixed-use structures that will line the eastern edge of the project. North across Harbour Road from the commercial buildings, a new shoreline park has been created at Point Ellice, including a kayak launching point.

Subsequent neighborhoods will extend Dockside Green's development south toward downtown Victoria. The final neighborhood, the Village, will feature more retail and office development and a boutique hotel, all at a higher density reflecting its proximity to downtown. The promised sustainability center will face a large circular plaza and open-air amphitheater.

Green Infrastructure and Accolades

With an upfront commitment to a high level of green design and greenhouse gas neutrality, Dockside Green needed to experiment with somewhat unproven methods and technologies. The developers also committed to paying a $1 million penalty if the development did not reach LEED Platinum designation. The Federation of Canadian Municipalities made $350,000 available to support the development of infrastructure at the outset of the project. These funds offset the costs for LEED documentation (often a major hurdle to certification) and helped with the costs associated with developing and obtaining approval for an unprecedented wastewater treatment system. As BPW's Jim Huffman noted, during the design of Dockside's first phase new technologies were released "almost monthly," forcing the design team to constantly review and update its plans. When the project proceeds, there should be further energy savings and innovation by the time the final building is constructed.

The team's ambition for innovation clearly succeeded, because in 2008 Synergy was awarded Platinum with 63 points, making it the highest-scoring LEED-certified project in the world. In March 2011, Balance also received LEED Platinum certification with 63 LEED points. It includes standard elements for green building, such as fresh air ventilation, energy-efficient operable windows, low-energy appliances and lighting, greener (and healthier) building materials sourced as close to the site as possible as well as consideration of daylighting and solar orientation. A "living wall" was installed as 30-foot panels on either side of a plaza at Balance but it has since been removed–the location was bad for the plants due to wind and remediation including irrigation systems would have been costly for residents who voted to have it removed and a cable and vine system installed instead.

Dockside Green also received the first LEED for Neighborhood Development (ND) Platinum stage two designation, due to its brownfield location, reduced dependence on private vehicles due to car-sharing and access to trails and transit (including a harbor ferry), proximity to employment, walkable streets and onsite renewable energy sources.

The project takes an innovative approach to water treatment and recycling. Victoria has long dumped its raw sewage after preliminary screening directly into the Straits of Juan de Fuca, arguing that currents dilute it easily. Years of public pressure and environmental study have led to detailed planning for a new municipal treatment system. Dockside Green, however, has its own wastewater treatment system. Wedged between Inspiration and Synergy sits the Dockside Green's membrane bioreactor package wastewater treatment plant. Wastewater from sewage, bathwater and dishwater is treated onsite. Dockside Green residents will therefore be exempt from the hundreds of dollars of fees that will be assessed to pay for the new citywide system, currently estimated to cost over almost $800 million Canadian. Treated water is looped back into buildings to flush toilets and also irrigate site landscaping (although this is minimal, thanks to the use of climate-adaptive plantings). Heat recovery from the wastewater treatment plant was part of the original concept but was ultimately not financially feasible and, in fact, was unnecessary because the energy plant produces more than sufficient energy.

With the project's water-efficient appliances, the project will save up to 70,000 gallons of public water annually, a reduction of 65% over comparable conventional projects.

A series of terraced ponds, lush with wetland plants and interspersed with granite boulders, are interconnected throughout Dockside's central greenway. These ponds are a visual amenity and a significant public open space for residents and they also assist with onsite stormwater storage and act as a strip of wildlife habitat, even including introduced crayfish and stickleback fish. (If green roofs are included, 50% of Synergy's site is dedicated to open space.) The water levels in the pond are supplemented by treated wastewater from the nearby plant. Most paved surfaces at Dockside

A series of terraced ponds, lush with wetland plants and interspersed with granite boulders, are interconnected throughout the project's central greenway.

Photo: Lotus Johnson

Green are permeable surfaces to filter stormwater and most flat roof surfaces are vegetated, to slow rain runoff and help insulate buildings. The stormwater system incorporates artistic features such as rusted metal grates and concrete runnels along staircases exposing the flow of water for passersby. Townhouse units open directly onto the ponds with decks and docks, and a path winds its way across wood bridges, connecting with side stairs to adjacent streets and buildings.

Dockside Green also features an integrated energy system, which may provide an opportunity for the project to become a net-energy provider, together with units that are built 50% more efficient than code. The system includes a Nexterra biomass plant, operated by a new micro-utility, Dockside Green Energy. The plant converts locally sourced wood waste into a clean burning "syngas" to produce heat and hot water for the district (and beyond), eliminating the use of fossil fuel for heating buildings. The estimated overall impact of the plant is a reduction in greenhouse gas emissions of up to 3,460 metric tons per year.

Project Economics in the Global Economic Downturn

The project was not immune to trends in real estate, with a slowing in sales (about ten sales staff were laid off in 2011) coinciding with the global economic recession. Several large developments in the Victoria area were cancelled between 2009 and 2011, though Dockside has recently sold out all units, at a range of $500 to $900 per square foot (one-bedrooms to penthouses), roughly the same price point as local comparables. There is also clear evidence of the

Photo: Vancity

Prosperity is the first of a long row of several mixed-use structures that will line the eastern edge of Dockside Green.

savings available to residents from green building technology. The project features lower strata fees (a Canadian term roughly equivalent to homeowners' association fees) thanks to energy savings in common spaces. Residents will also save on regional wastewater assessments thanks to an onsite treatment system.

The project was initially envisioned to contain at least 10% affordable rental units for people with incomes as low as $15,000 and 26 units have been set aside at Synergy and Balance, priced under market value with some subsidy from the city. A three-story "attainable" housing building (a new, presumably less-stigmatized euphemism for "affordable"), with two levels of "micro-condos" (less than 400 square feet) over commercial/industrial space, designed by Number TEN Architectural Group, has recently been proposed.

Conclusion: An Inspiring Prototype

Dockside Green represents an inspiring prototype for green building on a neighborhood scale. The developers of the project, driven by a strong vision for urban regeneration that doesn't simply aim to maximize profit, are responding to larger social and civic concerns. Beyond simply striving for the highest LEED point totals, the Dockside Green team has built the first stages of a community that feels rooted in its context and expresses a strong contemporary aesthetic, while clearly competing well with less-innovative neighbors in a tough market.

If it's clear that a more sustainable future will require denser urban living, with alternatives to automobile use along with innovative and efficient ways to produce energy and reduce waste, then it's also clear that Dockside Green shows us all a bold precedent with lessons that we can apply to subsequent projects in our own communities. By the time of its ultimate buildout, we can hope that Dockside Green will have been joined by numerous similar projects across the continent.

DEFINING SUCCESS
Q&A with Kelly O'Brien, Marketing and Operations Manager, Dockside Green

What was the largest obstacle to obtaining project approval or buy-in and how was it overcome?
Building trust in the new technologies we were introducing into a residential environment: biomass plant, wastewater treatment plant located within close proximity to the residential suites and retail spaces, consumption meters in each suite. There have been some obstacles along the way, but as with any leader in an industry would do, we've been transparent with any major issues in an effort to educate the industry and residents.

What is an unexpected delight or success from the project?
The building of the community between the residents. As the developer, we make every effort to keep a strong focus on community (free yoga for residents, pedestrian pathways, gathering places); however, the added benefit is that the residents are taking this on themselves and developing their own initiatives. To name a few: Condo Crawl (cocktail party that moves from condo to condo), the new and improved recycling/garbage room (by putting up fun comic-like graphics showing what bins accept what materials and hosting a wine/cheese gathering in the room to show off their handiwork, residents transformed the room from a stale garbage collection point into a fun and attractive educational center); and monthly social gathering at local pubs.

What hasn't lived up to expectations or has required unanticipated change?
Locating a reliable and consistent fuel source for the biomass plant has been a challenge.

What continues to challenge or surprise you with the project?
The amount of international media coverage received on the project. And how many people are interested in a guided tour of the project (school and industry groups).

How do you define and measure success?
Absorption rate, resident feedback, community feedback.

Prairie Crossing
Grayslake, Illinois
by Simmons B. Buntin

Prairie Crossing in Grayslake, Illinois, is a conservation development centered around regenerated native prairie and working organic farms.

Prairie Crossing is a master-planned conservation development located 40 miles northwest of Chicago in the rapidly suburbanizing rural community of Grayslake, Illinois. The Conservation Fund and National Town Builders Association define conservation developments as projects that, through the use of traditional neighborhood development techniques, create communities in which compact development patterns are joined with permanent conservation and stewardship of significant land and water resources.

Based on a set of ten guiding principles, the project combines preservation of the regenerated prairie landscape, energy-efficient homes of a Midwestern vernacular, restoration of connections to local food production and opportunities for community involvement and lifelong learning. The development features a mix of clustered single-family homes and a pedestrian-oriented, mixed-use village center adjacent to two Metra rail stations. While landscape features physically define Prairie Crossing–Lake Aldo Leopold and wetlands at its center, the 100-acre organic farm at its edge and the adjacent, 5,800-acre Liberty Prairie Reserve conservation area–Prairie Crossing is also unique because of the institutional structures in place, ranging from the Liberty Prairie Foundation to the Prairie Crossing Charter

JUST THE FACTS

- Located 40 miles northwest of downtown Chicago
- 668-acre site developed beginning in 1992 using "conservation development model" criteria
- More than 60% open space, including wetlands, lake, ponds, trails and organic farms
- Anchors western end of 5,800-acre Liberty Prairie Reserve
- 359 single-family homes; 36 condominiums
- 72,500 square feet of commercial space (retail/restaurant/office)
- 135,000-square-foot Northwestern Lake Forest Hospital campus situated on 44 acres
- Adjacent to two Metra Prairie Crossing/Libertyville train stations: Milwaukee District North Line and North Central Service
- 100 acres of certified organic farmland
- protected by conservation easement, including a working farm, a farm business incubator and a learning farm
- The nation's first community-scale demonstration project of the U.S. Department of Energy's Building America program
- Horse pastures and stable
- Three onsite schools: nursery, charter elementary and Montessori adolescent program
- Progressive onsite stormwater "treatment train system"
- Developer: Prairie Holdings Corporation
- Planners include William Johnson, FASLA; Peter Lindsay, Schaudt Landscape Architecture, Inc.; Skidmore, Owings & Merrill; and Calthorpe Associates
- Architects include Tigerman McCurry, Worn Jerabek Architects and Serena Sturm Architects

School to the Liberty Prairie Conservancy.

History and Guiding Principles

Built on the rich soils of Lake County, Prairie Crossing began as a commitment from conservation-minded investors who sought to preserve and restore native prairie and farmland being lost to suburbanization. Their ambition was to build a new kind of development, one far different from the 1,600-house subdivision once approved for the parcel—which until 1986 was farmed on a rotation of soybeans and corn. In 1987, following a 15-year legal battle over the land's development that went as far as the U.S. Supreme Court, the property was acquired by printing company CEO and conservationist Gaylord Donnelley, who owned a farm in the adjacent Liberty Prairie Reserve.

With seven other families, Donnelley formed Prairie Holdings Corporation, Prairie Crossing's developer.

George Ranney, Jr., Donnelley's nephew and executive of Inland Steel Industries, and his wife Victoria Post Ranney, became officers of the company. After Gaylord Donnelley's death in 1992, they took over as developers at the request of his family; George was chair and Victoria became president in 2000.

According to Victoria Ranney, the developers agreed from the beginning that a set of principles should "provide the framework for a way of life that respects the environment and enables residents to experience a strong connection between community and the land."

The principles include:
- Environmental protection and

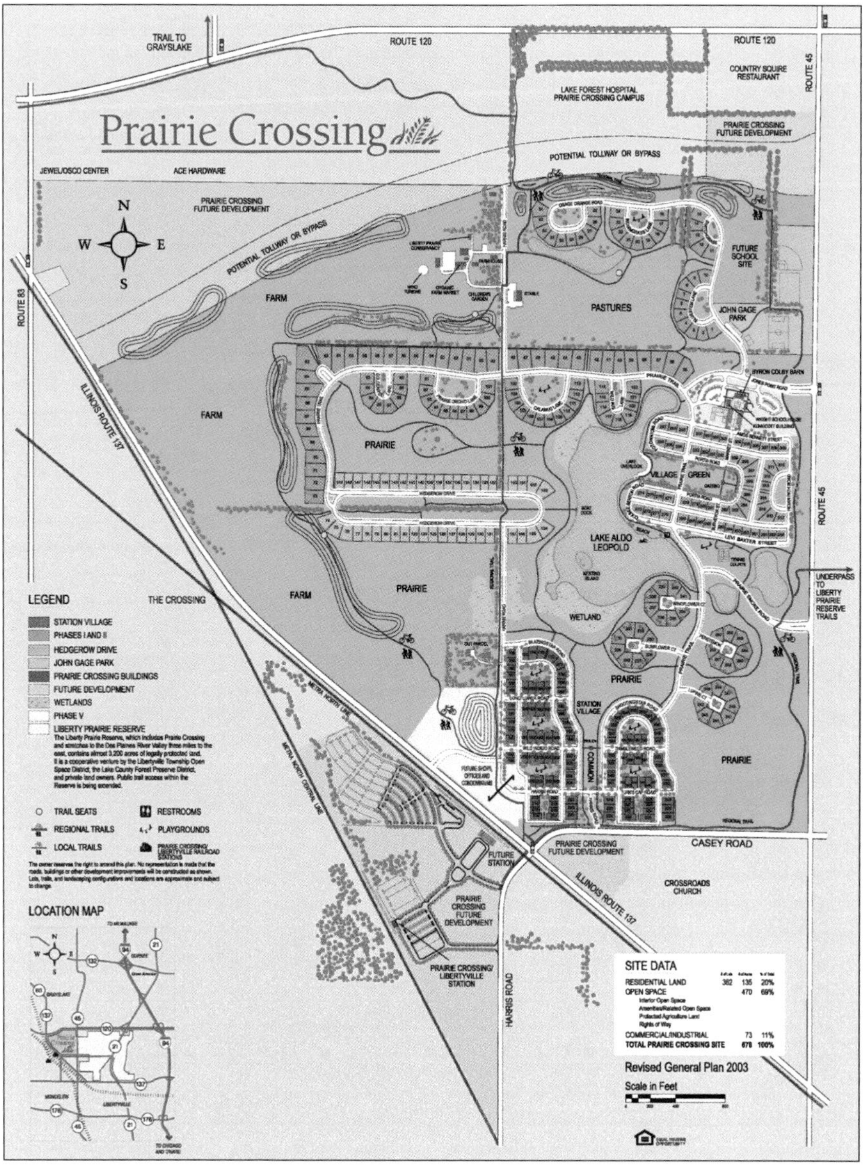

Prairie Crossing Site Plan

Graphic: Prairie Holdings Corporation

enhancement
- A healthy lifestyle
- A sense of place
- A sense of community
- Economic and racial diversity

- Convenient and efficient transportation
- Energy conservation
- Lifelong learning and education
- Aesthetic design and high-quality construction

- Economic viability

The last principle is just as important as the preceding nine, of course. "This is not a philanthropic project. It's a business venture," said George Ranney in 1995. Yet he also noted then–three years after groundbreaking–that Prairie Crossing aimed to "have social outcomes we hope will be noteworthy and affect public policy and business practice. We hope other builders will say, 'Someone else has done it, let's get into the market.'"

According to Bill Johnson, the landscape architect hired to plan Prairie Crossing, the developers' first vision was of a "farm village" –part of a several-thousand-acre preserve spanning the Des Plaines River to the Fox River.

"Giving form to that vision," writes Rene C. Kane in a 2003 article appearing in *Landscape Architecture*, "involved preserving the rural character of the land, creating a place that integrated an environmental ethic in its design and function. But it also had to succeed financially. If not, other developers would not embrace the underlying conservation principles."

Three architectural firms were brought in to create house plans that fit into the Midwestern vernacular and achieved superior energy efficiency. Along with Johnson, the developers hired Chicago landscape architect Peter Lindsay Schaudt from 1994 to 1999. Schaudt's task was to implement Johnson's overall design vision, providing specific design direction, particularly for prairie and wetlands integration.

The developers also formed the Liberty Prairie Foundation to work with other organizations and community members "to make Prairie Crossing a vibrant learning community," notes Linda Wiens, the foundation's project leader. In addition to managing events such as workshops and tours "relating to environmental education and stewardship, natural land preservation and restoration, conservation development and community design and sustainable agriculture," the foundation serves as a resource for organizational success, with expertise in conflict resolution, teambuilding, board development and governance and problem-solving–all essential elements of crafting sustainable community.

Place-Based, Energy-Efficient Homes

The initial dozen models of homes at Prairie Crossing represent the first community-scale demonstration project of the U.S. Department of Energy's Building America program. With whole-house comfort and efficiency as a baseline, these homes–averaging 2,700 square feet–used nearly half the energy of similarly sized homes of typical frame construction in the Chicago area.

According to the Building America program, "The systems engineering approaches used to develop the Prairie Crossing designs make maximum use of the interaction between the building envelope and its heating and cooling system." The homes demonstrated new framing, insulation, ducting and thermal barrier methods, including:

- Framing with 2" x 6" studs spaced 24" on center, providing more space in the wall cavity for extra insulation (R-26 walls, R-43 ceilings and R-19 foundation), as well as up to 30% less construction waste without a decrease in structural safety
- Extensive sealing and caulking of interior and exterior spaces to prevent air leakage
- Placement of ductwork on the building's interior to prevent leakage of heated and cooled air
- Double-glazed, argon-filled, low-e windows
- Ventilation fan controllable by occupants for fresh air exchange
- Direct-vent, sealed-combustion, 90% efficiency furnace and high-efficiency water heater
- Double air-barrier system that included

Photo: Simmons Buntin

Native prairie landscaping doesn't just serve as an ornamental buffer at Prairie Crossing; it is often the "lawn" itself.

gluing and clipping drywall to studs, providing a second airtight wall; and gluing rigid foam sheathing to the outside of the framing to seal the first wall, eliminating the need for polyethylene vapor barriers and housewrap
• Use of recycled wood products and nontoxic glues
• High-tech wiring

While many of these approaches have been adopted across the residential building market since these first homes went on the market in 1994, they were particularly innovative at the time. They were also cost-effective. A 1998 Rocky Mountain Institute study demonstrated that by limiting environmental impacts during construction, the developer saved about $4,400 per lot, for a total of $1.4 million.

The designs at Prairie Crossing are so efficient that Christine Ervin, then-deputy secretary for energy efficiency and renewable energy at the U.S. Department of Energy, told the developers, "I think you'll serve as a beacon to many communities across the country." And

initial Prairie Crossing builder Franklin A. Martin of Shaw Homes predicted early on that Building America's voluntary energy codes would eventually be standard procedure for many developers. Many of the same criteria are included in today's LEED system.

While energy efficiency is key, particularly in a cold-weather climate such as northern Illinois, what continues to attract homebuyers is the style of houses and the relatively pastoral setting, all with views of the lake and ponds, wetlands, restored prairies and hedgerows, pastures and the organic farm. The Midwestern vernacular of wide front porches, clapboard siding, gabled roofs and deep prairie colors "exude so much Americana they almost bring an Aaron Copland melody to mind," notes a 1999 article in *The New York Times.* Though there was early resistance from homebuilders to some of the design features, notably to the homes' bold colors (based on concerns that the colors would only appeal to a limited number of homebuyers), the developers hired an expert to create a palette that stems from the hues of the prairie. Since then, the colors of Prairie Crossing have been praised in such venues as

Prairie Crossing's Station Square features open space, condominiums, retail, and access to the region's Metra rail system.

The New York Times, Chicago Tribune, and *Landscape Architecture.*

Home sales went beyond architectural style, however. "We sold community from the start," said Eve Lee, who directed Prairie Crossing's first marketing efforts. Michael Sands, Prairie Crossing's environmental team leader and senior advisor to the Liberty Prairie Foundation, agrees. "People move to Prairie Crossing because of the farm and pastures, the authentic homes among an authentic, working landscape," he says. In today's struggling economy, that may be truer than ever. "If there is any market for new development in the near future," he writes in 2010's "Building Communities with Farms" report, "evidence indicates communities that distinguish themselves with integrated farms are gaining momentum in the

marketplace."

The initial homes marketed in 1994 were priced well above the $120,000 average home price of the area, ranging from just under $180,000 to $250,000. By 2000, homes ranging from 2,500 to 3,500 square feet were priced from $365,000 to $427,000–and before the economic downturn in 2007, sold as high as $650,000.

Even before the downturn, however, there were off-site factors that slowed sales at Prairie Crossing, including a proposed tollway–still a possibility–and a proposed power plant–no longer planned. Also adjacent to the site, just across Illinois Route 137, is a 200-acre landfill now operated by Waste Management, Inc. When Waste Management purchased the landfill in 2002, the company worked with

Prairie Crossing to meet the prior legal restrictions established between George Ranney and the previous owner. Ranney insisted that the landfill implement the best available technology to ensure that it would be a good and beneficial neighbor. "Geologically speaking," says Sands, "the landfill is where it should be, given the tight virgin clays." The landfill rises to the west of Prairie Crossing and can be seen from locations throughout the community.

To insulate developers and residents against potential negative impacts, Waste Management committed to responding quickly to concerns raised by homeowners. The company also accepted an existing home value contract with Prairie Crossing and homebuyers, guaranteeing that if a home couldn't be sold within 180 days, Waste Management would buy it from the original homebuyer for what that homebuyer paid. "Then the economy dropped out," says Sands. In a matter of a few months, 40 houses went on the market—more than 10% of Prairie Crossing's stock—and when most did not sell in that 180-day window, Waste Management purchased them. "That was an ugly time here," says Sands, as home values plummeted. Though the market has since picked up, Waste Management still owns dozens of homes in Prairie Crossing and is releasing them to the market slowly, or renting them.

Station Village, Station Square and Transit

When the housing market crashed around 2008, almost half of the 36 Energy Star-rated condominiums built as part of the mixed-use Station Square, located across from the train stations, had been sold. The rest were not sold until fall 2011. Initial prices ranged from $329,000 to $499,900 (1,600 to 2,700 square feet) when the condos were first offered in 2005 and 2006. Fifteen floor plans—named after birds in recognition of the high diversity of birdlife at Prairie Crossing—are located in three three-story buildings that flank the square.

Station Square serves as the community's public gateway—not only to the Metra stops, but also to Illinois Route 137 and nearby Casey Road. It houses the community's only retail and office space and Prairie Crossing's farmer's market. At buildout, Station Square will consist of the condos plus a total of 50,000 square feet of retail and restaurant space and 20,000 square feet of office space. Located at the intersection of Illinois Route 137 and Harris Road, Station Square's public plaza and fountain, and three-story condominium buildings (two with retail on the first floor) form a small village center. At one time a bookstore, café, children's clothing store, fair trade handicraft shop and knitting shop—all local businesses—occupied Station Square. After the economic downturn, however, only a yoga studio, nursery school and offices remained, though a café is in the works and office leasing appears to be on the upswing. More parking and up to three additional commercial buildings are still planned, as well.

Located adjacent to Station Square—and serving as a pedestrian-oriented link between the village center and the less dense clustered homes of Prairie Crossing—is Station Village, designed by Calthorpe Associates as a transit-oriented New Urbanist development of 103 homes on small lots with amenities that include a central commons, mid-block gardens and garages on alleys. Station Square was initiated after George Ranney persuaded Metra commuter rail system leaders to construct stations on both existing lines that cross adjacent to the community. To take advantage of transit stops, the developers eliminated some of the planned clustered enclaves in favor of the higher-density neighborhood near the train stations.

The proximity of Station Village to the train stations earned Prairie Crossing a 10% density bonus from the Village of Grayslake, which allowed for the construction of 36 additional condominiums, completed after 359 single-family homes were sold. Subsequently, the

Photo: Simmons Buntin

Single-family homes adjacent to Station Square display the community's strong Midwestern vernacular.

Station Village, including the Station Square, was certified as one of Illinois's first LEED-ND (Neighborhood Development) pilot programs.

When Prairie Crossing was initially planned, there was no commuter rail service. Both village representatives and Prairie Crossing residents expressed concern when the denser Station Village and Station Square were proposed. However, the concerns of the village were alleviated by opportunities for increased transit ridership, "There's certainly an appeal to the kind of development they're proposing," Grayslake's then-mayor Pat Carey said when the higher densities were proposed. "If a good deal of people walk across the street to take the train, that balances against the increase in density, in my mind." Today, Grayslake planners encourage developers to use Prairie Crossing's density and transit orientation as a model for other developments in the area.

The Prairie Crossing/Libertyville station serves the North Central Line, running between Antioch, Illinois, and Chicago. Growth along the line, which was completed in 1996, has been "phenomenal," say Metra officials. The second station, completed in

1999, serves the Milwaukee District North Line. Prairie Crossing's developers hoped for a "Main Street" between the two stations and purchased the land between the stations. Currently there are no plans to develop the land, though the excellent access by train from four directions makes buildout more likely in a development climate that values mass transit.

Sands estimates that about 20% of Prairie Crossing residents use the train on a regular basis and about 30-40% of the community's regular commuters take the train, which provides direct access to downtown Chicago (an hour away) and O'Hare International Airport (35 minutes away). Nearly 300 trains per week stop at the stations, "offering virtually unprecedented rail access for a suburban community," according to Prairie Crossing marketing materials.

At the other end of the development, the Northwestern Lake Forest Hospital's Grayslake comprehensive health and wellness campus was built on 44 acres. The facility was designed to be "physically inviting with a sense of healing and promoting a healthy lifestyle," according to Northwestern Lake Forest

Colby Barn, shown here adjacent to Prairie Crossing Charter School, serves as the community's center, both socially and historically.

Hospital board chairman Harold S. Jensen. Victoria Ranney agrees: "We're delighted with the interest of Lake Forest Hospital in serving this area," she said in 2000, "as well as the hospital's desire to develop plans that are compatible with the guiding principles of Prairie Crossing." The campus–which has an architectural style that differs considerably from the rest of Prairie Crossing–includes an urgent care center, medical offices, laboratories and other specialty offices and also offers a broad array of community education programs at its conference center.

Schools and Community Amenities

The Prairie Crossing Charter School–one of three onsite schools–has a goal of "lifelong learning," like the community itself. The K-8 campus serves 400 students and is integrated into the heart of the Prairie Crossing community, adjacent to the Byron Colby Barn. It features five buildings, the last of which was completed in 2006. The Wright Schoolhouse is an early 1900s one-room schoolhouse that was moved from its original location in Libertyville

to Prairie Crossing in 1996. Other facilities include an administrative center, classrooms, a gym, and a large common area bounded on one side by the Colby Barn. The Comstock Building was the first LEED-certified school building in Illinois, achieving LEED Gold status. Many of the school's building materials–including wallboard, classroom flooring, wood doors and bathroom tile–are made from recycled materials. Cisterns collect rainwater and snowmelt while a geothermal system, which uses a ground-source heat pump to move fluid through a series of ground wells 150 feet deep, provides heating and cooling for the classroom buildings. Inside the buildings, natural ventilation and daylighting help reduce electricity use and increase fresh air flow. Outside, native vegetation serves to reduce water use and plays an important role in the place-based education of the children.

"The cornerstone of the Prairie Crossing Charter School is excellence in education, grounded in experience of the local environment," says the school's website. The public charter school, which serves two adjoining school districts, admits students by lottery,

A wide courtyard connects Colby Barn to the charter school and provides a vista onto the community.

Photo: Simmons Buntin

according to Illinois law. With an emphasis on "good citizenship and conservation," students participate in hands-on learning, comprehensive multigrade-level themes, reading and creative writing, multicultural arts, math that is oriented toward problem-solving, and more.

In September 2011, Prairie Crossing Charter School received approval from the Village of Grayslake to construct a 2.4 kW wind turbine near the school's parking lot to provide power to the school's campus. Construction and operation will also serve as a learning opportunity for students; in fact, the turbine was proposed and researched as a project of two students. Groundbreaking for the turbine took place in October 2011.

Just inside the eastern entrance to Prairie Crossing and adjacent to the charter school campus, the Byron Colby Barn serves as a community centerpiece, providing Prairie Crossing's central gathering place. "The past suggests what is possible for the future," said early marketing materials. "In its proportions, its history and the common activities it will make possible, the barn is truly part of Prairie Crossing's design."

In 1992, the 100-year-old dairy barn located on Liberty Prairie Reserve's periphery had been scheduled for demolition to make room for a new housing development. Instead, Prairie Holdings Corporation asked the owner to donate the barn to the community. It was disassembled timber by timber, moved to Prairie Crossing and reassembled in a community barn raising in 1996. With a fitness facility on its lower level, a large and open room on its main level, and a loft and a caterer's kitchen, the barn hosts several hundred community events each year, ranging from homeowner meetings to an early music concert series (now in its tenth year), lectures and weddings. It also serves as the community's polling place and hosts regional activities such as the Prairie Pedal, an annual family bike event run by the Liberty Prairie Conservancy.

Other community amenities at Prairie Crossing include John Gage Park (a series of sports fields), the nine-acre Village Green with a gazebo used for weddings and concerts, neighborhood playgrounds, tennis courts, ice

The 100-acre Prairie Crossing Farm features a privately owned commercial family farm, a business development center, and a learning farm.

skating on Lake Aldo Leopold and miles of trails. A fishing and boating dock and popular beach are located on the shores of the lake, as well.

Prairie Crossing Farm : The Community's Organic Base

Prairie Crossing's largest amenity is the 100-acre Prairie Crossing Farm, a part of a 150-acre easement that permanently protects the original farmland. The farm incorporates three separate organic farming operations: Sandhill Organics, a privately owned commercial family farm leasing 40 acres; Prairie Crossing Farm Business Development Center, an entrepreneurial incubator program for new organic farmers; and the Prairie Crossing Learning Farm. Prairie Holdings Corporation saw the value of the farm to draw homebuyers nearly from the get-go. "At Prairie Crossing, we realized the potential of the farm early," says Sands. "Feature articles about the new local food farm helped to drive sales more effectively than ads in the real estate section of the *Chicago*

Tribune." In fact, Victoria Ranney says that Prairie Crossing was one of the first planned developments in the U.S. to incorporate food production.

Because the site of Prairie Crossing was farmed intensively (including the use of artificial fertilizers and pesticides) for some 50 years prior to development of the community, organic certification was introduced on the farm in 1992 as a method more compatible with residential living and healthy food production. In the common natural areas, the old farm drain tiles used to divert excess rainwater were removed, restoring natural wetlands. The land was planted with native prairie and wetland seeds, a part of the property's comprehensive onsite stormwater management system, where water flows from vegetated roadside swales laterally across the land to Lake Aldo Leopold, which was dug in the low-lying areas at the center of the site.

The Learning Farm and Farm Business Development Center operations fall under the oversight of the Liberty Prairie Foundation, which has owned and leased the farmland since 2006, when Prairie Holdings Corporation transferred ownership. While the budget for early farm operations was provided as a marketing expense for Prairie Crossing's residential development, the Foundation itself is supported by a transfer fee of 0.5% of the sale price of each new and resale home, as well as through funds generated by independent grants and other sources. Additionally, the Prairie Crossing Homeowners' Association contributes $10,000 per year "in recognition of the services the farm provides the community," says Ranney.

Sandhill Organics began operations in Prairie Crossing in 2004 and is owned and operated by Matt and Peg Sheaffer. The couple has a long-term lease on just over 40 acres of land and currently farms about 20 acres. According to the Liberty Prairie Foundation's report, "Building Communities with Farms", Sandhill Organics' lease and contract with Liberty Prairie Foundation "gives them independence from the Homeowners' Association, allowing them to operate with the flexibility required to achieve profitability." Yet the farm's proximity to homes "resulted in a re-creation of the traditional farming community. The Sheaffers created a new dynamic interaction between the typically separate residential and agricultural lands. Today they embrace this new level of interaction and continue to play an active role in the community, a stipulation that is required in a general way by their contract and welcomed by them."

Sandhill Organics, which grows more than 50 different crops and is certified organic by Midwest Organic Services Association, supports itself by selling at northern Chicago farmers markets as well as through a community supported agriculture (CSA) program that serves more than 300 families at Prairie Crossing and in Chicago's northern suburbs. From May through November, CSA members receive weekly deliveries of vegetables and/or eggs at the farm or host sites. In Sandhill Organics' CSA model, participants purchase weekly shares by the season. In 2011, all three growing seasons cost $830 for vegetables and $125 for eggs. Sandhill Organics' produce makes up about 90% of the weekly share. "We collaborate with several other local organic farmers in order to help protect our members from crop failure and to create a box that is as varied as possible from week to week," says Matt Sheaffer.

Power for Sandhill Organics is provided by a 120-foot-high wind turbine located on the farm. Erected in 2002 at a cost of $45,000, the 20 kW turbine powers irrigation pumps, compressors for a produce cooler, lighting and computers and is based on a net-metering model: any power generated from the turbine not used by the farm is sold back to the utility, ComEd. Typical of Prairie Crossing's community involvement, neighbors participated in erecting the turbine.

The Prairie Crossing Farm Business Development Center "supports the development of successful family farm enterprises that produce and market organic foods locally and regionally," says Victoria Ranney. Liberty Prairie Foundation leases up to five acres of land for up to five years, plus farm infrastructure, to beginning farmers. The farmers rent equipment and participate in organic farming and business development educational programs and are also provided a real-time community of other organic farmers. The Center works on a market-based fee structure, though Sands notes that the farmers only pay for what they use, enabling them to manage cash flow much better than traditional farmers who must invest considerably in farmland, equipment and supplies. Every winter, Liberty Prairie Foundation conducts a review of each participant's financials, which "truly helps them understand the business of business," says Sands.

Currently, several farmers participate in

The conservation development is crossed with miles of walking paths.

the incubator program, including Wild Goose Farm, Radical Root Farm, Topland Farm and Midnight Sun Organic Farm. In 2012, the Foundation made investments in irrigation and the site's wash-pack shed, allowing the Center to expand the incubator program.

Prairie Crossing Learning Farm was, according to Ranney, "founded with the purpose of educating and inspiring people to value healthy food, land and community through hands-on experiences on a working organic farm." It is located on a three-acre plot and includes a children's garden, mobile henhouse for egg-laying chickens, fruit orchard, greenhouse and hoop house. The Learning Farm operates as a project of the Liberty Prairie Foundation and offers farm-based education, farm camps, tours, the Great Garden Gang for K-5 students growing crops "from seed to table," and the Prairie Farm Corps, a paid summer internship for young adults interested in learning to farm and market their produce. Additionally, Prairie Crossing's community garden, which is located adjacent to the stables,

is maintained by the Learning Farm, which leases garden plots to people from both inside and outside of the community.

The Learning Farm also works closely with the schools at Prairie Crossing to integrate farming and an enhanced knowledge of food into the schools' curriculum, using the farm's facilities as outdoor classrooms.

Produce from all three farming enterprises is sold at the Prairie Crossing Farm Market, which was originally located at Prairie Crossing Farm but is now based in Station Square in order to draw from a wider area. It is open on Friday evenings from mid-June through mid-October. Sands notes that the foundation would also like to develop a portion of the farm along Illinois Highway 137 that would further connect the farm to the wider community, perhaps through a new farm-to-table restaurant.

Prairie Crossing also hosts a stable–operated by the Prairie Crossing Stable Cooperative–with 13 stalls, a tack room, outdoor arena, paddocks and pastures that are framed by the farm, wetlands and houses.

Environmental Preservation Begins with the Treatment Train System

Much of Prairie Crossing's notability comes from its conservation community design. The land was purchased primarily to safeguard its open spaces, which now range from prairie to wetlands, pastures to farmland. The 150-acre permanent conservation easement was facilitated through the nonprofit Conservation Fund. An additional 13 acres of wetlands, the 22-acre Lake Aldo Leopold and 160 acres of created prairies, along with the farmland and pastures, ensure that over 60% of Prairie Crossing is permanently preserved as open space. Greenways have been constructed and homes placed to protect native vegetation and wildlife corridors and the land has been contoured to properly manage stormwater with minimum use of concrete culverts and other manmade stormwater discharge systems.

Prairie Crossing's stormwater collection system acts as a "treatment train system," with several open space components–swales and wetlands, prairies and pastures–that work in sequence to treat stormwater before it enters Lake Aldo Leopold and leaves the site. The train system is a four-step process, according to an analysis detailed in "Using Ecological Restoration to Meet Clean Water Act Goals", written by Steve I. Apfelbaum, John D. Eppich, Thomas H. Price and Michael Sands:

1. Stormwater runoff from residential areas outside the village center is routed into swales planted with native prairie and wetland vegetation. These swales . . . convey runoff from roadways and residential lots into expansive prairies while providing a modest amount of infiltration and settling of solids.
2. The prairies slowly convey stormwater as diffuse overland flow to the wetland systems bordering the lake. The prairies are expected to infiltrate a substantial portion

of the annual surface runoff volume due to their very deep root systems and provide for additional solids settling as well as biological treatment.
3. The wetlands provide both stormwater detention and biological treatment prior to the runoff entering the lake.
4. The lake will provide stormwater detention as well as further solids settling and biological treatment.

The analysis, based on hydrologic modeling and 15 years of onsite sampling, shows that stormwater runoff volumes are reduced considerably over typical subdivision stormwater management practices.

Other design features further ensure good water quality, including shallow lake shorelines that reduce destabilization and in-lake sediment loading, use of organic and osmocote slow-release fertilizers only at peak grass absorption times, community composting to reduce dumping of landscape wastes and extensive native wildflower plantings and other low-maintenance landscaping for residential yards. The impact: more than 120 species of birds have been sighted at Prairie Crossing, as compared to the standard 15 species "typically found on conventional chemically farmed lands in the area," according to the Urban Land Institute.

The Illinois Department of Natural Resources uses Lake Aldo Leopold as a research site, having stocked the lake in 1998 with native banded killifish, the Iowa darter and blacknose and blackchin shiners, which are locally threatened or endangered. The lake now qualifies as a designated fish recovery site and, with adjacent ponds, is the primary source for fish restocking in other areas of the state, according to Sands.

The treatment train system works, but because of early stormwater management permitting standards the lake was designed at twice the size it needs to be. It remains full because of the amount of rain the region receives, but the water doesn't turn over as quickly as "ideal," says Sands. Because it takes twice as long as "normal" bodies of water, any excess nutrients take longer to flush out of the system. "So we emphasize managing the quality of the water on the inflow," says Sands, "and that is working very well."

The work of Michael Sands and the Liberty Prairie Foundation are essential to environmental protection, but just as essential is the Prairie Crossings Homeowners' Association, which maintains its Environmental Management Plan, updated annually. In 2011, the HOA was responsible for maintaining 252 acres of common area and 27 acres of ponds and the lake. The Management Plan is divided into landscape types, with objectives and strategies. For example:

Turf and Landscape Trees
Objective: Maintain lawns as aesthetically pleasing and comfortable recreational surfaces, using minimal irrigation, fertilization and pesticides.

Tasks/Practices include:
Test compost tea as an alternative to synthetic fertilizer on Village Green. Prepare and distribute "PC Environmental Handbook". Conduct appropriate homeowner education programs.

Prairies
Objective: Facilitate the development of stable, functional native ecosystems with broad plant diversity and minimal weed pressure that provide quality habitat for desired wildlife and aesthetically pleasing vistas.

Tasks/Practices include:
• Do spring burns on priority areas.
• Do fall burns on priority wetlands.
• Selectively remove invasive woody vegetation.
• Monitor use of nesting structures.

Objectives and tasks/practices–with feedback based on activities of the previous year–are also included for wetlands, hedgerows, lakes/ponds and trails.

Invasive species removal and controlled burning of the prairies and wetlands occurs at Prairie Crossing regularly, mimicking natural fires that historically served to regenerate soils while burning off excess organic materials. About 150 residents trained by the Liberty Prairie Conservancy conduct burns on common areas and individual home yards each year.

Over ten miles of crushed gravel surface trails exist at Prairie Crossing–internal trails are maintained by the HOA while external trails from Northwestern Lake Forest Hospital to the train station and along Harris Road are public regional trails that were conveyed to the Village of Grayslake. Additionally, developers spent nearly $500,000 to construct a trail underpass beneath Route 45, linking the eastern edge of Prairie Crossing to Liberty Prairie Reserve's network of trails.

With funding from the Liberty Prairie Foundation, Prairie Crossing's development team, residents and local community leaders established the nonprofit Liberty Prairie Conservancy in 1995. The conservancy's core purpose was to protect, enhance and educate people about the 5,800-acre Liberty Prairie Reserve. Three-thousand two-hundred acres have been permanently protected from further development due to the efforts of the Ranneys, residents and the conservancy. In 2004, the conservancy became a countywide land trust– "an organization that acquires land or conservation easements on land through voluntary transactions with people who wish to preserve their properties' conservation values," according to conservancy representatives. Land is preserved both in its natural state and for organic farming, ensuring Lake County's natural and

Prairie Crossing's extensive ponds, wetlands, and lake system are part of an integrated stormwater system designed to help restore native prairie.

agricultural legacies.

Conclusion: Living More Sustainably on and from the Land

As landscape architecture professor Janet Silbernagel Balster has written, "[t]he design for Prairie Crossing is not one of false utopia, or even New Urbanism." Which is to say, it doesn't follow the pattern of a "typical" neo-traditional development. And yet, Prairie Crossing is far more progressive in its principles and practices of sustainability than nearly every other development in the U.S., whether New Urbanist or conservation development or something in between. "It is a continuation of the rural Lake County native landscape and working farmland," Balster concludes.

Two decades after development began, Prairie Crossing's guiding principles remain innovative and practical. "I'm surprised and delighted to see that if you lay out guiding principles, the debate tends to be whether you're meeting them," Ranney said more than a dozen years ago. "People are taking up the cause of Prairie Crossing in ways I would never have guessed." Thanks to these people and the developers, the community of Prairie Crossing continues to be visionary and viable, setting an inspiring and essential example of how to live more sustainably on–and from–the land.

DEFINING SUCCESS
Q&A with Victoria Ranney, President, Prairie Holdings Corporation

What was the largest obstacle to obtaining project approval or buy-in and how was it overcome?
No one had seen or heard of a conservation community such as we were proposing at Prairie Crossing. Because it was a new concept, we presented it as a planned unit development and worked carefully with the local officials to answer their objections. The result was acceptance in a record number of weeks, though many details continued to be worked out as each phase was developed.

What is an unexpected delight or success from the project?
An unexpected delight has been the way residents of Prairie Crossing understood and supported the ten guiding principles of the community and carried them out beyond what we as developers initially imagined.

What hasn't lived up to expectations or has required unanticipated change?

When the project was almost completed and all our single-family homes had been sold, the collapse of the housing market meant that some of the condominiums were not sold on the anticipated schedule.

What continues to challenge or surprise you with the project?
What continues to surprise me is the resilience of the concept of living in concert with the environment, that people take great satisfaction on a daily basis in living in the midst of open land, eating healthy organic food grown right here, taking care of the native landscape and actively participating with their neighbors in developing the community.

How do you define and measure success?
We measure the success of the community against the ten guiding principles we established at the beginning of the project.

Civano
Tucson, Arizona
by Simmons B. Buntin

The community of Civano in Tucson, Arizona, combines quantifiable sustainability goals with New Urbanism.

Once planned as a 1,200-acre development comprised of four neighborhoods, a town center, environmental technology business park, 2,700 homes and nearly one million square feet of commercial and light industrial space, the New Urbanist community of Civano located 16 miles southeast of downtown Tucson has been scaled down to only its first neighborhood and largely unbuilt town center. Despite the fact that Civano did not build out as initially planned, it has been called "the largest high-performance, mixed-use community in the United States" and was named the "Best New Community" by *Sunset* magazine in 2004. The result of nearly two decades of planning, the community has morphed from the "Tucson Solar Village" to "Civano: A Model Sustainable Community" to the "Community of Civano", which celebrated its grand opening in 1999.

During its development, the master-planned community was mired in controversies oriented around the City of Tucson's financial commitment, the eventual sole ownership by the Federal National Mortgage Association (Fannie Mae), and the place-based politics of a passionate residency. Today, the neighborhood of 650 resource-efficient homes, an architecturally iconic mixed-use neighborhood center, lush desert landscaping, and the nation's "greenest" school continues to evolve, meeting its goal of serving as a model project for sustainable development while exceeding goals for reduced energy and potable water use. Civano remains the region's most distinct integration of sustainable development and New Urbanism. While its suburban location, minimal transit, and struggles to bring successful retail into the neighborhood center have hampered its success, Civano boasts a remarkable sense of place—an integration with the natural Sonoran desert environment that is more than

JUST THE FACTS

- Located 16 miles southeast of downtown Tucson
- 270-acre New Urbanist neighborhood with adjacent 55-acre "town center"
- Neighborhood is nearly built out; town center still in early stages of buildout
- Designed around principles of sustainability, with quantifiable goals for energy and water reduction, solid waste recycling, onsite job creation, reduced automobile use and housing affordability
- Two-acre mixed-use neighborhood center, including activity center/meeting hall and adjacent live/work residences
- Town center includes super-efficient light industrial manufacturing building and the nation's greenest Valero gas station; "green" Rincon Community Hospital at Civano scheduled to be built in several years
- 650 high-efficiency homes, many with carriage homes
- 35% open space in a mix of natural desert, landscaped parks, sports field, community gardens and paths and trails
- Extensive pre-construction tree and cactus salvage effort resulting in a 90% transplant success rate
- K-5 Civano Community School named "Greenest Grade School in America"; Civano Middle School (6-8) based on expeditionary learning model
- Developed through public/private partnership including the Trust for Sustainable Development; Case Enterprises; Community of Civano, LLC; Civano Development Company; CDC Partners, LLC; Fannie Mae's American Communities Fund; Jump Enterprises; and the City of Tucson
- Designed by Wayne Moody, Duany Plater-Zyberk & Company and Moule & Polyzoides

the sum of its diverse architecture, network of trails and public spaces, and extensive native landscaping.

Civano's Early History

In 1981, Arizona governor Bruce Babbitt participated in a showcase of locally built, solar-powered homes. His comment to the builders? "This is great. What are you going to do next?" That sparked a discussion that resulted in a vision for a new community that could significantly reduce resource consumption and adverse environmental impacts compared with standard subdivisions.

By 1987 the idea had evolved into the Tucson Solar Village, a community of 1,000 solar-powered homes. In 1988 the State of Arizona provided a grant of $210,000 to plan the village. Its concept was to "develop a whole community as a 'showcase' to demonstrate ways in which solar energy could be utilized to reduce overall energy consumption and result in a more harmonious environment," said planner Wayne Moody. That year, funding and siting for the solar village were authorized by the governor and Arizona State Land Department.

The conduit for funding and organizational activities behind the Tucson Solar Village was the Tucson-Pima County Metropolitan Energy Commission (MEC), which entered into a contract with the State Land Department and the Arizona Department of Commerce's Solar Energy Office. The MEC established ambitious goals for the site that included reducing energy consumption by 75%

compared to standard developments, reducing water consumption by 65%, reducing air pollution by 40%, reducing solid waste production by 90% and providing one job onsite for every two homes.

In 1989, a request for proposals for planning consultants was issued and Wayne Moody was selected as planner and project manager. Moody, who served until 1992, was driven by the idea of sustainability, according to friend and fellow consultant Paul Rollins, and he evaluated many models of sustainability in their application to the solar village.

In 1991, the project's name was changed from Tucson Solar Village to Civano: A Model Sustainable Community. "Civano" refers to the golden era of the late classic period of the Hohokam, the native peoples who developed sophisticated social, economic and agricultural systems in the Tucson region from 650 to 1450. According to Lee Rayburn, then-director of planning and design for the Community of Civano, LLC, the name change was the result of input from nearly 60 public meetings held in 1991 and 1992. During those meetings, participants recognized the need to broaden the project's focus from solar energy to sustainability.

The State Land Department committed 818 acres of undeveloped desert on the southeast side of Tucson and the city approved rezoning for a master-planned community. In order for the land to be sold, the State Land Department stipulated a comprehensive planning process that included extensive public involvement. The city's rezoning likewise set aggressive resource conservation goals and performance requirements. The result was the Civano: Tucson Solar Village Master Development Plan, which was created by Wayne Moody and approved in May 1992 (and revised as the Civano Master Planned Area Development in 2005). The original plan states:

The development of the Village of Civano is an attempt to demonstrate our ability to accomplish the broad goals [of]

the use of the sun as our primary source of energy; the conservation and multiple uses of water; the configuration of uses on the land which minimizes the use of fossil fuel- and time-consuming automobile travel; the reduction of waste in both product and time; and the development of a sense of community, social interaction and place.

The innovative plan incorporated a background summary, site and area analysis, market analysis and marketability study, energy and resource conservation features and techniques (including performance targets for energy, water, solid waste, transportation and employment) and a development plan summary.

Following a series of planning and marketing studies conducted by John Laswick, the city's project manager for Civano, the 818-acre parcel went up for auction in July 1996. David Case of Case Enterprises and David Butterfield of the Trust for Sustainable Development, working together as the Community of Civano, LLC, placed a bid of $2.6 million, the minimum asking price and the only bid received. Case came from Connecticut and Butterfield from British Columbia, and soon after they were joined by Kevin Kelly, who moved from Massachusetts.

Earlier in the year, the Arizona Energy Office granted $300,000 from oil overcharge funds to the City of Tucson to contract with the Arizona Solar Village Corporation—then called Civano Institute—to develop the Civano Builder Program and a sustainable design plan book to assist builders at Civano in creating residences that would meet the Master Development Plan's ambitious performance targets. The performance targets were codified in 1995 as the Civano Integrated Method of Performance and Cost Tracking (IMPACT) System, which remains in place to this day.

Once the land was purchased, the city agreed to support Civano with $200,000 in sewer credits and $3 million in infrastructure funding for water, sewer and roads–including a new line to supply reclaimed water for irrigation, the city's first and most comprehensive effort to use treated wastewater to offset potable water use in a residential development. The city's seed money was leveraged by developers through a commitment of an additional $20 million in private funding. City funding came after a 4-3 city council vote, at which, according to an *Arizona Daily Star* article, supporters said the expenditure "is justified because the project will show other developers how energy-efficient construction, pedestrian-friendly design and recycling can work in central city areas." Critics, however, claimed the city "has no business putting public funds into a private development when the city has so many other pressing needs." In 1997 the city agreed to loan Civano developers an additional $250,000 to help offset design costs–a move that drew more criticism.

Defining and Measuring Sustainability "The planning process for this project has been extensive and encouraging," said developer Kevin Kelly as construction began. "Civano is a fundamentally new approach to community planning. The goals are to connect people to each other and to their environment, instead of simply maximizing short-term profits by increasing building lot counts. All 'sustainable' planning principles require an analysis that incorporates the social, environmental and economic impact of a development."

Six quantifiable sustainability goals were set:

1. Reduce home energy consumption by 50% over the 1995 model energy code.
2. Reduce potable water consumption by 65%.
3. Reduce internal vehicle miles driven by 40%.
4. Create one job onsite for every two residences.

5. Reduce landfill-destined solid waste.
6. Provide 20% affordable housing.

Three agreements guided the developers, in partnership with the City of Tucson, in implementing these sustainability goals: the Development Agreement, signed in 1992; the Memorandum of Understanding (MOU) between the developer and city; and the IMPACT System. The Development Agreement addressed energy conservation and sustainability goals, rights and responsibilities of parties, Civano infrastructure improvement and financing and development rights.

The MOU began by stating, "The goal of the Civano project is to create a mixed-use community that attains the highest feasible standards of sustainability, resource conservation and development of Arizona's most abundant energy resource–solar–so that it becomes an international model for sustainable growth." It also established the development process, monitoring and evaluation process (including reporting and periodic review by the master developer), strategies and responsibilities, specific procedures for implementation, master developer requirements, development and building plan review process, demonstration projects and certification of compliance.

The IMPACT System codified the annual review of Civano sustainability goals and accomplishments, setting performance targets, requirements, implementation responsibilities and monitoring for building energy demand, building energy supply, water use, solid waste recycling, transportation, land use balance, and housing affordability.

The 2010 IMPACT System Monitoring Report and the latest annual Energy and Water Use in Tucson and Civano Report indicate that Civano meets or exceeds the building energy demand, building energy supply, water use and housing affordability goals. The community did not meet the solid waste recycling goals for construction, though is meeting the

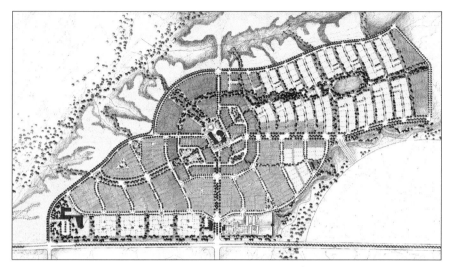

An early version of the Civano site plan, with its Neighborhood Center District (red), Neighborhood General District (orange), and Neighborhood Edge District (yellow).

goals for recycling of consumer waste. Architect Gallagher Witmer, author of the IMPACT monitoring reports, concludes that Civano will meet the transportation and land-use balance goals only after buildout of the town center is complete.

Designing Civano: From Charrette to Specific Plan

From 1996 to 2000, the developers worked with more than two dozen consultants and organizations to formulate Civano's design. The town plan itself was created at a three-day design charrette held in September 1996. Wayne Moody facilitated the charrette, which brought together New Urbanist designers Andrés Duany and Stefanos Polyzoides, plus the developers, city representatives and other stakeholders. Unlike other New Urbanist charrettes, however, Civano's consisted of public meetings for Civano "pioneers" and city officials interspersed with intense, closed-door design sessions that did not involve the wider public.

Two separate site plans were developed by two different design teams–led by Duany

Plater-Zyberk & Company and Wayne Moody, respectively–and these were critiqued every few hours. A third team of designers (Moule & Polyzoides) worked specifically on the first neighborhood center, streetscapes and home designs, as well as the creation of individual architecture and planning elements for the differing house types. By 9 p.m. on the final night, according to Rollins, no acceptable design concept had emerged and some participants wanted to finish design work from home. "But we weren't allowed to leave and by 3 a.m. the Civano site plan was blessed into existence by a tired but happy group," Rollins says. Overnight, Stefanos Polyzoides and his team created a new, holistic plan that combined aspects of the two plans created by Duany and Moody, for Monday morning's scheduled presentation to Tucson city officials.

A year later, the charrette led to the development of the Neighborhood 1 Specific Plan, which set forth three land uses or intensities within Civano's first neighborhood: Neighborhood Edge District, Neighborhood General District and Neighborhood Center District.

The Specific Plan–which was based on

the concepts of building community, connection with the land, respect for climate and generation–included the Development Design Guidelines, a phasing plan, a circulation plan, interpretations and variances and visual representations of streets and street sections, parking, landscaping, parks and trails. The entitlement work on Civano's first neighborhood, however, occurred before the Specific Plan was adopted. "The ideas that were codified in the Specific Plan were promoted and advocated during the long civil engineering design and review period," says Rayburn.

The Controversy of the Master Developers

In 1997, Fannie Mae's American Communities Fund became a 16% equity investor in Civano with a $3 million commitment that increased to $5 million by the time the development opened in April 1999. "The fund invests in leading-edge, catalytic developments that expand opportunities for homeownership and the revitalization of communities across the nation," said American Communities Fund executive managing director Kenneth J. Bacon at the time. "Civano is truly a first of its kind, a bellwether in real estate development. Fannie Mae believes Civano is a worthy investment in America's new generation of housing and fully supports its innovative efforts to balance community and residential needs."

This was the first step in Fannie Mae's largely unanticipated move to become Civano's sole developer. After the 1996 design charrette, David Butterfield and his Trust for Sustainable Development sold its interest in the Civano project to the operating partner, Case Enterprises. In 1998, the American Communities Fund bought out developer David Case, gaining a controlling ownership interest at 66%.

By the time Civano officially opened on April 16, 1999–with an initial 70-acre, 195-home first phase–it included an innovative neighborhood center, a series of highly efficient model homes and a thin-film photovoltaic manufacturing facility. The grand opening brought together hundreds of people, including U.S. Congressional representative Jim Kolbe, Department of Energy assistant secretary of energy efficiency and renewable energy Mark Ginsburg and Arizona governor Jane Hull, who hailed Civano as "the poster child for better planning."

Despite the fanfare, criticism of the project by outsiders persisted: "Problems finding someone to develop the project, bankers' reluctance to finance it and the slow development and high cost of new solar energy technologies resulted in most of the solar elements being stripped away," contends an *Arizona Daily Star* article published the day after the grand opening. The development was also knocked for its approach to site planning, as the articled noted "the ground has been scraped bare and leveled" and that other, smaller projects could just as easily meet Civano's energy and water goals without city funding. Responding to the criticisms, Ginsberg agreed that smaller developments may use similar energy efficiency and renewable energy technologies, but "Civano demonstrates how it can be done on a large scale," saying that solar energy would be used more at Civano as the development matures–a prediction that has come true.

Shortly after the grand opening, Fannie Mae became the sole owner and master developer, as the Community of Civano, LLC, when it bought out Kevin Kelly. Though Fannie Mae's financial investment kept the project alive, it also resulted in the erosion of Civano's ideals. Planning and design director Rayburn worked to balance Civano's guiding documents and original intent with the expectations of a growing, vocal residency and a master developer in Fannie Mae that demonstrated, with increasing frequency, that it was more interested in removing itself from the development process than ensuring Civano's design lived up to its New Urbanist principles.

The Civano Neighborhood Center hosts a mix of businesses, the homeowners' activity center, and a plethora of social events. It also serves as a pilot project for building and energy technologies.

The sale of the land that would have become Neighborhoods II and III by Fannie Mae to Pulte Homes in 2004 effectively limited the original New Urbanist plan for Civano to Neighborhood I, as the national developer constructed a subdivision of cul-de-sacs, non-native landscaping, fenced retention areas and cookie-cutter houses quite different from what was originally intended.

Neighborhood Center and Town Center: The Heart of Civano

Civano's heart lies in the community's neighborhood center, a two-acre complex of commercial buildings and open-air courtyards and plazas designed by Moule & Polyzoides and constructed in the middle of the neighborhood. "Civano represents for New Urbanism one of the first projects where community-building initiatives, which focus on anti-sprawl, are being carried out in tandem with an environmentally ambitious design program," says Polyzoides. "The overlap of social and environmental ideals that are the hallmark of Civano can be best isolated and understood

in the design of its neighborhood center."

Constructed prior to Civano's grand opening, the neighborhood center initially housed a café, art gallery, offices and the model home center. After the café and gallery closed in 2001 from lack of business, various businesses used the office space, including the developer. The café space was converted to an HOA activity center and ultimately–just before Fannie Mae left the project–the round meeting hall and adjoining buildings were turned over to the HOA to be the public space they were designed for. "In its form, particularly the kiva-inspired cylinder and enclosed courtyard," says Polyzoides, "it provides a place for the citizens of Civano to live in public."

For several years, however, Fannie Mae's onsite manager discouraged resident use of the community center, which the developer subdivided and attempted to sell as separate commercial condominiums. Considering the center's wide patios, shallow amphitheater, lush landscaping and distinct architecture highlighted by the meeting hall's rich adobe brick and concrete block cooling tower, its lack

187

of use as a civic center was frustrating. From 2004 through 2009, when Fannie Mae sold the neighborhood center to resident and Civano Nursery owner Les Shipley and his family, a number of editorials were written and neighbor meetings held to discuss bringing the neighborhood center back to the community.

Once the Shipleys purchased the neighborhood center, however, they immediately offered it for neighbor events and regular neighborhood use. The Shipleys actively marketed the neighborhood center and within months had landed an Italian restaurant, fitness center, hair salon, bicycle shop and new office uses, including an optometrist. Though the restaurant lasted just one year–due in part to the downturn in the economy–today the neighborhood center, combined with the HOA activity center in the rotunda, serves as the community's central gathering place. "If we didn't have this little community meeting space, there would be no community," says Shipley. "There would be no coffee meetings, there would be no book club, there would be no teen night. There would be nothing."

The neighborhood center is distinct not only because of its mix of services, but also because it was designed as an environmental technology showcase. The activity center (meeting hall) features adobe construction for thermal mass and a three-story cooling tower that can take advantage of evaporative cooling. The system is tied into the courtyard's fountain. A mix of building construction materials–from straw bale to RASTRA recycled polystyrene-concrete to wood frame and stucco–along with passive solar siting, fosters efficiency and a unique architectural styling. The neighborhood center also features solar hot water heating, active solar photovoltaic panels, super-efficient windows and recycled carpet. Like the rest of the neighborhood, it takes advantage of xeriscaping using native plants.

The neighborhood center is located within the Specific Plan's Neighborhood Center District. It is surrounded by dense, single-family courtyard homes and live/work units–many of which required additional negotiation with the city or, in some cases, retrofitting to accommodate their commercial components, including the newly opened and popular Harriett's Café. Tom Doucette, owner of Doucette Communities, built the two-story live/work units that house such businesses as Ballet Rincon, Shoppes at Civano, Zona Gardens Bed & Breakfast and the Inn at Civano. "The city made it so difficult to do the mixed-use in the neighborhood center," says Doucette, "yet Civano's plans clearly advocate mixed uses."

Resident Bruce Rhoades, who owned and operated Uno Bicycle Studio in the neighborhood center, moved his business to Tucson from Colorado. He also expresses concerns about the city, though in his case the concern is "the amount of hoops you have to jump though just to get open–it's a huge disappointment." But he has been pleased with the support he has received from Civano residents and the Shipleys, particularly as he has expanded his space with the increasing success of his custom bicycle business.

Civano-based businesses are not restricted to the neighborhood center. The CivanoNeighbors.com website lists over 90 businesses, most home-based, though even here a mix of retail services–hair salon, massage therapy, skin care–are allowed. Additionally, a two-acre area of mixed-use zoned land on the southeast corner of Civano is owned by Doucette Communities. Though the current economic market doesn't justify development, Doucette hopes to build boutique-style, "high-design" leased housing above street-level retail, such as a coffee shop and fitness center. Civano otherwise does not offer any multifamily housing.

Each of the project's four neighborhoods were envisioned to have a mixed-use neighborhood center, while at the core of the overall project was a 110-acre town center, a full circle

Civano's homes are inspired by a regional desert vernacular, including these barrio-style houses, while landscaping features native trees and cactus.

Photo: Simmons Buntin

of live/work, commercial and light industrial uses bridging the east and west portions of the development along Houghton Road, a busy north-south arterial. Today, a 55-acre town center on the east side of Houghton is still in the works and was included in the Civano Master Planned Area Development. The first building constructed (in 1997) was the Global Solar thin-film photovoltaic manufacturing facility. The 31,000-square-foot building was lauded as Arizona's most energy-efficient industrial building when it opened. It features skylights equipped with mirrors that rotate to follow the sun and more than 20 other improvements over Model Energy Code standards, saving the tenant an estimated $46,000 per year in water and energy use.

The second building in the town center was not completed until 2010 and it was controversial not in its energy or water use, but in its service: a gas station. The Valero service station and "Corner Store" on the northeast corner of Houghton and Drexel—the street on the neighborhood's southern edge—meets the town center's stringent environmental and design guidelines, but the irony of having a gas station anchoring a corner of a pedestrian-oriented community is not lost on Civano's residents. Still, the station is Valero's greenest

in North America and features solar hot water preheating, skylights and photocells, waterless facilities, reclaimed water for irrigation, xeriscaping and an 11 kW photovoltaic system.

Representatives of the developer of Civano's town center, Jump Enterprises, have met with residents several times and continue to communicate about possibilities for the northern half of the town center, including a small-footprint grocery store. Along the southern half, Tucson Medical Center (TMC) plans to build the state's greenest hospital, called Rincon Community Hospital at Civano. Initial indications are that the hospital will be a 90-bed, three-story building that will be designed to LEED-Silver certification standards. Originally slated to open in 2010, TMC has purchased the land and installed underground infrastructure, but with the downturn in the economy has not moved further on the project. TMC now expects to first build medical offices, followed by the hospital, though the time frame for either is not set.

Homes of a Desert Sensibility

In 1998, Civano was named one of five Partnership for Advancing Technology in Housing (PATH) national pilot developments, chosen because of its "highly innovative technologies

A rendering of Civano's Desert Country area (Neighborhood Edge District), which is inspired by Davis, California's Village Homes: winding paseos in front, alleys in back.

as well as for new approaches for land planning and design [that allow it to] serve as a model for the U.S. residential construction industry," according to the U.S. Department of Housing and Urban Development. In living up to this standard–and meeting the requirements of the Civano IMPACT System–Civano's builders teamed up with Tucson Electric Power to take advantage of the utility's Guaranteed Comfort program, which certifies individual homes based on such practices as duct sealing, insulation, air conditioning efficiency and the like. Homes also feature solar hot water heating, low-e windows, low-flow water fixtures and other resource-efficiency measures that resulted in the homes costing 10% to 15% more per square foot than a typical Tucson house, yet save homeowners 50% on electricity costs.

Civano also served as a national demonstration site for the American Lung Association's Health House Project, the first nationwide program to provide consumers with a standard building practice and verification of a home's performance relating to the minimization of indoor air pollution sources and energy consumption. The Health House criteria focused on moisture control, ventilation and filtration. Two custom homes, which were completed in 1999, were tested and their performance verified; the design, construction and verification processes were then made available to other Civano homebuilders.

At the 1999 grand opening, 17 model homes by five builders were available, ranging in price from $90,000 to more than $200,000. Though most homes used 2x6 traditional wood (or recycled steel) framing, others were constructed of structurally insulated panels, RASTRA block, or straw bale, averaging an efficiency rate of R-28 for walls and R-42 for roofs. Other typical systems incorporated into the homes include solar control glazing, architectural overhangs and air handlers and ducts located inside the thermal envelope. Over the life of the project there have been eight builders, plus a number of custom homes.

Photo: Simmons Buntin

The Sonoran desert landscape allows for a rich mix of colors, such as the purple on this solar-powered bungalow.

More unique than the builders, perhaps, is the range of home types that occur at Civano–a result not only of the Specific Plan and variety of homebuilders, but also of design work and advising to the builders provided by Moule & Polyzoides. KE&G, for example, built single-story, Craftsman-style bungalows with wide front porches, tile or metal roofs and detached garages on alleys. The homes were modeled after historic bungalows near the University of Arizona. T.J. Bednar built Santa Fe-style homes with low curving walls, beehive fireplaces and shared driveways in a barrio-style area, as well as Santa Fe variations of the KE&G bungalow once KE&G pulled out of the Tucson market. SolarBuilt constructed custom homes in Civano's "Desert Country" area, defined in the Specific Plan as the Neighborhood Edge District. SolarBuilt homes apply principles of high thermal mass and passive solar energy collection to control interior temperature and reduce reliance on mechanical heating and cooling systems. The homes are primarily solar-powered, with photovoltaic systems, water harvesting systems and a modern desert architecture. RGC courtyard

homes incorporated structurally insulated panels into a vertical urban design. The homes, which bridge the neighborhood center with (moderately) less dense areas of the neighborhood, were completed by local builder MW2 after RGC went out of business.

In 2001, Doucette Communities began offering homes in Civano. Doucette acquired lots originally slated for RGC, First Homes and KE&G. In their place, Doucette built new variations on the courtyard homes (ranging from 900 to 1,600 square feet), the live/work two-story homes around the neighborhood center and the Sol models, which took their architectural cue from the flat-roofed Territorial style of historic homes found throughout Tucson. Now that those portions of the neighborhood are complete, Doucette offers clustered homes in the Civano Presidio–adjacent to the Civano Community School at the southern end of the neighborhood–and the Civano Orchards, Arizona ranch-style homes that front the wide pedestrian path along the neighborhood's eastern edge. With the exception of the Presidio homes–which share driveways and have variable lot lines–all of the Doucette

Civano's central greenway system serves many purposes, from stormwater management to recreation. A south sports park is particularly popular on mild days.

homes place garages on alleys or behind the home and offer carriage home options.

Both ContraVest Properties and Voyager Homes offered single-family homes designed to meet specific design criteria. In the case of ContraVest, houses with a decidedly urban façade were built. The ContraVest homes are the only production residential units that do not include solar hot water. Voyager Homes built a series of single- and two-story homes around Mary Webber Park, the oval park that provides an unobstructed view from the neighborhood center to the Rincon Mountains to the east. Their architecture and siting is reminiscent of a walled Mexican town, with the park serving as a central commons.

The final production builder at Civano is Pepper-Viner Homes, controversial in both of its Civano locations. In the Desert Country area–a lower-density region of Civano modeled after the path-fronted Village Homes concept of Davis, California–the developer allowed the builder to front homes to the alleys rather than the paseos. Though the homes of modernist desert architecture are attractive and

sold well, their siting was a point of contention for many neighbors. At Civano North Ridge, Pepper-Viner inherited a parcel that many believed would hold perhaps two dozen mini-estates. The Master Development Plan, however, allowed for up to 85 homes and original North Ridge owner T.J. Bednar platted the land accordingly. Following a lawsuit filed by a resident, Bednar sold the land to Pepper-Viner. The city approved the plat and Pepper-Viner has built about 50 of 75 homes, filling in a number of arroyos and dismissing the neighborhood's New Urban street grid for a series of cul-de-sacs. What the homes lack in neo-traditional design, however, they make up in resource efficiency, boasting the neighborhood's most innovative and energy-efficient production homes–including a LEED Platinum-certified BASF high-performance demonstration home constructed in 2009.

While Civano is arguably the most energy- and water-efficient production development in the country, its custom homes take resource efficiency to a new level. The home of Rich and Susan Michal, for example,

Thanks to the diligent efforts of Canadian transplant Les Shipley and family, Civano's tree salvaging efforts have been highly successful.

incorporates rammed earth walls, insulated block walls, a cooling tower, active and passive solar systems, an outdoor "cowboy" shower, greywater use, rainwater collection and reuse, passive solar orientation, super-efficient appliances and an evaporative whole-house cooling system. At the time of its completion in 2005, the 1,750-square-foot house with sizable outdoor porches may have been the country's most efficient on-grid home, resulting in a $113 per year total electric bill for heating and cooling for a family of five. Other custom homes incorporate straw bale, extensive photovoltaic systems, rainwater harvesting, locally produced adobe and other features that enable them to far exceed IMPACT System requirements. Homeowners have also increased their resource efficiency over the years by adding photovoltaic systems (some as large as 12 kW) and participating in cistern raisings to harvest rainwater for irrigation.

"One of the glorious things about Civano Phase 1," says Rayburn in *Inside the Civano Project*, "is that the houses look like they belong in Tucson, [which] creates a sense of place." Indeed, Civano's often boldly colored homes seem to have grown from the landscape just as the mix of native landscaping has grown around them. Builders may have come and gone, but their legacy of a walkable community of distinct, resource-efficient homes remains.

Parks, Gardens, Trails and Amenities

Civano began by setting aside 33% of the community for natural and enhanced open space, defined predominantly by a central spine of linked open spaces that channel water into the center of the neighborhood for onsite stormwater management. The central greenway links the neighborhood center to a large grassy park and adjacent pool and then the school on the south. To the east, the elliptical Mary Webber Park provides a view toward Saguaro National Park and the Rincon Mountains beyond. Another smaller grassy park with a tennis court and pool is located just north of the neighborhood center. Pocket parks and natural areas are nestled throughout the community, particularly along the north and eastern edges of the development, where a series of arroyos that run to Pantano Wash are located. The neighborhood's proximity to the wash–a wide, dry riverbed that runs only after monsoon and other rainstorms–serves as a highway for wildlife and it is not uncommon to see javelina and coyotes, as well as bobcats, ringtails, snakes and a stunning variety of birds among the lush landscaping of the neighborhood.

Civano's landscaping is often its first accolade and the vitality is intentional. Before Civano broke ground, Les Shipley and his sons moved from Victoria, British Columbia, where he had retired as a successful horticulturalist. The Trust for Sustainable Development's David Butterfield recruited Shipley to develop a new method for salvaging mature trees and cactus and Shipley began by taking plant classes at Pima Community College. His first job was to salvage native mesquite, palo verde and cactus. Prior to their arrival, transplanted native species had a 50% survival rate. Over several years, Shipley and his sons perfected new methods of salvaging desert trees that included hand-digging the root ball and boxing the trees, resulting in a 90% success rate.

Having mature native trees is "vital to the Civano philosophy," says Shipley. "It's the balancing of human needs with the natural environment. That's why we can't disregard the value of preserving these precious resources." Shipley and his family salvaged and replanted over 8,000 palo verde and mesquite and 3,000 barrel cactus and saguaro, many 100 years old. Civano is home to more than 2,100 trees in the 1.2 million square feet of the common areas and rights-of-way alone, including a mesquite bosque in the central greenway. The Shipleys founded Civano Nursery, located at the main entrance to Civano at Houghton and Seven Generations Boulevard. The nursery and garden center offer native and near-native stock as well as classes on xeriscaping and desert gardening as part of the nursery's ongoing

workshop and demonstration programs.

Civano's native landscaping is also the product of comprehensive landscape guidelines implemented under the homeowners' association. The guidelines provide a list of allowable native and near-native plans while restricting a wide variety of plants that, with enough water, would grow in Civano but do not meet Sonoran desert character.

Other environmental features include a wide pedestrian and bicycle path that skirts the neighborhood along Pantano Wash; a series of paseos that run through the central greenway and throughout the Desert Country area; HOA-managed community gardens with plots available to rent, complete with irrigation; a tot lot; and wide, densely landscaped medians with sloping curbs, allowing runoff to collect in the medians and percolate into the soil while watering the plants. All common spaces and most homes are irrigated with reclaimed city water, as well.

Civano Community School : The Greenest Grade School in America

In January 2008, the 66-student Civano Community School was named the "Greenest Grade School in America" by Ellen DeGeneres. It was selected from among more than 3,000 schools that participated in the "Go Green with All Small & Mighty" contest. The school, which was founded in 1999 as a public charter school in the Vail School District, was awarded $50,000–money set aside to build a school kitchen "so that we can make lunches with food grown in our organic garden," says Pam Bateman, schoolmarm. The kitchen and attached pavilion–which uses trusses salvaged prior to the demolition of a big box store in Tucson, thanks to the collaborative efforts of Civano residents–were completed in 2011. Once temporarily housed in one of the ALA Health Houses, the 3,910-square-foot school moved into its energy-efficient permanent

Civano residents fill the neighborhood center during the community's annual Spring Picnic and Earth Day Celebration.

Photo: Simmons Buntin

location on the south side of Civano in 2003. The shared-grade (K-1, 2-3 and 4-5) public school features extensive daylighting created in part by donated windows that create a distinct if not funky collage, thermal massing, a 2kW solar photovoltaic system donated by Tucson Electric Power, learning gardens, rainwater harvesting, xeriscaping, comprehensive recycling and a wealth of other environmental features that also serve as hands-on educational opportunities for students.

"Civano Community School is rooted in the concept of community—a community of learners encompassing students, family and staff," reads the school philosophy. "We are centered around a child-initiated approach to learning and committed to the progress of all members." Just as the neighborhood center serves to foster community at Civano, the school likewise supports community, both by involving parents in its experiential-based curriculum and by providing the school for community meetings. Each day begins with "community time," bringing together students in a

sharing of information and energy representative of the school's unique, place-based learning model.

"We took a huge risk when we opened this school," says superintendent Calvin Baker. "It was 180 degrees from what other districts were doing." Civano Community School embodies the neighborhood school model, in which schools are an active part of the community—in design and function—rather than a sprawling campus placed on leftover land.

Civano Middle School opened across the street in its own resource-efficient building. Like the grade school, which was also designed by architect Phil Swaim, it takes advantage of daylight so that electrical lighting is not needed on most days. Other features include rainwater and air-conditioning condensate harvesting, reclaimed water use for irrigation and secondary plumbing (toilets), recycled denim insulation, low-VOC paints and adhesives, high-efficiency HVAC system with heat recovery and onsite stormwater retention without a basin. During construction 90% of the waste was

Most of the homes in Civano are alley-loaded, yet even in these secondary spaces, lush landscaping, diverse architecture, and lovely views are easy to find.

recycled and prior to construction the architect met with students to help design the building. "The students really get it," says Swaim. "It's a part of the way they live."

Creating Community from and beyond Design

"With all its technological advancements, the most important element of Civano is its sense of community," says David Case. That sense of community is evident both in design and in the wide variety of social activities and events that occur at Civano. At the Annual Community Celebration in May 1998, to provide a design example, many of the neighborhood's streets were named in dedication to those worthy of recognition from across Tucson. George Brookbank Place reminds residents of the urban horticulturalist who, for more than 50 years, brought the science of desert botany to the residents of Tucson by teaching desert gardening. Joseph Parella Lane honors the police officer who dedicated his services to helping low-income Tucson neighborhoods become drug-free. Cele Peterson Lane pays tribute to the Tucson businesswoman who advocated

civic pride and improvement for more than 60 years.

While design fosters community in other ways–the running joke at Civano is that it takes an hour to check the curbside mailbox because of all the neighbors out on their front porches along the way–neighbors have been active in communication throughout project development. In October 2002, the first issue of *The Town Crier*–the community newspaper supported by the neighborhood association–was published. Since then, the paper has been the leading source of regular information, mailed to every home and business within the community. Featuring news, editorials, reviews and events, the paper is now published online.

The neighbors' website was created as soon as homeowners began gathering, even before breaking ground on their homes. Located since 2002 at civanoneighbors.com, the website features an active discussion forum, calendar of events, historic neighborhood information, links to guiding documents and design guidelines, business and resident directory, opportunities for purchasing Civano merchandise (with proceeds benefiting the neighborhood association) and the Civano Resource Exchange, a listing of services, equipment and the like loaned for free, neighbor to neighbor.

Over the last dozen years residents have conducted a variety of events, ranging from weekly book club and card game gatherings to monthly potlucks and a speakers series. Larger annual events—such as the Civano Picnic and Earth Day Celebration, Spring Arts & Crafts Fair and Quilt Raffle and Independence Day Parade—are managed by neighbor volunteers and often sponsored by local businesses. Impromptu gatherings are just as common: bonfires and sing-alongs in the community garden, wine tastings, campouts in Mary Webber Park and lining the streets with luminaries before Christmas, to name just a few.

Finally, the neighborhood association has spawned several ongoing working groups, though none as active as the Aging in Community organization, which provides free medical equipment, services such as driving for doctors' visits and at-home assistance on a volunteer basis to the neighborhood's elderly.

Conclusion

While designers and activists continue to debate whether Civano is truly a New Urbanist community due to its minimal transit (limited bus service began only in December 2012) and slowly evolving commercial components, few can debate its authentic sense of place and community. Despite its rocky development and the coming and going of developers and builders, the neighborhood continues to serve as a model for community-wide, quantifiable sustainable development. Nearly all of the homes are built and only a mixed-use parcel owned by Doucette Communities and the town center await buildout. Once those are completed—and given Tucson's struggling economy, that may take several years or more—the community is likely to come closer to reaching its comprehensive sustainability goals, including onsite jobs and air pollution reduction.

At the 1999 grand opening, developer Kevin Kelly said, "We are proud that Civano has become the model for building a livable community for the coming century. Civano has been a group effort from the very beginning, involving the community, government, private business, academicians and experts in planning and environmental engineering to create a classic town setting that meets residents' economic and social needs, in balance with the natural surroundings." More than a dozen years later, his statement is as true as ever.

DEFINING SUCCESS
Q&A with Lee Rayburn, former Director of Design and Planning, Civano Development Co. / CDC Partners, LLC

What was the largest obstacle to obtaining project approval or buy-in and how was it overcome?
Obtaining approval and buy-in from the City of Tucson. This was a complex public/private partnership. So much of what Civano attempted to do and, in some cases, was required to do by the terms of its Development Agreement with the City of Tucson, was untested; especially at the scale of Civano and with the mandate of being "affordable." The resource conservation goal methodologies and the New Urbanist planning concepts we used did not have—at that time—a body of codified success and standards that reviewing agencies could turn

to. We were, in effect, asking dedicated civil servants to step well outside their experience and training and to take risks: something that does not come naturally to governmental entities and especially review agencies. We overcame this by being persistent; by being consistent in what we said and promised and what we did. Eventually, we could point to actual built examples of what we had been promoting and show successful implementation. Things got a bit easier after that. Having said that, Civano suffered from a disconnect between a city government that created complex and innovative development demands for the project and then proceeded to review them by established rules.

What is an unexpected delight or success from the project?

Meeting and working so closely with Stefano Polyzoides and other New Urbanist designers. Hosting hundreds and hundreds of visitors to Civano who always went away inspired to go back to their communities and struggle for their own versions of sustainability and a return to human-scaled development.

What hasn't lived up to expectations or has required unanticipated change?

Not a one-sentence, or one-paragraph, or one-page answer. I will just pick one thing: the lack of coordination among key documents: CC&Rs, Specific Plan and design guidelines. They were all created under time pressure and were not coordinated and that lack continues to cause problems in fulfilling Civano's objectives. The failure to create a full "form-based code" is included in this comment.

What continues to challenge or surprise you with the project?

Whatever the history, whatever the things achieved or not achieved, when I look out on the project and see how the community is growing and evolving–the architecture that speaks of its place in the Sonoran Desert, the lush landscape and the social activity going on everywhere–I realize that all the academic talk is merely secondary commentary of the reality of this vibrant community.

How do you define and measure success?

In my own terms and in the case of Civano, I would say:

1. Was there an honest attempt to meet the goals set? Yes.
2. Did the project take the evolving discussion on and practice of sustainable development forward? Yes.
3. Does it continue to show what any and all vibrant entities demonstrate growth and evolution around core realities? Yes.
4. Can I look back on the time and effort I put into this thing, without shying away from the hard parts of the things that may have happened and be glad? Yes.

Acknowledgements

The authors wish to thank the following people for their invaluable assistance during the creation of this book: Liz DiLorenzo and Paul Rice (Belmar); Lee Rayburn, Stefanos Polyzoides, Tom Doucette, and Phil Swaim (Civano); Kelly O'Brien (Dockside Green); Walter Brown and Pam Sessions (Glenwood Park); David McGowan (Lenox Village); David Ford and Romy Mortenson (NorthWest Crossing); Michael Sands and Victoria Ranney (Prairie Crossing); Kiki Wallace, Mark Sofield, and Andrés Duany (Prospect New Town); Geraldene Moyle (River-Place); David Levy and Cindy Cotte Griffiths (Rockville Town Square); Fred Evins (Second Street District); and April Wooden, John Kearns, and Scott Corey (Suisun City Waterfront District). Simmons would also like to thank Jeanne Bennett, Annie Harris, Carey Shane, Jana and Ted Dawson, Yvette Meltzer and Allen Ramsier, Adele and David Buntin, Miles Buntin, Andrew Bone, Shannan and Jason Reese, Carolyn and Joe Dooling, and Karen Yurch for their hospitality.

The authors also wish to thank the following project sponsors:

- Ingrid Anderson and Dan Weber
- Teague Bohlen
- Christopher Cokinos
- Elizabeth Dodd
- Boyd and Laurie Foster
- Deborah Fries
- Andrew C. Gottlieb
- Linda and Rick Hanson
- Grant Humphreys
- David Rothenberg
- Lauret Savoy
- Ernest J. Yanarella

About the Authors

Simmons B. Buntin is the founding editor-in-chief of *Terrain.org: A Journal of the Built + Natural Environments*, an online magazine publishing a mix of literary and technical work, including the Unsprawl case studies. He has published prose and poetry widely, including two books: *Bloom* and *Riverfall*. Simmons holds graduate degrees in urban and regional planning and creative writing and serves as web program manager at the University of Arizona. He lives in the community of Civano in Tucson, where he founded the neighborhood association and led the community's speaker series for several years. Before that he lived in Denver and Westminster, Colorado, where he served on the planning commission.

Ken Pirie is an associate with Walker Macy Landscape Architects in Portland, Oregon. Originally from Quebec, via Scotland, then Seattle, Ken works on urban design and campus planning projects up and down the West Coast. He recently helped prepare a master plan for Cottonwood Canyon, Oregon's newest state park, on the Wild & Scenic John Day River. He has also been working with the development team behind NorthWest Crossing on an expansion to that community. Ken teaches a graduate class in planning at Portland State University and loves to hike and ski when he's not supporting the Portland Timbers.

References

Chapter One:
Prospect New Town, Longmont, Colorado

Asner, Marci. "Prospects good for neo-urbanism." *Boulder County Business Report.* June 1997.

Associated Press. "In search of the 'Holy Grail' of planned communities." August 10, 2006.

"Best New Town: Prospect, Colorado." *Sunset.* March 2001.

Bortnick, B. Scott. "Longmont landmark moving down road; Johnson's Corner will not be razed." *The Denver Post.* June 24, 2003.

Bressi, Todd W. "Prospect: Expectations and Enthusiasms." *Places: A Forum of Environmental Design.* 14.3. Spring 2002.

Buntin, Simmons. "Denver: America's Great Urban Canvas, Part I." *Next American City* (online). August 4, 2008.

Business Report Staff. "Prospect project will be wind powered." *Boulder County Business Report.* November 7, 2007.

Business Report Staff. "Sugar's closes retail shop in Longmont." *Boulder County Business Report.* December 27, 2007.

Callahan, Patricia. "Denver: A study in New Urbanism Conference to address city sprawl." *The Denver Post.* April 26, 1998.

Campbell, Greg. "Welcome to Pleasantville: Local builders find that planning a new urbanist development is anything but a black-and-white issue." *The Daily Times-Call.* April 4, 1999.

City of Longmont. "15.03.060 – Planned unit development (PUD) districts." *Municipal Code.* Accessed on October 31, 2011.

City of Longmont. "15.03.150 – MU mixed use district." *Municipal Code.* Accessed on October 31, 2011.

City of Longmont. "Mixed Use District." Accessed at www.ci.longmont.co.us/planning/ mixeduse_tod.htm on October 31, 2001.

City of Longmont. "Prospect, Neighborhood Groups." Accessed at www.ci.longmont.co.us/cnr/ neighborhood_groups/prospect.htm on October 31, 2011.

Cox, Jack. "Longmont's Prospect neighborhood is both friendly and flamboyant; like Mayberry...

REFERENCES

but hip." *The Denver Post.* April 21, 2002.

Dennis, Bill. "Peer Review: Of Pot Roast and Sushi." *Council Report III.* Congress for the New Urbanism and *The Town Paper.* 2003.

DestinationProspect.com. Accessed on October 31, 2011.

Duany, Andrés (Principal, Duany Plater-Zyberk & Company). Interview and email communications with Simmons Buntin. November 21 and December 2, 2011.

Duany, Andrés and Elizabeth Plater-Zyberk. *Prospect Urban Regulations.* The Kiki Wallace Co. and Park Engineering Consultants. May 14, 1996.

Duany Plater-Zyberk & Company. *Prospect Architectural Regulations.* The Kiki Wallace Co. 1997 (revised January 13, 1998).

Duany Plater-Zyberk & Company. "Prospect, Colorado." Tear Sheet. n-d.

Filmanowicz, Stephen. "Modern mixed-use building at Prospect." Photo credit with narrative caption. Congress for New Urbanism Image Bank. Accessed at www.cnu.org/resources/imagebank on October 31, 2011.

IonPlaceColorado.com. Ion Place Prospect. Borst Company. Accessed October 31 and November 13, 2011.

Jacobs, Kerrie. "Something Happened." *Dwell.* April 2002.

Kostovny, Mark. "Solar Village Prospect: America's Coolest Neighborhood." Article/Fact Sheet. Accessed at www.solarvillagehomes.com on October 31, 2011.

Lichtenstein, Grace. "Younger Buyers Want Better, Not Bigger." *The New York Times.* May 7, 2006.

Lieber, Ron. "Is This Your Beautiful House?" *Fast Company.* December 19, 2007.

MarkSofield.com. Accessed in August, October and November 2011.

ProspectArtistsAssn.com. Prospect Artists Association. Accessed on October 31, 2011.

ProspectNewTown.com. The Kiki Wallace Co. Accessed August 2000 and September, October and November 2011.

Potter, Beth. "Milestones Icon: Prospect New Town." *Boulder County Business Report.* September 15, 2011.

Ryberg, Erica. "Building the New Urbanism." *Smithsonian.* August 1, 2006.

Sofield, Mark. *Prospect Architectural Regulations*, Revised. The Kiki Wallace Co. October 10, 2003.

Sofield, Mark. "Prospect: Project Evaluation." *Council Report III.* Congress for the New Urbanism and *The Town Paper.* 2003.

Sofield, Mark (Prospect Town Architect). Interview and email communications with Simmons Buntin. September 26 and 28 and November 17, 28 and 29, 2011.

Solar Village Homes. "Solar Village Prospect Announces that Condo Performance Data Exceeds Expectations." Press Release. Solar Village LLC. 2007.

SolarVillageHomes.com. Solar Village Homes. Accessed on October 31, 2011.

Speck, Jeff (Principal, Speck & Associates LLC). Email communications with Simmons Buntin. November 18, 2011.

Steuteville, Robert. "Going modern in Colorado." *New Urban News.* January/February 2001.

Stewart, Randolph. "Peer Review: The Prospect Vernacular and Charter Principles." *Council Report III.* Congress for the New Urbanism and *The Town Paper.* 2003.

Wallace, Kiki (Prospect Developer). Interview with Simmons Buntin. August 2000 and September 26 and November 28, 2011.

Walter, Claire. "Prospect New Town Loses 2nd Food Retailer." *Culinary Colorado* (blog). January 3, 2008.

Chapter Two:
NorthWest Crossing, Bend, Oregon

Aulwess, David (Landscape Architect, Walker Macy). Interview and Informal Discussions with Ken Pirie. February and March 2006 and June 2011.

Binsacca, Rich. "Tree-Lined Green." *Builder.* June 2010.

BuildingABetterBend.org. Building a Better Bend. Accessed in February and March 2006 and June, July and October 2011.

City of Bend. "NorthWest Crossing Overlay Zone." 10-10.22D of *Bend Code.* May 2, 2001 and amended on October 1, 2003 and December 17, 2003.

REFERENCES

EarthAdvantage.org. Earth Advantage Institute. Accessed in February and March 2006 and June, July and October 2011.

Ford, David (General Manager, West Bend Property Company LLC). Interview and Email Communications with Ken Pirie. February and March 2006 and May, June, July, August, September and October 2011.

Kennedy, Heidi. "Issue Summary: Discussion, public hearing and first reading of the West Bend Property Company, LLC application request (PZ04-551)." Department of Community Development, Planning Commission and City Council, City of Bend. April 20, 2005.

Macy, J. Douglas (Principal, Walker Macy). Interview and Informal Discussions with Ken Pirie. February and March 2006 and June 2011.

Mortensen, Romy (Vice President for Sales and Marketing, Brooks Resources Corporation). Interview and Email Communications with Ken Pirie. May, June, July, August, September and October 2011.

NorthWestCrossing.com. West Bend Property Company LLC. Accessed in February and March 2006 and June, July and October 2011.

NorthWestCrossing.com/blog. *NorthWest Crossing Blog*. West Bend Property Company LLC. Accessed in June, July and October 2011.

NWXBiz.com. NorthWest Crossing Business Association. Accessed in July and October 2011.

Pirie, Ken. "A regional New Urbanism takes shape in Oregon." *New Urban Network*. June 1, 2007.

Urbsworks, Inc. *NorthWest Crossing Prototype Handbook*. West Bend Property Company. February 2005.

Walker, Ruth. "Finding a Home Among the Trees." *New Towns*. December 2007.

West Bend Property Company LLC. *Master Declaration of Covenants, Conditions and Restrictions for NorthWest Crossing*. December 20, 2001.

West Bend Property Company LLC. *Rules & Design Guidelines: Residential Architectural Standards*. May 2008.

West Bend Property Company LLC. *Street Tree Guidelines*. May 2006.

Zillis, Mike (Principal, Walker Macy). Interview and Informal Discussions with Ken Pirie. February and March 2006 and June 2011.

http://stonebridgehomesnw.com/news-events/building-stability/

Chapter Three:
Lenox Village, Nashville, Tennessee

"$43M building sets financing in Lenox." *Nashville Business Journal.* April 20, 2008.

Blackwood, Suzanne Normand. "Local farmers, residents benefit from Lenox Village market." *The Tennessean / Brentwood Journal.* July 22, 2009.

Burch, Bonnie. "Dining options multiply on Nolensville Road." *The Tennessean.* October 7, 2009.

Covington, Keith. "Stars in Alignment over Nashville." *The Commonspace.* July 2002.

Cousins, Juanita. "Wave of businesses open in Lenox Village." *Brentwood Journal.* January 19, 2011.

"Demand prompts expansion at Lenox Village." *The Tennessean.* November 17, 2006.

LenoxLiving.com. Lenox Village Homeowner's Association. Accessed October 2011.

LenoxVillage.com. Regent Development, LLC. Accessed in August 2004, September 2011 and October 2011.

LenoxVillageTownCenter.com. Regent Development, LLC and Regent Realty. Accessed October 2011.

Loggins, Sarah (Lenox Village Town Center Condominiums Manager). Interview with Simmons Buntin. August 22, 2011.

Looney Ricks Kiss, Inc. *Lenox Village Urban Design Overlay.* Nashville / Davidson County. Adopted May 15, 2011 and Amended July 15, 2003. Available at www.nashville.gov/mpc/urban/udo/lenox.asp.

McGowan, David (Regent Development, LLC President and CEO). Interview with Simmons Buntin. June 22 and September 8, 2004 and August 19, 21 and 22 and October 6, 2011.

Metropolitan Government of Nashville and Davidson County. *The Community Character Manual 2008.* Planning Department. Adopted August 14, 2008 and amended January 13, 2011.

Metropolitan Government of Nashville and Davidson County. "Memorandum to Metro Planning Commissioners: Metro Planning Department Application of Alternative Zoning Districts." July 18, 2011.

Metropolitan Government of Nashville and Davidson County. "Ordinance No. BL2005-762: 'Specific Plan' (SP)." September 24, 2005.

Nannie, Phillip. "Regent plans 'Urbanism' approach for Lenox Village project." *Nashville Business Journal.* August 10, 2001.

Nashville.ApartmentHomeLiving.com. Apartment Home Living (Apartments.com). Accessed on February 6, 2012.

"Smart Growth Awards Presented to Mayor and Lenox Village." *The Nail.* January 2004.

Southeast Watershed Assistance Network. "Case Study: Lenox Village." n-d. Accessed at www.watershed-assistance.net on October 27, 2011.

U.S. Environmental Protection Agency. "Receipt of an Application for an Incidental Take Permit for the Lenox Village Development Site, Nashville, Davidson County, Tennessee." *Federal Register.* Vol. 67, No. 55. March 21, 2002.

Watson, Courtney. "Farmer markets adapt as season changes." *The Tennessean.* September 13, 2009.

Yearwood, Ron and Gary Gaston. *Healing the Pikes.* Nashville Area Metropolitan Planning Commission, Nashville Civic Design Center, Tennessee Department of Transportation and Federal Highway Administration. November 2010.

Zeitlin & Co. "Neighborhood Focus: Lenox Village." *Zeitlin & Co. Realtors Blog.* Accessed on October 27, 2011.

Chapter Four:
Rockville Town Square, Rockville, Maryland

Boorstin, Julia. "A Genetic Map: Biotechs Flock to Rockville." *Fortune.* November 27, 2000.

Brachfield, Melissa J. "Several more businesses close in Rockville Town Square." *The Gazette.* June 12, 2009.

Brenner, Elsa. "A Piazza for a Maryland Suburb." *The New York Times.* November 22, 2006.

Briggs, Don. Presentation and discussion for walking tour of Rockville Town Square on behalf of the Congress for New Urbanism. June 23, 2007.

Carrick, Nathan. "Super Fresh backs out of lease in Town Square." *The Gazette.* March 26, 2010.

Chernikoff, Helen and Al Yoon. "Special Report: Smart money in real estate is on smart growth."

Reuters. August 3, 2010.

City of Rockville. *Town Center Master Plan.* October 2001.

City of Rockville. "Rockville Town Center: The Countdown is On — Grand Opening May 2007." Brochure. n-d.

Congress for New Urbanism. "Rockville Town Square Profile." January 28, 2008.

Crisostomo, Contessa. "Town Square doing well, retail and residential managers say." *The Gazette.* May 6, 2009.

Doane, Alan David. "Rockville Mall: Rockville, MD." Deadmalls.com. March 24, 2007. Accessed at www.deadmalls.com/malls/rockville_mall.html.

Federal Realty Investment Trust. "Rockville Town Square Profile." n-d.

Griffiths, Cindy Cotte. "Choice Hotels is Moving to Town Center."*Rockville Central.* October 25, 2010.

Griffiths, Cindy Cotte. "The Papery's Kaput but What's Still Open."*Rockville Central.* July 15, 2010.

Griffiths, Cindy Cotte. "Possible New Grocery Store in Town Square." *Rockville Central.* December 14, 2010.

Levy, Claudia. "Rockville's Moribund Mall." *The Washington Post.* June 4, 1981.

Lenhart, Jennifer. "Faith in the Library's Future." *The Washington Post.* November 29, 2006.

Metropolitan Center for the Visual Arts. "VisArts at Rockville." n-d.

Montgomery County Public Libraries. "About the New Rockville Library." www.montgomerycountymd.gov/library. Accessed March 2011.

Norris, Sean Patrick. "Rockville blog moves to Facebook only." *The Washington Post.* March 10, 2011.

"Report of the Town Center Summit on April 21." *Town Center Action Team Blog.* May 4, 2009.

Razak, Matthew. "Rockville Finds Its Heart." *Potomac Almanac.* July 19, 2007.

Rockville Economic Development, Inc. "Business Directory: Incubator: The Rockville Innovation Center." n-d.

REFERENCES

Rothenberg, Pamela V. "Pondering Public Use: Consider possible business development opportunities generated by Court's ruling." *Journal of Property Management.* November/ December 2005.

Ryan, Kate. "Development at Rockville Town Square disappearing." WTOP.com. June 5, 2009.

Shaver, Katherine and Miranda S. Spivack. "It takes more than stores to build a winning town center." *The Washington Post.* February 28, 2010.

Shay, Kevin James. "Merchants buying into 'buy local'." *The Gazette.* September 25, 2009.

Slattery, Chris. "Of corks and chords: Rockville's wine and music festival." *The Gazette.* September 23, 2008.

Stern, Julie D. "Rockville Town Square." *Development Case Studies.* Volume 39, Number 06. The Urban Land Institute. April-June 2009.

Walerysiak, Mark. "Rockville Town Square, Maryland... An example of a successful downtown revitalization." *Bristol Rising.* January 12, 2011.

The Whiting-Turner Contracting Company. "Rockville Town Square Profile." 2010.

Chapter Five:
Glenwood Park, Atlanta, Georgia

BeltLine.org. Atlanta Development Authority. Accessed on October 30, 2011.

Benfield, Kaid. "Meet Glenwood Park, Atlanta's new showcase neighborhood of smart growth and green design." *Switchboard: Natural Resources Defense Council Staff Blog.* July 22, 2009.

Brewer, Charles (Green Street Properties Founder). Interview and Electronic Communications with Simmons Buntin. April 24, July 1, July 31, August 5 and September 4, 2005.

Brown, Walter (Green Street Properties Vice President of Development and Environmental Affairs). Interview with Simmons Buntin. August 23 and October 31, 2011.

Dewan, Shaila. "The Greening of Downtown Atlanta." *The New York Times.* September 5, 2006.

Dover, Kohl & Partners. "Glenwood Park, Atlanta, GA." Project Sheet. n-d. Accessed at www.doverkohl.com on October 28, 2011.

EarthCraft.org. EarthCraft. Southface Energy Institute. Accessed on February 25, 2012.

Flanders, Danny C. "Urban Warrior." *Atlanta Homes & Lifestyles.* February 2008.

Fleming, Adina. "Glenwood Park: Growing up." *Creative Loafing Atlanta*. June 4, 2008.

GlenwoodPark.com. Green Street Properties. Accessed in August and September 2005 and August, September and October 2011.

Grillo, Jerry. "Building Green." *Georgia Trend*. April 2008.

Mijanovich, Ann. "Glenwood Park Town Center: Retail Space Available for Immediate Lease." The Meddin Company. Retail flyers. n-d. Accessed at www.meddin.com on October 28, 2011.

Nyren, Ron. "Orienting toward Transit." *Urban Land*. April 2009.

Sessions, Pam (Hedgewood Homes Principal). Interview with Simmons Buntin. August 23, 2011.

Saunders, Tinah. "Green Living." *The Atlanta Journal-Constitution*. June 3, 2005.

Zarroli, Jim. "Atlanta Community Offers Amenities of Earlier Age." *NPR*. National Public Radio. April 12, 2006.

Chapter Six:
Belmar, Lakewood, Colorado

BelmarColorado.com. Belmar. Continuum Partners. Accessed on November 2 and 20 and December 1, 2011.

BelmarLab.org. The Lab at Belmar. Accessed on December 1, 2011.

"Belmar/Lakewood." Visit Denver, The Convention & Visitors Bureau. Accessed at www.denver. org/metro/neighborhoods/belmar-lakewood on September 24, 2011.
BelmarSquareLofts.com. The Lofts at Belmar Square. Residential Investments, LLC. Accessed on December 1, 2011.

"Belmar Community." Lakewood Economic Development Green Projects. City of Lakewood. Accessed at www.lakewood-colorado.org/sustainability/projects.htm on November 20, 2011.

Buntin, Simmons. "Denver: America's Great Urban Canvas, Part III." *Next American City*. September 8, 2008.

Button, Andrew. "Villa Italia: Lakewood, CO." DeadMalls.com. Accessed on November 20, 2011.

City Council Staff. "Request for Council Action: Ordinance O-2002-5 (Item 15)." City of Lakewood. February 11, 2002.

REFERENCES

Colorado Brownfields Foundation. "Case Study: A Declining Mall Reborn." Colorado Department of Public Health and Environment. Accessed at www.coloradobrownfields.org/resource_center.htm#casestudies on November 20, 2011.

ContinuumPartners.com. Continuum Partners. Accessed on November 2, 2011.

Continuum Partners. *Belmar Design Standards and Guidelines.* City of Lakewood. March 21, 2002 (revised June 2005).

Continuum Partners. "Belmar Events + Culture." Flyer. n-d.

Continuum Partners. "Belmar Residential Information." Brochure. 2007.

Continuum Partners. "Belmar Solar Array." Fact Sheet. n-d.

Continuum Partners. "Sustainability Initiatives." Fact Sheet. n-d.

Continuum Partners. *Villa Italia Modification No. 3 Official Development Plan.* City of Lakewood. January 4, 2002.

Development Research Partners. "Economic and Fiscal Impacts of the Belmar Reinvestment Project: Impacts in the City of Lakewood, CO 2002-2008." Lakewood Reinvestment Authority. City of Lakewood. August 2009.

DiLorenzo, Liz (Development Associate, Continuum Partners). Interview and email communications with Simmons Buntin. November 7, 8, 9, 21, 22 and 28 and December 8, 2011.

Dunham-Jones, Ellen and June Williamson. *Retrofitting Suburbia: Urban Design Solutions for Redesigning Suburbs.* Wiley. Updated Edition: 2011. 304 pp.

Environmental Demolition, Inc. "Villa Italia Mall: Scope of Work: Asbestos Abatement, Universal Waste." Accessed at www.edicolorado.com/index.php/102/villa-italia-mall on November 20, 2011.

Folger, Tim. "The De-Malling of America." *OnEarth.* May 28, 2008.

Garcia, Valentina. "Belmar solar panels will generate power to 225 homes." *KGUN 9 News.* April 7, 2008.

Harvard Communities. "The Courtyards at Belmar." Accessed at www.harvardcommunities.com/belmar.php on November 20, 2011.

Jackson, Richard J. and Stacy Sinclair. *Designing Healthy Communities.* Jossey-Bass. 2011. 304 pp.

KB Home. "Lakewood – Paired Homes Now Open for Information." Flyer. 2011.

KB Home. "Belmar in Lakewood, CO." Accessed at www.kbhome.com/ Community-CommID-00840740.aspx on December 1, 2011.

Lakewood.org. City of Lakewood. Accessed on November 20, 2011.

"Lakewood Opens New Downtown Area." *TheDenverChannel.com*. May 14, 2004.

Max, Sarah. "Malls: Death of an American Icon." *CNNMoney*. July 24, 2003.

Miller, Jason. "Another Greyfield Gone: Belmar in Lakewood, Colorado." *New Towns*. Fall 2005.

Office of Solid Waste and Emergency Response. "Brownfields Success Story: Colorado Coalition, Colorado." U.S. Environmental Protection Agency. October 2005.

Owings, Kimberly. "Complicated Villa Italia deal took years to finally get done." *Denver Business Journal*. June 9, 2002.

Pecsok, Roger (Development Director, Continuum Partners). Interview and email communications with Simmons Buntin. May 22 and 23, 2012.

Piercy, Susan. "Staff Report: Rezoning Case No. RZ-01-006." Development Review and Code Enforcement, Lakewood Planning Commission, City of Lakewood. December 13, 2001.

Rice, Paul (Planner, City of Lakewood). Email communications with Simmons Buntin. November 7 and 23, 2011.

Saviano, Eva. "So Fresh and So Green." *303 Magazine*. July 2008.

Shaer, Matthew. "After the mall: retrofitting suburbia." *The Christian Science Monitor*. May 22, 2009.

"Smart Growth in Action: Belmar's Walkable Downtown – Pedestrian-Friendly Redevelopment, Lakewood, Colorado." Smart Growth Online. National Center for Appropriate Technology. Accessed at www.smartgrowth.org/action on November 2, 2011.

Sobel, Lee (Real Estate Development and Finance Analyst, U.S. Environmental Protection Agency). Email communications with Simmons Buntin. November 7, 2011.

Sobel, Lee S., Steven Bodzin, John Norquist, Ellen Greenberg and Jonathan Miller. *Greyfields into Goldfields: Dead Malls Become Living Neighborhoods*. Congress for the New Urbanism. June 2002. 92 pp.

Stern, Julie and David Takesuye. *Urban Land Institute Award Winning Projects 2006*. ULI–the

Urban Land Institute. 2006. 138 pp.

Swope, Christopher. "After the Mall." Governing. October 2002.

Tatum, Christine. "Belmar set for public debut." *The Denver Post.* May 9, 2004.

Titus, Stephen. "Belmar project takes Lakewood downtown: city center rises in Villa Italia's wake." *ColoradoBiz.* August 2005.

Chapter Seven:
RiverPlace, Portland, Oregon

American Society of Landscape Architects. "Merit Award – Design: South Waterfront Park, Portland, OR." 2001.

Bureau of Planning. *Central City Plan.* City of Portland. 1988.

Bureau of Planning. *Central City Plan Fundamental Design Guidelines.* City of Portland. 1988.

The Center for Brownfields Initiatives. "EPA Region 10 – South Waterfront Redevelopment Project, Portland, Oregon." University of New Orleans. www.brownfields.com/Feature/Feature-Awards2003-region10.htm. Accessed on October 8, 2011.

Center for Livable Communities. "Model Projects: RiverPlace, Portland, OR – Redevelopment." Local Government Commission. 1995.

City of Portland. "Sustainable City Guidelines." November 1994.

Frank, Ryan. "Slowdown hits city, PDC, RiverPlace." *The Oregonian.* June 9, 2008.

Heichelbech, Ashley and Craig Sweitzer. "The Strand @ RiverPlace." Urban Works Real Estate. October 29, 2008.

HighRises.com. "The Strand Condos." Accessed on October 9, 2011.

Kauffman, Roy. "U.S. DOT, Secretary LaHood Invest $23 Million in the PDX Innovation Quadrant." Press Release. Office of Mayor Sam Adams. City of Portland. February 17, 2010.

Moyer, Geraldene (Portland Development Commission Senior Project Manager). Interview and Email Communications with Simmons Buntin. November 7 and 8, 2011.

Outreach and Special Projects Staff. "Brownfields Showcase Community: Portland, OR." U.S. Environmental Protection Agency. Quick Reference Fact Sheet. November 1998.

Portland Development Commission. "2100 River Parkway Building at a Glance." Fact Sheet. City of Portland. n-d.

Portland Development Commission. "Construction Underway on The Strand at RiverPlace." City of Portland. Press Release. March 1, 2005.

Portland Development Commission. "Development Opportunity: RiverPlace Parcels 8 & 3." City of Portland. Request for Proposals #06-26. 2006.

Portland Development Commission. "North Macadam Urban Renewal Area." Fact Sheet. City of Portland. n-d.

Portland Development Commission. "RiverPlace Area." City of Portland. www.pdc.us/ura/riverplace/riverplace.asp. Accessed in January 2000 and June, September and October 2011.

Portland Development Commission. *RiverPlace Development Strategy*. City of Portland. July 24, 1997.

Portland Development Commission. "RiverPlace Parcel 8." City of Portland. Proposed Development Concept Presentation. n-d.

Portland Development Commission. "South Waterfront Park." City of Portland. Fact Sheet. n-d.

Portland Development Commission. "South Waterfront Park Redevelopment Area: Region 10 Phoenix Award Winner 2003." City of Portland. Fact Sheet. n-d.

Sanders, Steve. Interview with Simmons Buntin. Portland Development Commission. March 4, 1997.

Sedway, Paul. "They Planned, It Worked." *SPUR Newsletter*. San Francisco Planning + Urban Research Association. November/December 2005. Available at http://www.spur.org/publications/library/article/theyplanneditworked11012005.

Urban Land Institute. "RiverPlace, Portland, Oregon." *Project Reference File*. Vol. 18. No. 3. 1988.

Chapter Eight:
Second Street District, Austin, Texas

2ndStreetDistrict.com. AMLI Austin Retail. Accessed September 2006 and October 2011.

AMLI.com. AMLI Residential. Accessed on October 30, 2011.

AshtonInAustin.com. UDR, Inc. Accessed on October 30, 2011.

REFERENCES

Black & Vernooy + Kinney Joint Venter. *Downtown Great Streets Master Plan*. Planning and Review Development Department, City of Austin. December 2001.

Block21Residences.com. CJUF II Stratus Block 21 LLC. Accessed on October 30, 2011.

Breyer, Michelle and Shonda Novak. "The rebirth of downtown." *The Austin American-Statesman*. December 21, 2003.

City of Austin. Art in Public Places. Accessed at www.ci.austin.tx.us/aipp in September 2006 and October 2011.

City of Austin. *Downtown Austin Plan*. Draft: November 2010. Accessed at www.ci.austin.tx.us/downtown in October 2011.

City of Austin. R/UDAT Austin. Accessed at www.ci.austin.tx.us/downtown/rudatuastin.htm in September 2006 and October 2011.

City of Austin. Second Street Streetscape Improvement Project. Accessed at www.ci.austin.tx.us/downtown/ssdsip.htm in September 2006 and October 2011.

Coppola, Sarah and Shonda Novak. "Advocates question affordable housing plans for Green redevelopment downtown." *The Austin American-Statesman*. April 4, 2012.

Coppola, Sarah. "Civic building is Austin's latest icon." *The Austin American-Statesman*. November 19, 2004.

Cultural Arts Division. *CreateAustin Cultural Master Plan*. Economic Growth and Redevelopment Services Office, City of Austin. 2009.

Design Commission. "Urban Design Guidelines for Austin." City of Austin. January 29, 2009.

Dinges, Gary. "ACL Live becoming a popular pick for special nonmusic events." *The Austin American-Statesman*. June 25, 2011.

Dinges, Gary. "High-profile W Austin Hotel turns 1 year old." *The Austin American-Statesman*. December 17, 2011.

Dinges, Gary. "Second Street District hoping for a lift from new arthouse movie theater." *The Austin American-Statesman*. April 23, 2011.

DowntownAustin.com. Downtown Austin Alliance. Accessed in September 2006 and October 2011.

Evins, Fred (Redevelopment Project Manager / Architect, Austin Economic Growth and Redevelopment Services Office). Personal Interview and Electronic Communications with

Simmons Buntin. August 14, 18 and 28 and September 7, 2006, August 21, 2011, and June 8, 2012.

Gonzales, Rodney. "Press Release: Austin's 2nd Street District Redevelopment Receives Global Economic Development Award." Economic Growth and Redevelopment Services, Office, City of Austin. September 26, 2011.

Green Roofs for Healthy Cities. "2008 Awards of Excellence: Austin City Hall." Accessed at www.greenroofs.org on May 6, 2012.

Neighborhood Planning and Zoning Department. "Downtown Austin Design Guidelines." City of Austin. May 2000.

Novak, Shonda. "After years of delays, construction in sight for areas in Seaholm District, official says." *The Austin American-Statesman*. October 18, 2011.

Novak, Shonda. "City's 2nd Street block appraised at $9.2 million." *The Austin American-Statesman*. March 13, 2004.

Predock.com/Austin/Austin.html. Antoine Predock Architect, PC. Accessed on May 6, 2012.

Seibert, Janet (City of Austin Civic Arts Coordinator). Personal Interview with Simmons Buntin. March 10, 2006.

Seibert, Janet. "The Arts and Austin's Second Street District." *Terrain.org: A Journal of the Built & Natural Environments*. Summer/Fall 2007.

Spong, John. "Street Smarts: A Quickie Guide to… Second Street District, Austin." *Texas Monthly*. February 2009.

TheAustonian.com. Moreland Properties. Accessed on October 30, 2011.

WHotels.com/Austin. W Hotels Worldwide. Accessed on October 30, 2011.

Chapter Nine:
Suisun City Water District, Suisun City, California

The American Architectural Foundation. *Back from the Brink: Saving America's Cities by Design*. Hosted by Charles Royer, created by Kevin E. Fry, produced by GVI. 57 minutes. 1996.

Applied Development Economics. *Transit-Oriented Development Feasibility Study*. City of Suisun City. April 16, 2009.

Association of Bay Area Governments and Metropolitan Transportation Commission.

REFERENCES

"Downtown Waterfront District." *FOCUS: A Development and Conservation Strategy for the San Francisco Bay Area.* Accessed at BayAreaVision.org on October 24, 2011.

Berke, Arnold. "Turnaround Town." *Historic Preservation.* March/April 1996.

Bragdon, Suzanne. "It's the economy, stupid!" *Suisun City Discovery.* City of Suisun City. April 2011.

California Department of Water Resources. "Suisun Marsh Program." Accessed at www.water. ca.gov/suisun on October 9, 2011.

Center for Livable Communities. *Livable Places Update.* Local Government Commission. May 1996.

City of Suisun City. "1996 in Review: Suisun City shining brighter than ever." *Suisun City Discovery.* December 1996.

City of Suisun City. "A Redevelopment Success Story." *Suisun City Discovery.* April 2011.

City of Suisun City. "Successor Agency to the Redevelopment Agency." Accessed at www.suisun. com/Successor-Agency.html on May 6, 2012.

City of Suisun City. *Suisun City Amended Downtown Specific Plan.* 1990, 1995 and 1999.

Coastal Services Center. *Adapting to Rising Tides.* National Oceanic and Atmospheric Administration and San Francisco Bay Conservation and Development Commission. Accessed at risingtides.csc.noaa.gov on October 9, 2011.

Corey, Scott (Suisun City Marketing Manager). Interview with Simmons Buntin. July 6, 2011.

Corey, Scott. "Suisun City RDA Delivers $1.3 million to State as Required." *Suisun City Patch.* May 12, 2011.

Community Development Department. "Notice of Preparation: City of Suisun City *General Plan* Update – Draft Program Environmental Impact Report." City of Suisun City. October 24, 2011.

Kearns, John (Suisun City Associate Planner). Interview with Simmons Buntin. July 6, October 11 and October 24, 2011.

Kearns, John and April Wooden. "Agenda Transmittal" and "Attachment 5: Guiding Principles – Suisun City General Plan Update." Planning Commission. City of Suisun City. July 6, 2011.

Lockwood, Charles. "Small Town: The Rebirth of Suisun City, California – Neotraditional Town Planning Comes to the Real World." *Hemispheres.* United Airlines (Pace Communications, Inc.). November 1995.

Metropolitan Transportation Commission. "Downtown Suisun City." *Pedestrian Districts Study.* January 4, 2006.

OneBayArea.org. *One Bay Area.* Association of Bay Area Governments, Bay Area Air Quality Management District, Bay Conservation and Development Commission and Metropolitan Transportation Commission. Accessed on October 9, 2011.

Peirce, Neal R. "What Suisun City knows about revival." *The Sacramento Bee.* September 6, 1995.

ProtectOurLocalEconomy.com. *Redevelopment: Mend It, Don't End It.* League of California Cities and California Redevelopment Association. Accessed on October 9, 2011.

Shone andrea. "Community is reborn by going back to its roots." *USA Today.* December 27, 1996.

Suisun.com. City of Suisun City. Accessed on October 9, 11, 24 and 25, 2011, and May 6, 2012.

SuisunCityBusiness.com. City of Suisun City. Accessed on October 9, 2011.

SuisunWaterfront.com. *Suisun City Waterfront District.* Suisun City Historic Waterfront Business Improvement District. Accessed on October 9, 2011.

Suisun City Historic Waterfront Business Improvement District. *Downtown Suisun City Self-Guided Historic Walking Tour.* November 2009.

Thompson, Ian. "Construction Takes Off In Suisun City." *Plant Your Business In Solano County!* Blog at SolanosGotIt.Blogspot.com. September 20, 2007, accessed on October 9, 2011.

Upton, John. "Bay Area Adopts Historic Climate-Change Rules." *The Bay Citizen.* October 6, 2011.

Wooden, April and Suzanne Bragdon. "City of Suisun City Agenda Transmittal." City of Suisun City. January 18, 2011.

Wooden, April (Suisun City Community Development Director). Interview with Simmons Buntin. July 6, 2011.

Chapter Ten:
Dockside Green, Victoria, British Colombia

Benfield, Kaid. "Is This the World's Greenest Neighborhood?" *The Atlantic.* August 25, 2011.

City of Victoria. "Dockside Lands Request for Proposals." September 10, 2004.

City of Victoria. "Master Development Agreement between the Corporation of the City of Victoria and Dockside Green Ltd." September 7, 2005.

CRD.bc.ca. Capital Regional District. Accessed in February 2010.

DocksideGreen.com. Dockside Green LP. Accessed in February and March 2010 and August, September and October 2011.

DocksideGreenEnergy.com. Dockside Green Energy. Accessed in February and March 2010 and August, September and October 2011.

Dockside Working Group. *Development Concept for the Dockside Lands.* City of Victoria. May 2004.

Fosket, Jennifer and Laura Mamo. *Living Green: Communities that Sustain.* New Society Publishers. 2009.

Hart, Sarah. "Case Study: Dockside Green, Victoria, B.C., Canada." *GreenSource.* 2009.

Huffman, Jim (Associate Principal, Busby Perkins+Will). Interview with Ken Pirie. February 2010.

Miller, James (Director, Dockside Green LP). Interview with Ken Pirie. February 2010.

Moresco, Justin. "Dockside Green: Setting a New Standard for Green Building." *RenewablEnergyWorld.com.* August 19, 2009.

Nexterra. "Dockside Green Residential Development." Accessed at www.nexterra.ca/industry/dockside.cfm in February 2010 and September and October 2011.

VictoriaWest.ca. Victoria West Community Association. Accessed in February 2010 and October 2011.

Chapter Eleven:
Prairie Crossing, Grayslake, Illinois

Abderholden, Frank. "Prairie Crossing leads nation into energy-efficient future." *The News-Sun.* April 19, 1996.

Apfelbaum, Steve I. and John D. Epplich, Thomas H. Price and Michael Sands. "The Prairie Crossing Project: Attaining Water Quality and Stormwater Management Goals in a Conservation Development." *Using Ecological Restoration to Meet Clean Water Act Goals: 33-38.* 1995.

Apfelbaum, Steve I. and Michael Sands, Tom Price, John D. Eppich, Peter Margolin and David Hoffman. "On Conservation Developments and Their Cumulative Benefits." A National Symposium: Assessing the Cumulative Impacts of Watershed Development on Aquatic Ecosystems and Water Quality. March 19-21, 1996.

Brown, Patricia Leigh. "It Takes a Pioneer to Save a Prairie." *The New York Times*. September 10, 1998.

Buck, Genevieve. "Serene and clean." *Chicago Tribune*. June 3, 2000.

Cohen, Nevin. "The Suburban Farm: An innovative model for civic agriculture." *UA-Magazine*. December 2007.

Community Stewardship Exchange. "Community Garden Case Studies: Prairie Crossing." n-d.

The Conservation Fund. "Model Conservation Development Criteria." Accessed at www.conservationfund.org/model_conservation_development_criteria on May 19, 2012.

Dunlap, David W. "Developing a Suburb, with Principles." *The New York Times*. July 11, 1999.

Erb, Madelyn. "Prairie Crossing - Grayslake, Illinois." January 21, 2000.

Fatsis, Stefan. "New Communities Make It Easy Being Green." *The Wall Street Journal*. November 10, 1995.

Gause, Jo Allen and Richard Franko, Jim Heid, Jr., Seteven Kellenberg, Jeff Kingsbury, Edward T. McMahon, Judi G. Schweitzer and Daniel K. Stone. "Case Study: Prairie Crossing, Grayslake, Illinois." *Developing Sustainable Planned Communities*. Urban Land Institute. 2007.

Handley, John. "Experiment on the Prairie." *Chicago Tribune*. September 29, 2002.

Holt, Nancy D. "How 'Green' Is Your Household?" *The Wall Street Journal*. May 22, 1998.

Kane, Rene C. "Prairie Flower." *Landscape Architecture*. October 2003.

Lake Forest Hospital. "Lake Forest Hospital to Develop Prairie Crossing Campus in Grayslake." Press Release. October 2000.

Leinberger, Christopher B. "Marketing Overview of Current Product Program of Prairie Crossing, Grayslake, Illinois." Charles Lesser & Company. 1999.

Liberty Prairie Foundation. "Sandhill Organics." *Building Communities with Farms*. September 2010.

REFERENCES

Long, John K. "No wasted energy in these homes." *Chicago Tribune.* April 19, 1996.

Office of Building Technology, State and Community Programs, Energy Efficiency and Renewble Energy, U.S. Department of Energy. "Case Study: Prairie Crossing Homes: Building America houses that use half as much energy." Building America Program. n-d.

Prairie Crossing Farm. "Meet Our Farmers." n-d.

Prairie Crossing Homeowners' Association. "Environmental Management Plan – 2011." Accessed October 2011 at www.pchoa.com.

PrairieCrossing.com. Prairie Holdings Corporation. Accessed September 2000 and October 2011.

PrairieCrossingCharterSchool.org. Prairie Crossing Charter School. Accessed September and October 2011.

Ranney, Vicky. "Overview." *Building Communities with Farms.* Liberty Prairie Foundation. September 2010.

Ranney, Vicky. "Prairie Crossing." *Building Communities with Farms.* Liberty Prairie Foundation. September 2010.

Ranney, Victoria. Personal interview with Simmons Buntin. August 22, 2000.

Revsine, Barbara. "Farm market gets its own building–and two farmers." *Chicago Tribune.* Muly 29, 2004.

Roszkowski, John. "Metra plans third rail station here." *Libertyville Review.* September 14, 2000.

Sands, Michael. "'Just Hire a Farmer': Putting Intent into Practice." *Building Communities with Farms.* Liberty Prairie Foundation. September 2010.

Sands, Michael. Personal interview by Simmons Buntin. July 25, 2011.

Stangenes, Sharon. "Convenience is part of the deal at these condos." *Chicago Tribune.* February 11, 2006.

Terra Firma. "Station Square at Prairie Crossing." Retail/Office Space Leasing Flyer. n-d.

Village of Grayslake. "Agenda Brief." Village Board Meeting. September 20, 2011.

Wisby, Gary. "Blowin' in the wind." *Chicago Sun-Times.* July 6, 2002.

Chapter Twelve:
Civano, Tucson, Arizona

Altschul, Craig. "Neighbors Support Pulte as Developer; Homebuilder Pledges to Continue Dialogue." *The Town Crier*. Civano Neighbors Neighborhood Association. March 5, 2003.

Bateman, Pam. "Civano Community School Expansion." *The Town Crier*. Civano Neighbors Neighborhood Association. October/November 2010.

Beal, Tom. "Civano: New Urban life Civano is eco-living." *Arizona Daily Star*. June 30, 2002.

Buntin, Simmons B. "Civano: The Dark and the Light." *Terrain.org: A Journal of the Built & Natural Environments*. Fall/Winter 2004.

Buntin, Simmons B. "The Town That Wouldn't Be? Civano and the Rise and Fall of New Urbanism in the American Southwest." Presentation to the University of Colorado Denver College of Architecture and Planning. September 25, 2005.

Burchell, Joe. "4-3 council vote approves $7 million for solar village." *Arizona Daily Star*. July 2, 1996.

Burchell, Joe. "City promises more funds to Civano builder." *Arizona Daily Star*. June 25, 1997.

Burchell, Joe. "'Future community' is now." *Arizona Daily Star*. April 17, 1999.

Bustamante, Mary. "Civano school is greenest in the land (and $50K richer)." *Tucson Citizen*. January 19, 2008.

CivanoNeighbors.com. Civano Neighbors Neighborhood Association. Accessed weekly from December 2003 through November 2011.

Civano Development Company. "Civano Neighborhood 1 Overview." n-d.

Civano Development Company. "Civano: Discover. Explore. Enjoy. Grow." Marketing Brochure. n-d.

"Civano Provides Sustainable Alternatives." *FieldWorks*. U.S. Department of Housing and Urban Development. March/April 2001.

Curd, Sally. "Kids: It's easy being green." *Tucson Citizen*. April 22, 2008.

Davis, Tony. "Don Diamond negotiating for share of Civano." *Arizona Daily Star*. July 12, 2000.

Doucette, Tom (Owner, Doucette Communities). Interview with Simmons Buntin. November 2, 2011.

REFERENCES

Editors. "Civano: remote but vital." *Arizona Daily Star*. April 21, 1999.

Gregory, Daniel and Peter O. Whitely. "Best New Community: Civano." *Sunset*. January 2004.

Grubbs, Nicole R. "Civano lots can't hold business traffic flow." *Arizona Daily Star*. May 31, 2003.

Haggerty, Colleen and Lynn Hudson. "PATH National Pilot Civano Opens First Sustainable Neighborhood Homes . . . Tucson Community to be the Nation's Largest Sustainable Living Development." Press Release. U.S. Department of Housing and Urban Development. April 19, 1999.

Heltsley, Ernie. "Onlookers' cheers greet Civano sale." *Arizona Daily Star*. July 25, 1996.

Holeman, Tim. "Letter RE: Valero #1665 Civano Development, Tucson, Arizona." Letter to Scott Lantz, Commercial Areas Working Group, Civano Neighbors Neighborhood Association, from Valero Retail Holdings, Inc. December 7, 2009.

Juarez, Jr., Macario. "The best-laid plans." *Arizona Daily Star*. February 18, 2001.

Juarez, Jr., Macario. "Civano looks to others for help." *Arizona Daily Star*. October 20, 2001.

Juarez, Jr., Macario. "Future worries Civano residents." *Arizona Daily Star*. August 15, 2000.

Machelor, Patty. "'A better way to live' proves irresistible." *Arizona Daily Star*. February 2, 2007.

Nichols, Al. "Energy and Water Use in Tucson and Civano: January 2007 – December 2007." Al Nichols Engineering, Inc., Pulte Homes and City of Tucson. July 10, 2008.

Nichols, C. Alan and Jason A. Laros. *Inside the Civano Project: A Case Study of Large-Scale Sustainable Neighborhood Development*. McGraw-Hill. 2010. 299 pp.

Pallack, Becky. "Pulte steps in at Civano." *Arizona Daily Star*. January 6, 2004.

Pepper-Viner Homes. "Green Building: Pepper-Viner Has Gone Green!" Accessed at www.pepperviner.com/green-building.asp on November 4, 2011.

Rayburn, Lee (former Director of Design and Planning, Civano Development Company). Interview with Simmons Buntin. November 3 and 21, 2011.

Rhoades, Bruce (Uno Bicycle Studio Owner). Interview with Simmons Buntin. November 4, 2011.

Rollins, Paul. "Birthing Civano… the Design Charrette." *The Town Crier*. Civano Neighbors Neighborhood Association. September 2005.

Sorenson, Dan. "From ground up, new home is model of energy efficiency." *Arizona Daily Star.* October 17, 2009.

Swaim, Phil (Principle, Swaim Associates). Interview with Simmons Buntin. November 23, 2011.

Swedlund, Eric. "Civano to add state's 1st 'green' hospital." *Arizona Daily Star.* November 28, 2006.

Vail.k12.az.us/~civano. Civano Community School. Accessed in October and November 2011.

Vail School District. "Civano Community School." Brochure. n-d.

Witmer, Gallagher. "IMPACT System Monitoring Report #16 - 2010." Pulte Homes and City of Tucson. October 4, 2011.

25849896R00131

Made in the USA
Charleston, SC
17 January 2014